The
Professional
Astrologer

The Organization for Professional Astrology (OPA) is a non-profit organization 501(c)(6) that advances the cause of professional astrology by developing programs, publications, and community support to help students and practitioners foster their understanding of astrology and launch and enhance their astrology practices.

OPA supports astrology in its different streams and advocates tolerance, ethical practice, high standards, and continual growth of the profession. We are a community, we are friends, we live in different nations, and we bring together different schools of thought.

OPA offers completely unique programs and publications to foster education, community, and professional practice in the field of astrology.

You can find further details about OPA's activities on the website

www.opaastrology.org

Supporting and advancing beginners, intermediate, and professional astrologers everywhere — since 2000.

Join a Vibrant Community,

Make Astrology Stronger

The Professional Astrologer

Building a
Successful Astrology Practice

Initiated and Compiled by

Published by the Organization for Professional Astrology—OPA
www.opaastrology.org

ISBN 978-0-9968077-0-8

Project Manager: Maurice Fernandez
Editors: Julian Wise, Maurice Fernandez, Arlan Wise
Cover design: Sara Fisk
Layout: Maurice Fernandez

Survey initiated by OPA through SurveyMonkey
www.surveymonkey.com

*"They tried to bury us,
they did not know we were seeds"* Use

Mexican proverb

"Millionaires don't use astrology, billionaires do." Use

J.P. Morgan

This book is dedicated to those who support, learn, and practice astrology, across time, cultures and traditions, despite the establishment's best advice.

OPA would like to express immense gratitude to all the contributors of this book, including the people who participated in the survey, the authors of the chapters, the astrologers who shared their personal stories, Sara Fisk our designer, Julian Wise our supervising editor, Leann Plank for the layout guidance, and all OPA members who have supported the organization and astrology through the years.

Contributors

Chapters

Donna Young – Maurice Fernandez – Sandra Leigh Serio –
Chris McRae – Georgia Stathis – Anne C. Ortelee –
Robert Woodliff and Leisa Schaim (AFAN) – Wendy Stacey –
Monica Dimino – Jacqueline L. Janes – Arlan Wise –
Frank C. Clifford – Alexandra Karacostas – Kay Taylor

Interviews

Steven Forrest – Melanie Reinhart – Kim Marie –
Chris Brennan – Linea Van Horn – Aleksandar Imsiragic –
Caroline W. Casey – Madalyn Hillis-Dineen– Donna Woodwell –
Hakan Kirkoglu – Ray Merriman

References

Nancy Beale

Contents

Introduction

For a Future Generation of Astrologers

Maurice Fernandez

President, OPA

I was first exposed to astrology as a young child, reading a well-written book that helped parents understand their child by their Sun ✳ sign. If my parents would have read that book as they intended upon purchasing it, it might have save us many tantrums and a great deal of time. As superficial as Sun sign books can be, it nailed me, and I was sold! Astrology uncovered for me insights no other in my reality *Expand* managed to get to; I felt better understood, and that provided inner solace. Yet, as truthful as astrology revealed itself to be, I hadn't in my wildest visions imagined myself becoming an astrologer. The universe had to hypnotize me, kidnap me, and position me on this path, while I was busy making other plans…and here I am, looking back and thanking "the universe" not only for being an astrologer today, but also for starting me on this path when I was 19 and not having to wait for astrology to be a second or third career.

Who knew back then astrology was a profession at all? The two most common responses I received when I shared my occupation with people were, for one, amazement and subsequent question about my telescopes (you get the point), and the other, a facial expression conveying "How am I getting out of this conversation now?" No one is to blame, this path less travelled was not advertised and people were bewildered about it, just as much as I initially was. Being an astrologer was, first of all, an important exercise in filtering out public opinion and tuning into internal guidance, as I consciously chose to be very open about it. I know these anecdotes are nothing unique, and many fellow astrologers will nod their head recognizing their own similar story.

As fascinating and adventurous as these pioneering years were, and still are in our days for professional astrologers, we at OPA do hope future generations will have better options. We do want parents to seriously read the Sun sign books about their kids and gain perspective on their needs and orientations, or better yet, get a professional reading for that purpose. Perhaps this will divert some teenagers from destructive experiences, or save people wasted years with the wrong crowd or the wrong profession. We do want young people to have more readily available options to choose astrology as their first career path, and professional astrologers to feel more secure and globally respected for their services. We do believe astrology will contribute to a better world, with well-educated, compassionate, and competent practitioners. We do see the time for that is now.

An earlier version of this book was published in 2001, soon after OPA's incorporation. OPA founder Bob Mulligan had the insight to address the lack of a support system for astrologers. We know the conventional world can be cynical to astrologers, yet even within the astrological community very few opportunities exist to properly guide those who audaciously feel called to this vocation. Astrology schools may provide high quality knowledge about the stars, but seldom about the humans involved. This volume is the revamped version of the original book, adapted to an evolved reality where the profession of astrology is fast developing, bolstered by more rigorous educational programs, and the internet revolution that has opened many new avenues for practitioners.

We have gathered a wide variety of professional practitioners, each with a different background and experience, to share their insights and their story. You may read conflicting suggestions as you go through the different chapters, highlighting the fact that the paths to a successful and fulfilling practice are diverse. OPA does not endorse everything proposed. The purpose of the book is for readers to gain perspective and examine options.

Whether you are in your initial steps and contemplate becoming an astrologer, or you are a seasoned professional, we sincerely hope you will gain insights from the contribution of every author and inter-viewee, for they have walked the path. This can serve as an inspiration to take this professional path more seriously.

We thank you for your involvement and keeping this flame burning, started perhaps by a rattling galactic lightning that ignited our consciousness. We cannot backtrack or falter; together, as astrologers, we are here to stay, serve, and enlighten more.

With blessings,

Maurice Fernandez
President, OPA
October, 2015

Ethical Guidelines for the Professional Practice of Astrology

By OPA

Preamble

Astrology has diverse uses, among them using the birth chart to analyze personal development, timing procedures and events, projecting economic, political and societal trends, and understanding the meaning of cycles and time as a whole. Astrologers are equally diverse, taking into their astrological practice a variety of additional skills and educational backgrounds.

Astrologers recognize the apparent synchronicity between life cycles on the earth and cycles of the cosmos. They identify the mythological associations to celestial bodies and their physical order in outer space, combining astronomical measurement with symbolism in their interpretation. Astrologers strive to provide a service that enriches and enhances life, and protects human dignity. They can contribute to the ongoing evolutionary process of astrology by providing quality service and continually increasing their own proficiency and mastery of the practice through ongoing studies, research, and the support of other astrologers.

The Ethical Guidelines governing personal, public, and professional conduct in the practice of astrology must lend dignity to the profession, without stifling creativity, individuality and future growth. Astrology does not lend itself to a rigid set of rules outlining all of its functions and procedures. However, a guide of acceptable conduct is paramount to its respectability.

Definition of a Professional Astrologer:

A Professional Astrologer, for the purpose of this code, is one who is able to accurately generate a horoscope and interpret it by verified and generally accepted standards of procedures, and one who adequately performs any of the following functions to generate an income:

- Using astrological interpretive skills to consult clients.
- Organizing, researching, or developing verified astrological information and presenting this knowledge in print, in speech, or on the internet.
- Teaching astrology.

Ethical Guidelines

1. Responsibility to the client

a. All horoscopes must be calculated using standard methods of procedure based on accurate data. It is critical to have a recorded time, date, and place of birth that is as precise as possible. If a rectified time or an alternative method such as a Johndro Locality, Solar Chart or Natural Chart is used, this should be stated and its limitations, if any, described.

b. Astrologers must use reasonably verified and credible astrological knowledge in their interpretation and test their competence through regular practice.

c. The terms of the consultation need to be stated and understood prior to the appointed time. This would include fee, duration, style and what the client has a right to expect.

d. Astrologers respect the dignity of the client regardless of any personal belief, political affiliation, or bias the astrologer or client may have. In the event that they feel conflicted with their client's beliefs in a way that would undermine their neutrality during a consultation, they must acknowledge that and suggest alternative options to the client.

e. Confidentiality regarding the exchange between the client and the astrologer must be maintained. There will be no use of client charts for lectures, articles, or in sharing a database with other astrologers unless prior permission has been obtained in writing and/or names have been eliminated.

f. Astrologers must take full responsibility for the information they impart, and acknowledge the autonomy the client has over their life decision and processes. Every client needs to be treated in a thoughtful manner. This includes refraining from making statements that are rigidly deterministic, such as predicting someone will never marry, never have children, or die at a specific time.

g. Clients must not be misled in any way, including emotional, sexual or financial exploitation and harassment.

h. If modalities and disciplines other than astrology are used in an astrology consultation, then it must be mentioned and agreed upon prior to the meeting.

2. Responsibility to the general public

a. All astrological work is expected to be performed with the highest standard of integrity and personal competence.

b. Astrologers are expected to practice good citizenship, and not use their skills to take advantage of others or work against the common good.

c. Astrologers should not mislead by making unfounded promises, or exaggerated claims.

d. Any advertisement about the professional practice must be truthful and factual. This means the astrologer must be honest in stating proficiency and scholastic degrees, and must deliver what is advertised.

e. Astrologers are expected to practice only in areas of their competence and qualifications and avoid making unfounded claims or assessments in the name of astrology. This includes but not limited to medical, psychological, financial or legal advice. The astrologer may make suggestions, but openly state that he or she is not a professional in those fields. When a client's needs are beyond the capability of the astrologer, the client must be referred to appropriate agencies or other professional services.

f. When dealing with horoscopes of public figures using commonly published data, observations should be made in a way that is educational, and in such, refrain from gossip and unfounded assumptions.

3. Responsibility to other astrologers and the profession of astrology

a. Astrologers are expected to make a conscious effort to continue their professional growth and education. This can be done by taking courses, reading literature, attending conferences and seminars, conducting research, etc.

b. Astrologers must remain tolerant to personal and astrological differences where there is no breach of ethics. If unethical conduct is noted, it should be dealt with in an appropriately professional manner.

c. Astrologers are encouraged to give support to the efforts of other astrologers, so that everyone benefits from our collective knowledge, experience, and insights.

d. Research and any related presentations are to be conducted in a rigorous manner with objective references, always maintaining strict professional integrity. It is appropriate to take credit for scholarly work and ethical to give credit to contributions made by others.

e. Copyright laws must be honored. This does not preclude the use of other astrologer's work providing the law is upheld and/or appropriate credit is given.

4. General

a. Astrologers are expected to maintain a personal image of cleanliness, competence, and social respect when representing astrology.

The Astrologer's Oath

The infinity of the sky has cohesion
The astral planes reveal a logic
To which nature fully resonates and aligns
If few are initiated in this art of interpretation
Of celestial science with existential meaning
I am one

I recognize the privilege and responsibility
To serve humanity as an astrologer
Be the channel between above and below
Remain grounded, clear of prejudice, and open hearted
Respectfully, gracefully, and truthfully
I pledge to assist those who seek higher guidance
Direct them to the space, the time, and the way
As depicted in the map of geocosmic cycles
I will enlighten them in the perspective
That despite trials and tribulations,
Their lives are intrinsic to an intelligent cosmic order
These suggestions shall be made
To the best of my humble understanding
Whether venerated or depreciated publicly in this task
I shall not falter, aware of the merit of this honorable calling

Part 1

The Survey

2015

The Astrology Practitioner Survey

In April 2015, OPA conducted a survey through Survey Monkey (www.surveymonkey.com) to assess the demographics of professional and amateur practicing astrologers, the financial parameters of their practice, their social concerns, and general educational backgrounds.

This survey can serve as a reference to some of the comments and insights made by the different authors of this book, as they discuss the situation and circumstances of the profession of astrology, particularly within the United States culture.

Question 1

Are you male of female?

Answered: 230   Skipped: 3

Answer Choices	Response	Units
Female	78.70%	181
Male	21.30%	49
Other	0%	
TOTAL		**230**

Close to 80% of astrology practitioners are female.

Question 2

What is your age?

Answered: 230   Skipped: 3

Answer Choices	Response	Units
18 to 28	0.87%	2
29 to 40	9.57%	22
41 to 56	35.65%	82
57 to wiser	53.91%	124
TOTAL		**230**

Most astrology practitioners are above their 40's, with a majority above age 57. We do not know at what the age they began to practice, but can have a sense that most people take on astrology as a second career or a practice for their retirement. Very few begin their career path as astrologers.

Question 3

Do you rely primarily on the income of your astrology practice to sustain yourself and grow?

Answered: 227   Skipped: 6

Answer Choices	Response	Units
Yes	29.96%	68
No	70.04%	159
TOTAL		**227**

Most people who practice astrology, rely on additional sources of income to sustain themselves.

Question 4

If you have additional sources of income or savings, are they what allows you to practice astrology?

Answered: 217   Skipped: 16

Answer Choices	Response	Units
Yes	68.66%	149
No	31.34%	68
TOTAL		217

Close to 1/3 of the practitioners are able to sustain themselves primarily from their astrology practice.

2/3 of practitioners must rely on an additional income to practice astrology.

Question 5

If you have an additional source of financial support, can you describe the source?

Answered: 196   Skipped: 37

Answer Choices	Response	Units
Additional part-time job	24.49%	48
Additional full-time job	29.08%	57
Partner's income	18.88%	37
Family funds and inheritance	15.31%	30
Other	33.67%	66
TOTAL		**196**

"Other" responses:

- My retirement funds
- Social Security
- Investments
- Alimony
- student loans

More than 53% of people who practice astrology while having an additional source of income, work at another job to sustain themselves.

Question 6

How much do you charge for an astrology reading?

Answered: 204   Skipped: 29

Answer Choices	Response	Units
10-80 US$	24.02%	49
81-120 US$	33.82%	69
121-175 US$	22.55%	46
176-250 US$	14.71%	30
More than 250 US$	4.90%	10
TOTAL		**204**

Readings are typically 60 to 90 minutes long, and require preparation time.

More than 57% of practitioners charge $10 to $120 for their reading consultations.

Question 7

What do you feel can be the most intimidating factor in being a practicing astrologer?

Answered: 209   Skipped: 24

Answer Choices	Response	Units
Difficulty making a sustainable living financially	44.50%	93
Lack of credibility and criticism from society and the scientific community	18.66%	39
It is considered blasphemous in my religion	0.96%	2
People do not know enough about the value of astrology	45.93%	96
Other (please specify)	20.10%	42
TOTAL		**209**

Financial concerns and lack of awareness about astrology are the greatest concerns of practitioners.

"Other" listed responses:

- Self-promotion
- I don't find anything intimidating in being an astrologer

Question 8

How long have you studied astrology before charging money for readings?

Answered: 204   Skipped: 29

Answer Choices	Response	Units
1-3 years	19.12%	39
3-5 years	20.59%	42
5-7 years	14.22%	29
7-10 years	15.20%	31
More than 10 years	30.88%	63
TOTAL		**204**

The time of transition from student to professional varies greatly.

We do not know if among those who have studied more than 7 years before they began charging for their service (46%), people had access to structured study programs.

Question 9

How have you studied astrology?
(Multiple options possible)

Answered: 213   Skipped: 20

Answer Choices	Response	Units
Self-taught (internet, books)	72.77%	155
Living room classes of a local teacher (or similar setting)	57.28%	122
Established certification program	46.48%	99
Other (please specify)	32.39%	69
TOTAL		213

"Other" listed responses:

- With a mentor
- Attending conferences and workshops
- Through doing charts for people and direct experience
- Through dreams

Less than 50% of astrologers have pursued a certification program.

Part 2

Understanding the Profession

and

Guidance for Success

Chapter 1

Different Orientations and Uses in the Practice of Astrology
Donna Young

The origins of astrology date back thousands of years; the precise number is difficult to prove. The Elder Pliny in the first century CE claimed that the Chaldeans had been observing celestial phenomena for 490,000 years. Documents written in the cuneiform script of the Sumerians and Akkadians, the oldest recorded evidence supporting celestial observations, date back to 2100 BCE. The Enuma Anu Enlil Babylonian tablets were found in the royal archives of Nineveh and are named after its opening words, 'When (the gods) Anu, Enlil [and Ea established in council the plans of Sky and Earth].' Of the 70 tablets containing over 7000 omens, the first 50 are inscribed with information on lunar, solar and meteorological omens, with the remaining 20 concerning planets and stars. These tablets are dated between 1922 and 1542 BCE.

These ancient astrologers would have practised omen-based astrology, but detailed calculations required for erecting a horoscopic chart would be established later.

The Babylonians tracked planetary positions and eventually accumulated a large enough body of knowledge by the 4th century BC to calculate the planetary positions and establish the foundations of a 360 degree circle with twelve 30 degree constellations.

The Hellenistic period from 1 BC–6 AD saw the accumulation of knowledge from the Egyptians, Babylonians and Persians and the first evidence of natal astrology. The more complex horoscopic astrology we practise today was firmly in place. The conquests of Alexander the Great established the famous library in Alexandria, which became the astrological epicentre of the Greco-Roman world. Unfortunately, although there is an evidenced body of knowledge, very little of the original documentation exists that can prove its exact origins.

A major decline in astrology's fortunes came with the onset of the scientific revolution during the 17th century CE. It was largely out of fashion until the turn of the 20th century when it was again made popular by astrologers such as Alan Leo and Marc Edmond Jones.

Among the Different Uses of Astrology

Mundane Astrology

Likely the oldest form of astrology, Mundane astrology began with the observation that celestial events had a relationship to the events on earth. Eclipses and major planetary cycles were of particular relevance, but the regular cycles of the inner planets and the Moon made it possible to start tracking regular patterns which eventually gave us the ability to make predictions. Its major importance is in the study of the collective influence through the charts of countries and their leaders, cities, political parties, etc. It is also used in Astro-meteorology to predict major weather cycles.

Electional Astrology

An Electional chart is focused on establishing the optimal time to embark upon a new business project, marriage, important purchase, journey, medical procedure, etc. If you have the luxury of being able to choose a date and time for such endeavors, it allows you to optimise the planetary energies available and minimize any potential negative outcome by choosing the *birth chart* for your endeavor. Electional astrology should be conducted in tandem with Natal astrology to achieve the best results.

Horary Astrology

Horary astrology is a form of oracular practise whereby a chart is erected at the exact time a client asks a question. The question must be specific, and the chart will be used to provide an answer to this question. For example, it can be used to locate lost objects, determine whether the house you are about to buy is a worthy investment, or to assist in important decisions. The question should be timely, relevant, and important. Lee Lehman lists three rules that should be adhered to:

1. The querent must be emotionally or mentally involved in the question

2. The question should only be answered once

3. The question must have a meaningful, verifiable answer

Horary astrology engages its own set of rules that are important to the delineation. It cannot deliver anything that is not promised in the natal chart - your gifts and talents will not change with a positive horary chart.

Olivia Barclay says that "the moment of the question is a moment of contact with a greater intelligence" and in this regard, Horary is considered akin to other ancient divinatory methods such as Tarot, and the I Ching.

Medical Astrology

Use

"A physician without knowledge of astrology has no right to call himself a physician." Hippocrates (born 460 BC)

The practise of using astrology as an indicator of physical characteristics dates back thousands of years. Each zodiac sign has a relationship to a physical party of the body starting with Aries (head, subrenals), Taurus (throat, neck, thyroid), Gemini (nerves, arms, lungs), Cancer (stomach, mammary glands;), Leo (heart, spine back), Virgo (intestines, nervous systems), Libra (kidneys;), Scorpio (sexual organs), Sagittarius (liver, hips, thighs), Capricorn (bones, teeth, skin), Aquarius (shins, ankles, blood circulation), Pisces (feet).

"No man ought to commit his life into the hands of that Physician, who is ignorant of Astrologic: because he is a Physician of no value." *Use* Nicholas Culpeper

The connection between astrology and medicine was firmly in place until the 18th century when they parted ways. Until that time, when an individual was unwell a chart was drawn for the moment *V. Imp* the patient succumbed to his illness. In this regard it acted much like a horary chart, but created specifically for the purpose of diagnosing and treating the illness.

Significations of the illness, as well as the drugs that would have been used to treat them, all relate back to signs, planets, and houses. The goal of treatment was to bring natural harmony back to the body. *Correspondences*

Since astrology represents every aspect of our existence, we can *Use* also associate astrology with our physical and mental conditions and predisposition. Today the study of medical astrology is a fascinating pursuit for our own learning and for taking preventive measures, but unless you are already a medical doctor caution should be taken when reading the charts of others and addressing their existing health conditions. In some countries, it is even illegal to provide medically related recommendations, unless the astrologer has some sort of medical training. As a rule of thumb, astrological advice on health matters should not be considered a replacement for professional medical advice; it's essential to suggest a person be tested by a medical physician.

Natal Astrology

Natal Astrology reflects the chart of a *nativity*, erected for an individual for the moment of birth. When time was recorded by means of sun dials and other rudimentary devices, most individuals would not have paid attention to the moment of birth that would have been essential for erecting an accurate natal chart. This was reserved for the birth of members of a royal family or important leaders.

Modern natal chart interpretation is based on the foundations that were established by traditional astrologers thousands of years ago. Techniques vary from astrologer to astrologer but the fundamental meanings of planets, signs and houses, elements, modes, aspect relationships, etc., remain constant.

The placement of the planets in the natal chart will tell us unique characteristics of the individual born at that particular moment in time. It needs to be taken into consideration with the place and circumstances of the individual's life. For example, the chart does not reveal the gender of the person, and with an identical chart, a child born in a third world country struggling for survival will have different challenges than a person growing up in a first world environment. Fundamentally, the energy of the natal chart remains constant throughout the life of the individual. However, from the moment of birth the planets continue to move, and through this movement we are able to glean additional information about the life of the individual.

Moving the Chart Forward

There are numerous ways of moving a chart forward for prediction measurement purposes. Outlined below is a brief summary of a few of the more common methods.

Transits

As the planets continue to move in the natural cycle after the moment of birth, they begin to "interact" with the fixed planetary placements of the natal chart. They make new contacts with other planets, points, and house cusps in the natal chart, and accordingly, activate certain aspects of the chart. This movement is called a planetary transit, and the connections these transiting planets make will activate important issues in our lives. Transits do not override the natal chart—the influence is to be interpreted in conjunction with the birth chart.

Solar Return

By casting a chart for the time the Sun returns every year to the exact position of the birth chart, the astrologer can create a Solar Return Chart. This chart can be read like a natal chart, but is only active for a year, some say starting a few months before the actual return date. Planetary connections between the solar return and natal chart are important considerations. This system can also be used for other planetary returns, such as a Moon Return Chart every month.

Secondary Progressions

Secondary Progressions use a formula that consists of associating roughly a day of one's life for a year of one's life. The chart for the next day after the birth of a newborn will reflect dynamics that may affect the whole first year of life, and so on with the following days to years. Without a computer, this can be calculated approximately by looking at an ephemeris and counting the number of days past the birth date that are equivalent to the current age.

In this system, the faster moving bodies have greater importance. For example, the Sun at zero degrees would take 30 years to change signs. The moon takes 2.5 years to change signs and moves approximately one degree per month, and the cycles of Sun and moon and their changing phase relationship can provide further significant information. The outer planets would most likely not change signs at all. When changes do occur by sign, house placement, by changing direction (going retrograde or direct), or by tight aspect connections to planets in the natal chart, these progressions can indicate significant changes in the life of the individual.

Solar Arc Direction

Much like Secondary Progressions, Solar Arc directions move the chart forward approximately a day for a year, but in this model the entire chart is moved forward one degree per year, at the pace of the Sun—thus, all chart factors are moved approximately one degree per year, at the rate of the progressed Sun. The chart patterns remains exactly the same as the natal chart, but as they are moved forward, the degrees, signs and house cusps will change. An approximate Solar Arc chart can be calculated with the naked eye by adding the number of degrees equivalent to the age of the individual to the original planetary positions.

V₁/m₀.

There are times of the year when the Sun moves slightly slower or faster than average so you will want to verify with a computer for complete accuracy. With this information you will see the current planetary relationships and what influence these might have on the life of the native.

Relationship Charts

Synastry

When the individual charts of people who are in relationship are put together by superimposing one chart over the other (creating a bi-wheel), the astrologer is able to see how the planets of one chart interact with the planets of the other and assess what kind of relationship dynamics are in play. Synastry reveals information about how one person is having an impact on another and the general chemistry between two people. We might find ourselves drawn to people who complement our own energy astrologically, but we might also be drawn to individuals who can compensate for an energy that is lacking in our own chart.

Composite charts

A composite chart is a third chart that is immediately derived from the charts of two people who are in a relationship. It is created by calculating the median point between each planetary pair and erecting an entirely new chart that represents the relationship. For example, to calculate the composite Sun, the average distance between the two individual Suns would create a third Sun that would represent the relationship. Analysis of this chart is essentially the same as for an individual natal chart. Some would argue that because the composite combinations can create impossible planetary scenarios they don't behave as naturally. For example, Mercury and

Venus would never be more than 1-1.5 signs away from the Sun in an individual natal chart, but in a composite chart they could end up opposite the Sun.

It's also possible to calculate a composite chart that would represent more than two people. A chart with all of the members of your family, or all of the partners in a business are possible, and would give an indication of how you operate as a group.

Davison relationship charts

In this model the birth date of two individuals is combined. The median longitude/latitude, time, and date of birth is calculated to create an entirely new chart. For example, a Davison relationship chart between someone born on August 1, 1950 in Paris, and another person both September 1, 1950 in New York City would be August 16, 1950 somewhere in the middle of the Atlantic Ocean. While the location could end up in the middle of the ocean, it is not relevant to the analysis other than to anchor house positions. This chart is considered the birth chart of the relationship, and can be moved forward in time and relocated in the same way that a natal chart would be.

Orientations of Astrology

Astrology is divided into two main zodiac systems to measure the position of planets: the *Tropical* and *Sidereal* zodiacs. These systems are measured with reference to the position of the Sun on the spring Equinox in both hemispheres (March 21 and September 22). The Tropical zodiac maintains a constant of zero degrees Aries position for the Sun on March 21, while the Sidereal zodiac's position varies according to the precession of the equinoxes, an astronomical phenomenon related to a gradual shift in the rotation of the Earth's axis that causes the Sun to change its position over time on the day of the Spring Equinox.

About 2000 years ago these systems were in alignment for a period of time and both had the Sun positioned at zero degrees Aries on March 21, but through precession of the equinoxes, the Sidereal zodiac has shifted over time. So astronomically, the Sun is currently around 6 degrees Pisces on the Spring Equinox (of the Northern Hemisphere).

Sidereal Astrology

The Sidereal zodiac is largely used by Hindu or Vedic Astrologers and places the planets in their observable fixed star constellations. They interpret the planets' position against the actual backdrop of fixed stars (constellations). However, most Vedic Astrologers divide each of the constellations into 12 equal parts, even though the actual constellations are not, astronomically speaking, equal in size.

Tropical Astrology

The Tropical zodiac was adopted during the Hellenistic period, and is now primarily practised by Western Astrologers. It uses the Vernal (Spring) Equinox—the interception of the ecliptic and the equator— as the starting point for the zodiac at zero Aries, without accounting for the precession of the equinoxes. Interpretations are based on seasonal changes.

There are many similarities in the interpretations between the Sidereal and Tropical systems, and excellent arguments to be made for the validity of either side. What they share is a rich history on which to weave a symbolic tapestry.

Astrology is a continually expanding field with research being done by dedicated individuals all over the world. The following is a very brief outline of some of the major practises of astrology in use today, but is by no means considered an exhaustive list.

Vedic Astrology

Largely because their religion has remain unchanged for thousands of years, Indian astrology did not suffer the loss of their astrological language in the same way that Western Astrology did. Vedic astrologers today practise an astrology that is little changed from the original masters. David Frawley describes Sidereal astrology as "cosmic astrology". "Its zodiac measures the relationship between our solar system, the fixed stars and the galaxy. It possesses good predictive powers and is good for spiritual astrology".

Vedic astrologers most commonly incorporate the visible planets (Sun to Saturn) and list them according to the days that they rule, starting with Sunday, and including Rahu (North node) and Ketu (South Node)

1) Sun, 2) Moon, 3) Mars, 4) Mercury, 5) Jupiter, 6) Venus, 7) Saturn, 8) Rahu, 9) Ketu

Their corresponding numbers relate to planetary energy, and each planet represents a stage in the development and distribution of solar energy.

In addition to astrological signs, Vedic astrology adds lunar constellations or Nakshatras of 13 degrees and 20 minutes to their interpretations.

Vedic astrology places the house cusp in the centre of the sign of the ascendant but calculates houses using both equal house and whole house systems.

Much about Eastern or Vedic interpretation is similar to Hellenistic Astrology, which is the root of modern Western Astrology. Without the interruption to their practise that Western astrology suffered through religious persecution and the scientific revolution, Vedic astrologers mastered the art of using remedial measures to balance planetary strengths and weaknesses. The use of gemstones, mantras and rituals to appease the planetary deities remains prevalent today.

Hellenistic Astrology

Hellenistic Astrology arose from the theoretical works of the 'Hermetic treatises' attributed to the Egyptian author Hermes Trismegistus (thrice great). The Egyptian God Toth possessed similar qualities, and as the Greeks identified the Egyptian gods as their own, the 'identification Hermes-Toth was made before the end of the fourth century'. Hellenistic Astrology was practised in the Western Roman Empire until its fall in 476 CE

This knowledge is the basis for modern Western Astrology. Although we are grateful that these teachings managed to survive throughout the ages, recent translations of the original Greek and Latin texts have made it apparent that, not surprisingly, much was lost through the translation of many languages.

Along with the basic interpretations of planets, signs, houses and aspect relationships, these translations have revealed a number of Hellenistic Astrology practises and techniques that have possibly not been used since the 7th century. These include the use of The Joys of the Planets, the use of Whole Sign House Division, the use of Time Lord Systems, additional sign relationships and rulership considerations, an expanded set of lots, solar phases and lunar phenomena, and a number of planetary combinations not considered in modern astrology.

Hellenistic astrology uses only the planets observable with the naked eye. There was much more of an idea of fate in this tradition, although the chart was seen as being able to foresee the underlying nature of the native along with eternal events that might be of influence.]

There is a vocabulary associated with Hellenistic Astrology that at first appears to draw fairly hard lines in the sand: Malefic and Benefic planets, good and bad places are all part of the vernacular. To the Hellenistic astrologer these conditions were helpful in determining possible outcomes with greater detail.[The idea of Sect comes from Hellenistic astrology. Sect is related to whether the chart is Diurnal (daytime) or Nocturnal (night time). Diurnal and Nocturnal charts both have planets that prefer to be above or below the horizon, and whether they meet these conditions give further indications about how the energy of the planet might be manifesting.]

Arabic Astrology

The transmission of knowledge into Baghdad ensured that the Hellenistic roots of astrology could continue to exist.[Arabic scholars translated Hellenistic material and further expanded it, developing it into four main branches of astrological practise: Natal, Electional, Horary, and Mundane] Important additions to the study included observation of the cyclical patterns of Jupiter/Saturn conjunctions, the Solar Return chart, the Aries Ingress chart, and increased usage of the lots.

Sun Sign Astrology

R.H. Naylor was the first recorded newspaper astrologer in 1930. The horoscope he wrote for London Sunday Express upon the birth of Princess Margaret proved so popular that he began a regular column. Within the next decade Sun sign columns were to be found in many major newspapers and magazines. Their popularity with the general population is in large part what makes it possible that almost every person we meet in the western world, whether they profess a belief in astrology or not, will know what "sign" they were born under.

This development in astrology seemed both a curse and a blessing. As much as it served to keep the masses interested in astrology, it would, at times, create division amongst astrologers themselves. Some felt that this much simplicity did nothing to enhance the reputation of astrology and did not consider it a serious practise. Nonetheless, fans continued to grow, and columns are seen in most periodicals to this day.

Just like the differences in interpretation that are possible between a cross section of astrologers, Sun sign astrologers employ different tools to base their interpretations. Much of this would be related to the knowledge of what their audience is interested in. A writer for a fashion magazine geared towards young teenage girls would be approaching the subject differently than one writing for an edgy alternative weekly entertainment guide or a mainstream conservative newspaper.

The chart, however, usually places the Sun sign in question on the zero degree of that sign on the Ascendant. Daily horoscopes would pay careful attention to changes of the moon and its movement through the houses and signs, and build from these foundations. Saying something original every day that would appeal to a mass audience seems like a challenging task, but there are some astrologers who have truly mastered this form of astrology.

Psychological Astrology

Psychological astrology stems from the concepts developed by Swiss psychiatrist and psychotherapist Dr. Carl Gustav Jung. Jung, a student of Sigmund Freud, was interested in Eastern and Western philosophies, including astrology. His beliefs on archetypal relationships and psychological types are connected to astrology, and his thoughts on synchronicity are supported by the astrological concept of "as above, so below".

The two initial categories of astrological types are *introvert* and *extravert*. Although we might self-identify as one or the other, we should remember that they are considered "completely equivalent and compensate one another. They supplement each other." Each division of introversion and extroversion has a conscious and an unconscious side. Although a man may be inclined to love his conscious life as an extravert or an introvert, his unconscious mind has the tendency to turn the opposite way."

Conscious or unconscious extravert and conscious or unconscious introvert along with the four functions of Intuition, Perception, Thinking, and Feeling give us Jung's eight psychological types.

The relationship between the four functions and the elements in astrology is fairly natural: Fire is intuitive, Perception is related to Earth, Thinking to Air, and Feeling to water.

Having explored the chart of an individual through these functions, the astrologer can now help their client explore whether they are consciously acting in alignment with their general disposition and character.

Unlike horary based astrology, the psychological astrologer will not necessarily attempt to provide absolute answers to a question, but will instead ask meaningful questions and see the influence of the planets as more of a process whereby the person has a role in their development, rather than as a fixed or predetermined outcome. Forearmed with the awareness of the psychological psyche based on the chart, the astrologer can help guide a struggling client to work towards a life that is more in alignment with their inherent nature.

Evolutionary Astrology

Evolutionary Astrology is a system of chart analysis that focuses on identifying the evolutionary journey and purposes of the soul. From this perspective a person can gain clarity on the spiritual reasons for certain circumstances to occur in his or her life, based on the soul's life lessons and karmic influences from past lives into the current incarnation. The purpose is not only to identify patterns or characteristics in a chart, but to source the reasons for them to occur.

This body of knowledge was partially inspired by the works of Dane Rudhyar who introduced eastern philosophies to western astrology and wrote about the different levels of consciousness to consider upon analyzing a chart in his book *Astrology of Transformation*.

Raymond Merriman first introduced the term and concept in his book called *Evolutionary Astrology* in 1977; however, the name is more commonly associated with the teachings of Jeffrey Wolf Green and his 1985 book *Pluto, The Evolutionary Journey of the Soul,* and in parallel with the teachings of Steven Forrest who developed a vast body of knowledge in this field since the 1980's. Later, Maurice Fernandez developed a sub-stream to this orientation: *Astrology and the Evolution of Consciousness*

Evolutionary Astrology recognizes there are different evolutionary levels of consciousness that define how a chart can be expressed. These are:

1. Consensus state – which comprises roughly 75% of the population, is characterized by the fundamental tribal need to belong and have security, thus following without much doubt the prescribed values, codes of conducts, and thoughts of the society in which the person lives.

2. Individuated state – which comprises roughly 20% of the population, is characterized by people who are able to develop their own inner authority, and seek to live more authentically without so much need for external validation. They will typically challenge and question traditional beliefs rather than take what is prescribed by society for granted, and can be change-makers.

3. Spiritual state – which comprises roughly 5% of the population, is characterized by people who fully integrate the spiritual notion of universal oneness and alignment of their ego with spiritual principles in their everyday lives. Their values are universal and their approach essentially heart-centered.

4. A fourth level of evolution is also considered by some evolutionary astrologers, and consists of dimly evolved souls who are not fully cognitively functional, (sometimes because they have devolved from other levels of consciousness), comprising roughly 2-3% of the population.

These levels of evolution cannot be identified in the astrology chart, and therefore two people may be born the same time and place, and have the exact same chart, but express their identical charts through different levels of evolution.

Financial Astrology

Financial market timing is a growing area of Mundane Astrology whereby investors can analyze planetary ingresses and stations, aspects, eclipses, etc. to aid them in determining the best time to buy or sell.

The popularity of this branch of astrology began in earnest when computer technology made it possible to easily analyze the massive amounts of data needed to connect astrological phenomena to historical patterns.

Before delving into the astrology of finances, it is important to understand the markets themselves. An investor should understand market trends and be able to do an in depth analysis of timing cycles and historical trades before they can begin to make predictions on future trading success or failure. But once you have a solid understanding of market cycles and historical patterns, you can combine this knowledge with basic astrological principles and begin to predict trends.

The signs of the zodiac can be related back to what they rule: Taurus, for example, will bring up security needs. Major planetary transits through this sign might suggest investing in things that are tangible and tactile and related to the comfort and security needs of this earthy sign. Because Taurus is a fixed sign, it might be advisable to hold onto what you have instead of shaking things up. These would be long term investments that will slowly build over time.

Of course, the transiting planets also assist in determining activity. Cycles of the moon would be far more valuable for a day trader, vs. the transit of Pluto, which would be a long term consideration.

Reference: Merriman, Raymond A. *Basic Principles of Geocosmic Studies for Financial Market Timing,* Seek-It Publications West Bloomfield, MI, 1995

Uranian Astrology

Alfred Witte was the founder of the Hamburg School of Astrology. During his time in the military, Witte observed that there were certain positions in the sky where there was significantly more fired artillery shots, and surmised that these positions "likely" contained undiscovered planets. Based on these observations he went on to develop an entirely new type of astrology in which hypothetical planets are included. It came to be known as Uranian or Symmetrical Astrology.

The eight hypothetical planets in this system are Cupido, Hades, Zeus, Kronos, Apollon, Admetos, Vulcanos, and Poseidon. The six points that are considered the most sensitive are the Sun, Moon, and Midheaven, which are considered inner or subjective individual characteristics, and the Aries Point, Node, and the Ascendant which indicate outer or objective characteristics.

Foundational to Uranian Astrology is the use of the 90 degree dial, which is a tool designed to quickly illustrate aspect relationships and symmetrical patterns.

Witte grouped planets together according to their symmetry and called them *planetary pictures.* These pictures are based on a formula similar to calculations of the Arabic Parts. These relationships are expressed in diagrams called trees, which serve to illustrate the planetary pairs. The use of midpoint calculations is a technique developed in this model, but now quite popular outside this field of study. Any planet landing at the midpoint between two others is considered to hold the focus and concentrate the energy of the two planets.

Uranian astrology uses the Meridian house system. Transits, returns, and secondary progressions are calculated for actual and hypothetical planets. MC, Ascendant and Node, and Solar Arc directions feature prominently in this system. Chart interpretations in this model are more focused on events than on psychological development.

Mayan Astrology

Although the true origins of Mayan Astrology have been lost, enough information has remained to permit the rich perspectives of these ancient people to be interpreted today.

Mayan astrology does not interpret celestial events, but refers to their calendar for the influence that the energy of a certain day might reflect onto the individual.

There are several calendar groupings within the Mayan Calendar, the most important being the 260 day tzolkin. As a calendar it serves many purposes, including divination and the timing of rituals and events. But perhaps its most important use, and one that is still valid today, is as a matrix of personality types.

Further personality breakdowns include a repeating 20 day period called a *Day Sign*, 20 blocks of 13 days called *The Trecena*, which are a subset of day signs and function much like the Western astrology moon sign, *The Lord of the Night*, which is a nine day repeating pattern named for the gods of the underworld, 52 year cycles related to solar years. *The Phase of Venus* is also an important consideration in the evaluation of the individual.

Chinese Astrology

Chinese astrology is based on a lunar cycle, the year beginning with the second new moon after the winter solstice.

Each year is given the name of one of 12 animals: **Rat, Ox, Tiger, Rabbit, Dragon, Snake, Horse, Goat, Monkey, Rooster, Dog and Pig.** Each of these years is also connected to one of the five Chinese elements: *metal, water, wood, fire and earth.* By combining these 12 animals with the five elements, it takes 60 years for a complete cycle.

In addition to the year of birth, Chinese astrologers also look at the specific date and time of birth to glean more specific information about an individual. Each animal is also assigned to a month, and this sign represents the relationship between the individual and those who have responsibility for him or her—parents, teachers, and in later adult life, employers. The animal is assigned to the day of birth, which reveals how the individual will relate to those their own age, and rules a two hour time period, which will reveal the relationship with children. Once these four animals have been established (one for year, month, day and hour) they can be evaluated for conflict or harmony.

The chart also considers the four directions, and astrologers will look for elemental relationships that are connected to these directions. Animals that share element are considered to be harmonious, as are those that are in the same element. Animals that are 90 and 180 degrees apart are considered unfavourable relationships, unless there is one on every angle which has a neutralizing effect and creates harmony.

When casting a chart, the astrologer creates a four column table incorporating the Hour, Day, Month and Year of birth. A calendar with a 10 day week is used. Each day is represented by a "stem" and the months and hours of the day are represented by "branches" that relate to the animal signs. Each of the stems and branches is also related to an element.

Chinese astrology as it relates to the elements is very connected to matters of health, but is also used to establish the future opportunities and life cycles of the individual.

Donna Young is a practicing astrologer based out of Calgary, Alberta. She is a graduate of Kepler College who currently instructs in their certificate program, while working as well with private students. At the local level she organizes a monthly group for those who wish to share their knowledge and speak the language of astrology. She is the Canadian Satellite Representative for OPA where, in her desire to strengthen the community and promote the professional practise of astrology, she hosts international speakers and helps to organize provincial and national conferences of Canadian astrologers. Email: youngestdonna@gmail.com

Chapter 2

Building and Sustaining
a Successful Practice

A Practical and Spiritual Guide

Maurice Fernandez

The Great Gift

Astrology is destined to become an essential resource and a prominent profession in modern society. Its truth, elegance, and effectiveness will be made evident to the mainstream, and subsequently, recondition collective consciousness to rebalance the interrelationship between humans, nature, and the cosmos. This is not an astrological prediction, but rather a call for every astrologer and enthusiast to engage in making this vision a reality, perhaps within our lifetime. Astrology is too important, necessary and accurate a tool to remain a passion for fringe groups. We cannot waste the treasure of astrology nor limit it to a hobby or part time retirement plan only. *It is not ours to keep; we owe it to humanity.*

The effort to integrate astrology into the mainstream should not be motivated by a need for validation, better social status, or approval from the scientific community; many astrologers succumb to the pressure of external critics, sometimes to the point of trying to overregulate the use of astrology, and choking natural and creative development in the field. The light of astrology will naturally shine and dissolve resistance if, and only if, astrologers, remain worthy stewards, practicing it competently and with confidence. The reference for a responsible practice is not the pleasing of critics, but in the fruit of the labor—results speak for astrology.

Astrology can have a central role in the advancement of humanity and civilization. It is not a mere system or a job opportunity, *in its science, astrology reveals the existence of a cosmic intelligence, an order within cycles, and that our life has a meaning.* When the world discovers the immensity of astrology, we may even anticipate a revolution of consciousness—many people had their life completely transformed when they discovered this system, and the same can happen collectively.

Many voices are advising for caution about a widespread use of astrology, saying it may be misused and diluted the moment it becomes too accessible to the public, and therefore, it should remain protected under the auspices of a responsible few. These warnings have complete merit, but the risk of misuse exists within any powerful and effective resource. Indeed, the superficial or malevolent use of astrology can end up doing more disservice than any good—for example, if practitioners still try to match lovers by Sun sign trines or develop prejudice against people born with particular configurations, we can expect poor results. Astrology itself is irrefutable, but our competence using it must continually improve and pass tests of credibility. This is a work in progress, but fortunately, we now enjoy better educational programs and a support system to advance the profession and do astrology justice.

The time for astrology

I personally anticipate that astrology is poised to gain greater recognition in the mainstream during the next Jupiter-Saturn cycle beginning in 2020 at zero degrees Aquarius. This conjunction sets the tone for the socio-political climate that will condition the following twenty years, and since it will take place in Aquarius, representing higher knowledge and astrology itself, we can expect a change of mentalities in this regard, stimulating more curiosity for modalities like astrology that are an amalgam of science and spirituality. The subsequent transit of Pluto in Aquarius in 2023 is an equally strong force to support this direction. I suspect the generation born under the Uranus and Neptune conjunction in Capricorn, and Neptune in Aquarius, will serve as the catalyst to further integrate astrology into the mainstream in this sequence of time.

Challenges and Maturation of the Astrology Practice

The existing prejudices against Astrology serve their purpose. This time as the "black sheep," serves practitioners to redefine their use and skills so that the practice can mature into a more substantial school of thought. The vilification of astrology by the scientific and religious institutions has served astrologers, for this time of rejection has been used for internal work. Astrologers needed to outgrow misaligned uses and practices of astrology, such as rigid, deterministic approaches or unverified and simplistic interpretations, not to mention internal battles about "deep existential issues," such as which house system is valid. A more serious and comprehensive approach is increasingly more prevalent. Furthermore, thanks to the work of dedicated professionals, astrology now possesses a greater sense of its origins as efforts have been made to recover its history and ancestral uses. Meanwhile, the expansion of the body of knowledge through research and natural growth takes astrology into the future with deeper contents and more effective uses. Our practice of astrology is expanding, and with more rigor in the practice and greater tolerance for the diversity of approaches, it may now be ripe to better serve humanity.

Uranus-Nodes transits and astrology development

The late astrologer Robert Blaschke shared on several occasions that many important developments in the field have occurred during the transits of *Uranus to the North Node* (I personally see this with all major aspects, the conjunction, square, or trine of Uranus to the Nodal Axis). In modern astrology, Uranus is commonly considered the ruler of Aquarius, and is associated with astrology because it represents our capacity to observe our lives from an objective distance, from above, from the stars. So when Uranus forms important aspects to the Nodal Axis, a crucial developmental axis, we can see how development and emancipation of the field can occur.

For example, some prominent astrologers who had an important role in the development and revival of Astrology in our era were born in **1946 when Uranus was conjunct the North Node in Gemini** (among them Stephen Arroyo, Liz Greene, Ray Merriman, and Jeffrey Green). Liz Greene published her classic book "Saturn, a New Look at an Old Devil" in **1976 when Uranus was conjunct the North Node in Scorpio**. This was followed by another classic title "Astrology, Karma, and Transformation" by Arroyo in 1978. The Uranus/North Node in Scorpio conjunction in the late 70's was an important marker for the surge of psychological and spiritual astrology, where concepts about the growth of consciousness and eastern philosophical concepts of karma were more firmly assimilated into chart analysis. **In 1984, when Uranus was conjunct the South Node in Sagittarius,** UAC (United Astrology Conference), the largest astrology convention that unified all streams of astrology and US based organizations, was conceptualized, and two years later, materialized for the first time in San Diego. **1991, when Uranus conjuncted the North Node in Capricorn,** was the time when astrologer Robert Hand and his team initiated a pivotal project to translate ancient astrology texts and make these buried treasures more accessible to modern scholars. This was also around the time Kepler College was conceptualized and established to provide academic standards in the formal study of astrology. **Uranus has transited the North Node in Pisces (2007),** a time when astrology's network and community dynamics have rapidly expanded with the emergence of Facebook and Youtube; there is a flourishing of astrological groups and material on the internet, where discussions, studies, and the sharing of knowledge is growing at an exponential rate. Before that, the only video available online on the subject was of Carl Sagan dismissing astrology. This expanding reach has brought astrologers from different schools of thought closer together and helped dissolve some of the intellectual polarization and isolation in the discipline. It is interesting to see that when **Uranus conjuncted the South Node in Aries (2015),** a new, top-notch film production about astrology has been announced. "The Change of Gods" is based on astrologer Rick Tarnas's well received book, *Cosmos and Psyche,* and has the potential to be a change maker in the collective understanding of astrology.

Credibility within and without

Today, aspiring astrologers have access to a richer and more detailed curriculum as better study programs are made available. With improved educational programs, growing awareness about ethical standards, and broader content, people have more reason to confidently affirm themselves as astrologers and "come out of the closet." The internet age has its negative side to reckon with, notably the availability of sporadic knowledge that gives readers the impression that astrology can be learned on the quick without the rigor of established study programs. For this reason it is vital we continue to strive for more seriousness and consistency in astrology education.

The professional expansion of astrology faces challenges, most notably engendered by the poor credibility astrology holds in the scientific community and the lingering miseducation of what it truly is. As mentioned earlier, I have faith that results will speak for themselves, without the necessity to "force-prove" its validity and usefulness. We must remember that, ultimately, it is the world of science that is lacking, and not astrology; while astrologers are not without reproach, the real issue lies in current scientific references not being adequate to recognize and validate astrology's truths. *In other words, science is failing astrology, more than the other way around.*

An important step towards reconciling scientific discrepancies in 'proving' astrology's credibility depends on recognizing that astrology is not solely based on astronomy, but is also archetypal. It combines measurement with symbolism. The most immediate illustration of this dynamic is in the fact that the zodiacal constellations are not truly the same 30 degree size on the ecliptic; while there is an astronomical reference to the placement of these constellations, their division into 12 equal parts is artificial, which is reflective of the symbolism of their equal importance in the dynamics of consciousness. The constant attempt to match astrology with precise astronomical measurements makes it look incoherent. Understanding these arguments can provide astrologers with greater confidence in affirming their professional position. The first step in creating a successful practice is overcoming social insecurities and taking pride in fulfilling such an important role. We are messengers who connect the heavens with earth as we translate coded cosmic information into human language. Such a task belongs to the ranks of high priests, and commands reverence.

Astrology needs astrologers; we are keepers of the flame who must gather the courage to take this path less travelled and stand strong when contrarian winds are blowing. If we forsake investing the time, resources, and thought into astrology during this time of lesser popularity, it will fade back to the ethers. Supporting the profession includes study and research, but also buying astrology books, attending conferences, and joining workshops—investment in the field kindles the flame; we empower what we spend our money on. Whether we are conscious of it or not, becoming an astrologer is a gesture that goes beyond personal gains and gratifications; it is a calling to support the greater endeavor to make this vast body of knowledge widely available again to humanity.

Marking Statement: *Astrology is a fusion between astronomy and symbolism. Using only astronomy's references to appraise astrology, as scientists often do, stems from a fundamental misunderstanding of its nature. Scientists fail astrology, and astrologers must be aware of that.*

Marking Statement: *The first step in creating a successful practice in Astrology is in overcoming social insecurities and taking pride in fulfilling such an important role. Astrologers belong to the ranks of high priests, and should command reverence.*

Earth – Practical Considerations

Making a living

The development of astrology as a profession and its eventual integration into the mainstream depends on making the profession lucrative for practitioners. Because astrology is still on the fringes, the practice doesn't reach its full remunerative potential. Most of those who choose it as a profession are often driven by their passion and are willing to make financial sacrifices. Just like starving artists living from high inspiration, free from the bondage to overly regulated schedules, and indeed starving, astrologers do not commonly prioritize financial stability and prosperity. The pool of potential clients who are already informed about the value of astrology is relatively small, and even though awareness of astrology's accuracy and usefulness is growing, it is an ongoing effort to raise awareness. Astrologers are not only challenged to market their freelance practice, but also need to spend energy and time educating people and dispel existing prejudices and misconceptions about their occupation. These challenges commonly impede the flow of income, prompting many practitioners to rely on parallel sources of income, family funds, social security, or accept the compromise of living on a relatively low income. Fortunately, this is gradually changing with the internet being a "game changer" in the profession and opening many doors. We see more astrologers managing to do very well financially and supporting themselves comfortably.

Demographic references

Financial challenges in the profession directly affect demographic facts. For example, we know that **the great majority of astrologers are in their forties or older**, with a greater percentage of them above their fifties *(refer to the survey section of this book)*. This reflects the fact that people tend to turn to astrology as a second career or a retirement plan. *Very few children know they want to be astrologers when they grow up.* The financial reason is naturally to be considered in this regard—people choose to practice astrology only after they made money through another profession and are past the financial pressure to raise children. But beyond that, these demographic facts also reflect the reality that many people find out about astrology, and what it truly can offer, only later in their lives. The profession of astrology is not an option discussed in schools or encouraged by parents, so few know that it is even an option when they are making vocational choices. These demographic extremes can be better balanced as the demand for astrological services continues to increase.

Another figure reveals that there is **a significantly greater number of female astrology students and practitioners**. To some degree, the reasons for this imbalance may be that women can more easily afford to delve into astrology because they have the financial security of their husband's income. Men, in turn, can be more status-conscious and therefore more impressionable when it comes to the credibility arguments against astrology, making them more reluctant to adopt the practice. When we look back at the epoch when astrologers were more revered and sometimes even advisers to the prominent leaders, we can see that astrologers were then usually males. If women are less conditioned to strive for social status, they are freer to pursue their authentic choices with less need to impress public opinion. When comparing the practice of male and female astrologers, we can generally see an equal quality of service and expertise, so the skills are not gender biased. The difference in the percentage of participation in favor of women may indeed be attributed to these social circumstances.

Financial security and success

Establishing a lucrative practice begins with pricing services adequately. Successful careers in astrology will naturally engender better study programs, better services, more research, and the growth of the industry. Yet, often we find astrologers underpricing their services, too insecure to charge adequate amounts, or presenting professional lectures for relatively meager pay. We must realize that this "poverty mentality" hurts astrology and stunts its growth. If professionals cannot make a comfortable living, the long-term future of the practice is uncertain. Obviously, the answer is not in exorbitant pricing, but rather a genuine assessment of the value of the time, service, and expertise inherent in the practice (possibly offering a sliding scale option to remain accessible for students, or unemployed people). Clients are willing to invest resources when they know they get quality. Pricing our services justly serves to educate the public about the value of astrology, diminishing associations with fanciful entertainment and a frivolous expense. Potential clients can realize that astrology services are a worthy investment that can help them improve their circumstances and lead better lives. They will value astrology if we authentically present it as a worthy discipline. Success results from commanding respect, not from begging for attention.

Marking Statement: *A great majority of astrologers come to it as a second career or a retirement plan, often because they discover astrology later in their lives, since it was not mentioned in their formative years. As the profession grows, more astrologers manage to do well financially and support themselves and their families, making it possible for younger people to become astrologers.*

Education and Mastery

To make a good living, we must offer worthy services. Quality is naturally attractive. In order to do astrology justice we must have skilled practitioners. Acquiring strong skills depends on the effectiveness of our own educational process. Ideally, our expertise will encompass *width, depth,* and *ascension.*

Width can be reflected in self-studies where the person exposes him or herself to the wide variety of views and subjects in astrology, exploring the different techniques and approaches through books, online material, and conference lectures. **Depth** comes from focused training and immersion under the closer supervision of a teacher or mentor who will organize knowledge, define boundaries, and bring rigor to the study and practice, possibly through a certification process. **Ascension** can be reflected in continued research once the person is fluent and professionally active. He or she makes new realizations from direct experience with client work. Once tested, the new insights add to the body of knowledge, to elevate astrology and enhance its use. The fruits of research and new insights not only enrich astrology as a whole, but can also differentiate a practitioner from another as unique perspectives are developed.

On an educational level, in this day and age of computerization in which charts are created with the click of a mouse, it is important for students to understand the building blocks of a chart. Aspiring astrologers will benefit from having a general knowledge of the history of astrology and learn how it grew into its present form. Accordingly, having a general background in astronomy and having an idea about how to draw charts manually is important. These foundational components serve a healthy development, even if they may not seem initially completely necessary for chart analysis. It is part of the process of making the connection between the two-dimensional chart wheel printed on paper and our physical understanding of the sky above us.

Marking Statement: *The development of astrology as a profession immediately depends on making the profession lucrative. Astrologers need to transcend a poverty mentality. The more they invest in the field, the more they will be able to eventually charge for their services.*

Marking Statement: *Success results from commanding respect, not from hiding, or conversely, begging for attention. Quality is naturally attractive.*

Building Blocks of a Successful Practice

DIY or professional help

Upon launching an astrology practice, the astrologer must also develop management skills to be able to lead a successful independent practice. As freelance practitioners, we normally have no boss, corporate system, or business partner to provide a framework and care for the numerous logistical details inherent in sustaining a practice. Such independence is a blessing that comes with a high cost. It can be wonderful to regulate our own schedule, conduct part of our work online from home, and have the freedom to choose our rhythm and developmental course. This freedom requires the astrologer to perform peripheral tasks, such as marketing, accounting, and sometimes even graphic design to maintain the practice. We can hire professionals to handle these tasks, but commonly our budget is limited in the early stages of our practice and it becomes more practical to perform them ourselves.

Today, many services can be performed independently as an abundance of Do-It-Yourself applications are available online. People can now build their own websites and do a significant portion of their promotion through social media platforms for free. However, we should not overlook the importance of hiring those who can offer expert services for us. Hiring a professional can make a significant difference in the client response we elicit. Remember that 'quality is attractive'—if we save money building our own website, but the website is too simplistic or looks amateurish, we have not truly saved money, but rather devalued who we are. Having a website is one of the most important career tools for astrologers today—it puts us on the map, it is our business card, our professional identity, and it has to represent us authentically. A website must be responsive to the smartphone and tablet formats, and include an online store. Every few years, new standards require an upgrade. Our work relies on the confidence our clients place in us, and a quality website inspires trust in our services. The website has to be easily navigable with clear information, offer valuable content, and look aesthetically pleasing. The better all these elements come together, the greater the potential business it can generate. It doesn't have to be glamorous, merely professional. If our design skills are not up to the task, hiring the services of a professional web designer and developer may be a worthwhile investment. Additionally, hiring a professional can help with wider search engine recognition and direct greater traffic to our website.

Marketing and visibility

With a website online, the next step is to proactively gain visibility. The website is passive; we must not solely rely on random visits but actively invite people to explore our services as we update our website content. One of the main difficulties I encounter with astrologers in the beginning stages of their practice is developing the confidence and skill to market themselves adequately. Gaining visibility and building a clientele takes time, patience and dedication.

The best marketing strategy is word of mouth; given the intimate nature of an astrology reading, potential clients will naturally respond to personal recommendations. Organic and gradual growth promises solidity, but at the same time, we need to sell our services assertively and confidently. One way to overcome shyness about promoting our services is to remember that it is not about us, but about the greater good that astrology can provide—we need to do it for astrology and for humanity. Being proactive, and tactful, in our promotional efforts naturally contributes to the growth of our practice, and simultaneously elevates the role of astrology.

Word of mouth begins close to home with family and friends. When we inform our peers that we can read charts, many of them will be curious, forget their own prejudices, and ask for a reading. There is a mystique to astrology that is very attractive to people, even if they have reservations based on the negative press or see it as little more than an amusing fortune-telling experience. For us, it is an opportunity to educate people about the deeper benefits of astrology and have test subjects to gain chart reading experience from. When we deliver a quality reading, the initially skeptical friend will likely share his or her experience with others. This can only succeed when we are completely open about the fact that we are astrologers and are not hiding behind substitute labels; doing a bit of 'chest thumping' doesn't hurt either. If we are self-conscious about charging friends or family a fee, making it donation-based can resolve that concern.

An important step in building a practice is to create a mailing list. Each client, student, or person inquiring about our services must be included in our data base under specific categories, so we may send them information about our workshops and activities. *Mailing lists are an asset*, and are essential to networking; as time passes, our mailing list grows, reflecting the expansion of our work.

The internet

We have to thank the internet for being a crucial catalyst in widening the scope of the profession of astrology and making it more lucrative. Astrologers are no longer dependent on their local environment to draw clients from, but can reach an international audience through the internet. Whether we create Facebook pages and share our blogs about current transits, or produce short videos or podcasts, we can now more easily gain visibility and reach the world, rather inexpensively. We can schedule phone readings via Skype, and charge for our services through online commerce, most easily through Paypal. While we may not appeal to everyone, our reach can be global.

It is important to keep knowledge circulating, as this naturally brings interest in what we do. Even if we do not sell services immediately by sharing our perspectives online or through publications, we enter the collective consciousness. Recurrent positive exposure increases the trust among the general public. However, as useful as social media platforms can be, we must be creative in the way we use them and focus on offering quality. Importantly, we must write well, informatively and with inspiration. Blogs in which too much astrological lingo is used and the information is abstract will drain the reader. People have relatively short attention spans, so we have to be concise, profound, and impactful.

The Mountain Astrologer magazine (and similar publications) is another important resource for astrologers, standing today as the most important astrology magazine in the market. It is available both in print and online versions and caters to professionals and beginners alike. Writing an article for The Mountain Astrologer is a constructive way to share our insights and expertise; however, unlike a blog that can easily be published online, submitted articles will undergo editorial scrutiny and will need to match the standards of the magazine. That makes the effort even more effective in elevating our credibility, for if we are published in The Mountain Astrologer it will expose our articles to a target audience. Placing ads in the magazine can also be effective, particularly if you target an audience who has some background in astrology.

By publishing our insights online or in articles, we may be concerned about other people stealing the content and taking credit. The risk is there, and readers may indeed "borrow" some of our ideas, and "forget" to quote their source; however, since they do not have the foundation that led to these ideas, their use is usually ephemeral. Knowledge also travels through the unconscious, and in some cases, people may tap into it literally through the ethers. As a general rule, when we release material to the world, whether freely or for sale, we must always make sure it comes with a *copyright* *disclaimer*. Overall, I believe that the benefits of sharing outweigh the risks of serious plagiarism. Releasing our observations and ideas to the world creates space within ourselves for new realizations to emerge into our consciousness.

Marking Statement: *We must find the proper balance between budgeting and retaining quality—knowing when to perform some managerial tasks ourselves, and when outsourcing can make a significant difference in the client response we generate. Spending time on tasks we are not proficient in can be time diverted away from remunerative client work.*

Marking Statement: *Make sure the material you publish online or in print has a copyright notice and that your website is listed. A copyright notice should contain:*
- *the word "copyright"*
- *a "c" in a circle (©) – (alt/ctrl/c)*
- *the year of publication*
- *the name of either the author or the owner of all the copyright rights*

Apply

Marking Statement: *With online platforms such as Skype (free phone for consultations), Facebook (free networking and community exchange), You-tube/Vimeo (mini-videos platforms), SoundCloud (audio podcasts) and Paypal (online payment service), it has never been easier to expand our practice internationally. Such extensive reach through the internet can be the lifeline for a full-time astrologer. (Note that the reader should do their own research to assess which online platform works best for them. The listed platforms are mere suggestions and should not be subscribed to without prior research).*

Multiple services to our practice

Relying exclusively on astrological consultations to generate income may not be enough to sustain us financially, particularly in the initial years of our practice while we are building a reputation and cultivating a returning clientele. In the light of the common 'single reading' format of astrological counseling, we need a considerable circulation of new clients. Returning clients commonly come back for readings every 6 months to a year. Therefore, expanding our range of services may be essential, particularly for those who would like to practice astrology full-time.

An important guiding principle is to never refuse clients, unless we feel unsafe or recognize that the client has become co-dependent. Once we open shop, clients choose us, not the other way around. For that reason, it is important to advertise our services correctly and precisely to attract the type of clientele that will truly benefit from what we offer. For example, if we do not wish to attract clients who seek a fortune-teller, our website must clearly describe the orientation of our practice. However, if a client is informed about our services and is willing to pay the listed fee, it is our role to be there for them and relinquish possible whims and biases that would deter us from taking the job. We must show up and deliver what we promise. Our devotion to the practice pays off as we generate a positive energetic flow to our work.

Readings consultations

To begin with, we can offer diverse types of readings. Some astrologers have different rates for personal chart readings and relationship, vocational, or transit analysis sessions, while others offer all-inclusive prices. We can encourage clients to come back for readings by reducing our fee for a second session within a certain period of time, or send them a note on their birthday suggesting a consultation to have a look at the planetary cycles for the coming year. Depending on personal expertise, astrologers can add Horary reading (erecting a chart for a specific question being asked), or Electional reading (finding an auspicious date for an event), to their menu.

Importantly, our *time to prepare for readings must be well managed.* Some astrologers, particularly beginners, can take hours, even days, to prepare for a reading. These long hours are not compensated adequately in the fee. While it is natural to require more preparation as we refine our skills, this may not be sustainable in the long run. As we gain confidence and expertise, our preparation time for readings must diminish without compromising quality. We must also remember that a good deal of information is revealed while we are interacting in real time with the client. We may discover that the reading has a life of its own, and find ourselves coming up with spontaneous new insights resulting from the synergy with the client. Something happens in the direct experience that cannot be anticipated during preparation time; it is important to trust this process, and our knowledge.

Writing

Beyond a reading practice, an astrologer can generate a regular income by writing periodic astrology columns; they can be published online, in a local newspaper, or, if the opportunity arises, in a major publication. The benefit lies not only in the possible pay for the column, but also in gaining exposure and attracting potential clients for readings. While we would discourage writing superficial entertainment columns that harm the credibility of astrology, these columns can be very valuable if written well and containing serious analysis.

Teaching classes and workshops

I often recommend that people launching practices teach astrology classes for beginners as a useful way to increase the volume of their practice. They may feel intimidated by such a suggestion, believing that they do not know enough to teach, however, to quote Yogi Bhajan, a yoga master, "If you want to learn something (well), teach it!" Creating a course curriculum requires us to organize our knowledge, and in the process, we may find out that there are holes to fill. By teaching, we inevitably deepen our own understanding on the subject, and that serves us to become more professional in every aspect of our practice. Moreover, from a financial point of view, teaching a beginner's class provides a more substantial income as participants commit for a longer period of time to study, whether it be a twelve week course or a year-long program. I remember teaching classes for two students in my living room, and these classes were extremely valuable experiences. I was passionate about introducing people to astrology, it gave me experience, and the extra income was welcomed. From living room classes with several students, the practice grew into an international career. However, small initial attendance was never a deterrent for offering the classes.

How to be an adult in a relationship

As our teaching skills are refined, we can eventually offer **weekend workshops** focused on a specific theme for more advanced students. You can choose an attractive and popular topic, such as *relationship dynamics* or *vocational direction*, and advertise the workshop through social media, your mailing list, or with the help of a local astrology organization. This workshop immersion format doesn't require an extensive commitment from participants, since it is a one-time meeting, and can be tremendously impactful.

Public speaking

Presentations can be organized through a local astrology organization, which commonly offers study meetings with a new speaker every month. These organizations are usually supportive of new talent, so it is worth submitting a proposal for an inspiring lecture, (you can see a list of astrology organization available at the end of this book). A strong first impression is critical, so an initial presentation should showcase your very best. If you have flexible options, choose a date for the event that is astrologically supportive for your chart.

Public speaking may not appeal to everyone. It is supposedly one of the most common fears people have, but I believe the discomfort and intimidation come from not addressing the issue correctly. To begin with, the astrology audience is not the most formal one out there, and people are usually supportive and encouraging. A good way to tackle public speaking anxiety may be to approach it as a conversation with peers. Having notes to rely on and using the aid of a visual presentation is always good strategy, but additionally, it may be beneficial to encourage questions from the audience and avoid conveying information in a dry fashion.

Public speaking opportunities can expose one to larger audiences through *astrology conferences*. Every astrologer can submit a proposal to present a lecture at these conferences; this is a good reason to become a member of astrology organizations as we can be kept abreast of announcements about upcoming conferences. Initially, the astrologer can be offered an introductory slot or a formal slot. These introductory slots are usually unpaid and are shorter in duration, but they serve as an entry into the international conference circuit.

Community, organizations, and the lone astrologer

Some astrologers build their practice without much contact with other colleagues and community members and pursue their career as loners. Others choose to be involved in the community of astrologers, whether they join an international organization or a local group. Joining a community serves the astrologer who is commonly very isolated in the mainstream—it is an opportunity to find other people who speak one's language. Moreover becoming a member of one or more organizations supports the profession and makes astrology stronger; it is a personal gesture for the collective good. These organizations also commonly organize events and conferences that can serve as important networking opportunities. They also typically produce magazines where astrologers can publish their articles and research. Ultimately, joining an astrology organizations does not interfere with one's individual practice, but usually adds to it.

Marking Statement: *We can expand the range of services for the practical aim of increasing our pool of clients and adding meaning to our practice. Our income can come from different sources, such as private reading consultations, weekly classes, column writing, or public speaking opportunities. The astrologer must test his or her skills and discover the best avenue of expression. Some astrologers will do well combining all these avenues, while others will do better focusing on one specific type of service.*

Whatever your choice of practice, make sure you bring meaning and creativity to it.

Marking Statement: *Saying 'Yes" to your practice and keeping a positive attitude can naturally invite clients. We must be aware of possible confidence issues that can sabotage our growth, such as when we make excuses for not seeing clients and rejecting public speaking opportunities. It is important to be available for anyone who responds to our services, unless there are security concerns. To avoid attracting the "wrong clients," make sure that you describe your approach and the nature of your services clearly on your website and in conversations.*

Sky – Astrology as a Spiritual Practice

Spirit and Matter

Most professions have at their core an incentive to serve and answer a need—whether we are cooks, lawyers, doctors, or construction workers, we contribute to humanity and its advancement. The service that astrology provides is to introduce a cosmic perspective to our lives. Astrology reveals that there is a Truth to our lives, connecting us individuals to an all-encompassing intelligent order encrypted in astral patterns. Few, if any, other professions provide the service to directly align our lives to the master plan of the universe.

The astrologer can only try to measure up to the endeavor of interpreting and communicating these symbolic planetary patterns. This task goes beyond intellectual training; in its highest forms, it requires the person to be a clean channel and strike a proper balance between spirit, mind, emotions, and matter. This does not necessarily imply that the astrologer is a psychic, for astrology is measurable and does not necessarily require extraordinary gifts of clairvoyance, per se. By 'clear channels' I speak of the need to remain as neutral as possible in our minds and hearts while maintaining a strong intention to serve the collective well-being.

Mind and Matter

Use

When we are clear channels, our perceptions and understanding of celestial knowledge are unclouded by personal biases and projections. We can therefore be more perceptive and accurate in our interpretations. As we learn from mentors and literature, knowledge must be verified though direct experience and not remain theoretical. Otherwise, not only will we rely on inaccurate information, but will keep passing it on to the next generation. For example, there is a widespread misperception among astrologers that the sign of Gemini represents superficiality, or that it relates to matters of the immediate environment; yet, if we check with the "real life" Geminis, *Use* we see they are often the deepest thinkers and multi-cultural world citizens who go way beyond their immediate environment. The reason astrological stereotypes persist is that too many astrologers regurgitate whatever information they took in without bothering to verify the knowledge in actual reality. Mind must meet matter; knowledge must be applied in experience to prove itself. If we employ and test our knowledge, astrology can remain vital and grow. *OuR CoNSciousness is evolving*

Moreover, good astrologers live and breathe astrology every day—it is not something they only spend a couple of hours a week on. This implies knowing the ongoing transits, checking the charts of events or people who make news headlines. If we happen to have a bad day, or meet someone special, we look at the charts and check to see how it shows astrologically. This helps us learn from observation.

Article

Love matters

To perform our role as astrologers, a lifestyle must be adapted to match this calling. To begin with, let us *practice what we preach* and conduct ourselves in an authentic, honest, and caring manner. It goes without saying that ethical standards of confidentiality and respect are essential. When we recurrently deal with client's vulnerabilities and misalignments, it is easy to become self-righteous and know 'what they ought to do.' Astrologers can sometimes forget that what seems obvious in a chart is not a magic formula that can instantly be applied to the client's life—we deal with humans, emotions, where change in real life is slower than the push of a button. To avoid preaching, caring and patience, with a good dose of humor about ourselves are essential. Our role as astrologers is to bring perspective and make suggestions, not to impose evolution or solutions on our clients.

Leading a healthy lifestyle is important to keep our channel clear. On a physical level, it can imply adopting mindful practices such as yoga or meditation, and nourishing our connection with nature. On an emotional level, it implies cultivating awareness of ourselves and developing our emotional intelligence. Astrologers can easily become overly cerebral as they perform in an analytic mode. Developing a more holistic lifestyle can activate other parts of the self for better balance.

Marking Statement: *the role of the astrologer goes beyond the mental application of our knowledge. As we serve as interpreters of a higher universal order, our way of living must support the performance of this delicate task. Mind must meet spirit, heart, and matter.*

Being an Astrologer

ARTICLE

We've established how valuable and important the practice of astrology is, but what does it really take to become a professional, and then how does that work realistically? Being an astrologer in this day and age requires a love for independence and the capacity to be self-motivated. It is a profession that can be successful when the passion for it exists, because as freelancers, we are our own engine and we need creative skills to make it work. This also implies that the astrologer needs to be fully visible, and will do best not hiding behind substitute labels, such as 'counselor;' they will likely attract more clients when **affirming confidently that they are astrologers**. This will also do astrology service.

The wonderful benefit of being an astrologer, besides doing something one truly cares for and enjoys, is the flexibility to work at our own pace. Since a great deal of the work is done online, it can be done from anywhere in the world where there is a reliable internet connection. Many astrologers work on weekends when clients are more available to come for classes or readings.

The lifestyle of an astrologer allows for a flexible schedule, and keeps people connected through the practice or community events. Fellow astrologers are usually interesting people because they typically are free-thinkers, creative, and non-conformists. A full time astrologer who develops a teaching or public speaking practice can also enjoy many travel opportunities. A good number of full-time astrologers find themselves traveling the world to teach and or speak, and in the process, encounter diverse cultures and form wide social and professional networks.

Include for Article

Are you?

Are you adventurous and willing to venture outside your comfort zone to find meaning?

Are you creative and self-motivated enough to manifest goals without external prompting or validation?

Do people interest you? Are you fascinated by life, and do you care about the well-being of others?

Are you humble enough to admit your own ignorance, laugh at yourself, and learn from every person and every moment?

Do you agree that there is a greater all-encompassing intelligent order in the universe, and that this order serves our ultimate freedom?

Are you able to see a whole life in a single drop, and timeless truth in one symbol? *holo gram*

Do you spontaneously look up at the sky when you are out at night?

Would you like to lead an international career, empower people, and elevate consciousness?

If so, you may very well be a natural born astrologer!

Follow the calling…a better world needs more astrologers.

Maurice Fernandez, currently serves as the OPA President. He is the author of the books Neptune, the 12th House and Pisces (New Edition), and Astrology and the Evolution of Consciousness—Volume One. He also has contributed chapters to books, such as The New Generation and Transpersonal Astrology. He has organized several astrology conferences, notably the River of Stars in Hawaii. Through his 25 years of practice, Maurice has forged a worldwide reputation of depth and excellence for his certification program, publications, and counseling work as an Evolutionary Astrologer. Website: www.mauricefernandez.com

Chapter 3

Consultations, Counseling, and Ethical Considerations
Sandra Leigh Serio

As working astrologers we are responsible for establishing practices that enable us to work with clients in a professional and courteous fashion. This chapter will cover the basics of setting up a practice, tips on conducting consultations in a professional manner and maintaining ethical standards and healthy boundaries for the client.

Setting up the Consultation

Your equipment
- Computer or Tablet
- Astrology Software — *Need*
- Telephones or (Skype) — *Need*
- Recording Equipment — *Need*
- Printers
- Private Office Space

Computer or tablet

Whether you need to generate charts or do more complex research, a computer is essential in today's astrology study and practice. You will need a reliable astrology software to make sure your calculations are accurate and the different daylight savings time are taken into consideration. Consider a laptop if you travel or a desktop model if you work in a single location. If you only have funds for one device, consider a large-screen laptop that serves as both a stationary and transportable piece of equipment. Many astrologers have a laptop, tablet and/or desktop computer (tablets may eventually replace laptops due to their efficiency, portability and ease of remote storage capabilities.)

Deciding on a PC or a MAC may come down to which astrological software you prefer. Some programs are not easily interchangeable between the two platforms. Research your options and decide what computer and software will best serve your needs. If deciding on a MAC, there are programs that are compatible with most, if not all PC software.

Landlines and cell phones

Many astrologers conduct readings over the phone. Decide if you want to use a landline or a cell phone to set up your appointments and conduct sessions. The advantage of a landline is that you can set it up as a business line, thereby giving you free advertising and easy accessibility when people search for an astrologer online or through telephone records. Landlines often have clearer connections with fewer dropped calls. However, you can't take your landline with you when you travel or leave your office unless you opt for a call forwarding feature from your telephone provider. Landlines can be an added expense because most people with landlines also have cell phones. However, having two lines (a landline and a cell phone) can have the advantage of defining one of the lines for business purposes, making it a tax deductible expense. If you decide to only use a cell phone, you're less likely to miss a call, as your cell phone will accompany you wherever you go.

If you don't want to give out your cell number there are providers that offer a free service allowing you to have a separate number for voice mail, email and texting. You can even have voicemails sent to your computer as an email message. From the variety of options, you can select which works best for your schedule and lifestyle.

Recording your session

Recording your session is recommended. Today's smartphones are equipped with sound recording options. For landlines, many astrologers use a digital recorder that can be connected to their landline so that both sides of the conversation are recorded. Recording the conversation is legal as long *as the client is aware of being recorded.* Some astrologers use Skype and record straight from their computers or from an online service. There may be minimal fees for a recording application. These services upgrade and change frequently, so it is best you do your research independently. Make sure that the quality of sound is adequate for your professional needs. You may also want to purchase a headset with a microphone to reduce background noise.

If you use a digital recorder you need a way to transfer the recording to the computer and email it to the client through a large file transfer service (such as hightail or wetransfer). You can also make a CD for the client (considering that CDs have a maximum capacity of 80 minutes, and are becoming outdated today). Either method may require appropriate software.

Recording policies

When you record your sessions make sure you have a policy set up ahead of time. If you are doing it as a courtesy to the client and the recording fails, you don't have to repeat the session as long as you make it clear in advance that the recording is not guaranteed. You can suggest the client take written notes in case the session fails to record properly. You can also allow the client to record the session on their end, thereby taking the pressure and responsibility off you. Quality equipment is a must if you are including the recording as one of the perks, because if the recording fails, you will have to make amends with the client, which may involve repeating the session.

Printers

Owning a printer can be useful, especially if you want to provide the client a printed copy of his or her natal chart. Being able to print material can also be useful for handout materials if you teach or lecture. There are wireless printers that have their own email address so you can email the chart directly to the printer.

Office space

You will need a suitable office space where you can conduct sessions in privacy, whether you see your clients in person or speak over the phone. Many astrologers prefer the convenience of working from home. Others prefer to work out of a rented office. The benefits of renting an office are that it sets a strong boundary between your private and professional lives and precludes interruptions that often occur while working at home. Research your options and see what is most suitable for your particular needs.

In either case, make the space comfortable, private, and secure. If working from home and you have pets, children or other people in your house, be sure to separate them from your office space. Decide if you are going to offer refreshments. The least you should offer is water and access to a restroom. You can also set up a nearby space for boiling water for tea, but refrain from over accommodating your clients. Keep it simple and to the point, as they are coming for a session, not a social gathering.

Booking appointments, fees, payment

You can schedule in person, over the telephone, or online, depending on which fits your lifestyle and professional image. When booking a client, request accurate birth information. Always ask for the source of the information: a birth certificate, mother's memory, or a third party? Stress the importance of accurate data for the best possible session; let them know they may be able to locate their birth time in the hospital where they were born, if it is not provided on the birth certificate. Additionally, make sure to explain to new clients what the reading is about, tell them what, if anything, to bring to the session and clearly explain your payment and recording policy.

Fees

Before you book your clients decide on the time allotment for your sessions and the fee. Some astrologers have sliding fees for their clients, but this can be a slippery slope as you cannot verify the financial status of your clients and their status can change over time. If you have a sliding scale, make it clear to the client that you want to keep this lower fee confidential. You could also have a 'friends and family' discount.

Setting your fees has to be in accordance with your level of expertise and where you live and work. Prices in New York City will be higher than in a small town in the Midwest. If you have authored books and are in high demand your fees will likely be higher than the average professional. Set fees you feel are worthy of your time. Be willing to review your fee structure every two or three years to see how it compares to the current cost of living and to the quality of service you offer. Are you now appearing regularly on radio or television or lecturing domestically and internationally? Have you written a book or column that is well received? Has inflation made an impact? The best advice I can give you is to *never* lower your fees, no matter what. Instead, you can offer occasional incentives and special offers. Many astrologers experience a slow period after the holiday season and offer discounts for a designated period of time. Others give birthday discounts.

I personally do not offer discounts or trades because I feel astrology services are comparable to legal advice, therapy, or health care. These professionals rarely offer discounts or trades, though quite a few lawyers will do pro bono work. Generally, it is not politically correct and, in some professions, illegal to do so. However, if you are starting out, offering specials may be appropriate to attract clients until you gain more experience.

Consider the length of the session and newness of the client when setting your fees. Many astrologers offer different fees for first sessions and subsequent visits depending on whether they will cover forecasting or just focus on the natal chart. Some astrologers who normally do hour-long sessions will offer 1/2 hour sessions as a follow-up, while others will always set a fixed time for the session and never deviate from that. Astrology sessions typically range from 45 to 90 minutes, with some running 2 hours. Astrologers with a strong emphasis on fixed signs or Saturn in their charts may naturally gravitate to longer sessions. Mutable sign astrologers may be more flexible and prefer shorter sessions. Overall, what matters is the quality and effectiveness of the session; how long it takes to make a good session depends on each astrologer.

Payment

There are several ways to process payments. Consider if you want to receive the entire payment before the session (this is usually a good choice) or prefer a deposit to hold the time slot and accept full payment when the session is complete. If you accept a deposit before the session, it will require more paperwork and bookkeeping for you. Additionally, decide on a cancellation policy. Some astrologers charge for the session whether the client shows up or not. Others are more flexible. If you have a 24 hour cancellation policy be sure the client is aware of it. Inquire how the client wants to pay when you are setting up the session so there aren't any misunderstandings. Many astrologers accept online credit card payments or use PayPal. A credit card processing device can also be plugged into computers, tablets or cell phones. Remember that credit card fees can run 3 - 4% per transaction per customer. And of course, you can always accept checks, money orders and cash. It is advisable to have the checks mailed to you ahead of time.

When setting up a credit card account for payment remember that some unenlightened credit card companies will not accept you if you are listed as an astrologer. They erroneously classify you as a fortuneteller. While it is important to be open about our occupation and serve as an example to the public, if you are running into roadblocks you can list yourself as a consultant. If you have any degrees or licenses that qualify, list yourself as a therapist or a psychotherapist. The term psychotherapist is broad and will be accepted, even without licensure but with graduate degrees. Be sure to check with your state to see what is legally acceptable.

If you have another business title, i.e. massage therapist, artist, accountant, programmer, software engineer, etc., you may be able to use that as your professional designation. Consider that the credit card company will want to see your business card. As a rule of thumb, if you have the choice, favor credit card processing companies that will not discriminate against astrology and stand proud of the service you provide. This is the way we will change mentalities about being an astrologer. Before the final approval, the credit card company sometimes sends a person to your place of business to check out its validity, so don't lie on your application.

The actual consultation

Preparing for a chart is important, as it gives you a *feel* for the person and information about the chart ahead of time. Some astrologers spend 20-60 minutes in preparation. New practitioners may spend a much longer time on the chart. As you refine your expertise, less preparation time is usually needed. Always keep within your established time limits. If you go over with a client, they may expect it every time they have a session with you. It is not a professional approach.

Once you complete the preparation, I personally suggest  breaking down the session into three sections:

1. **Welcoming the client** - introducing yourself and informing the client exactly what to expect in the session (if you have not already done so).

2. **The session** - analysis of the natal chart and personality tendencies and/or progressions, transits and other predictive techniques; conversation with the client, maintenance of ethical guidelines, honoring time limits.

3. **Closing the session** - making time for final questions, collecting fees if needed, information about follow-up sessions.

First things first

First impressions are crucial to a harmonious relationship between the client and the astrologer. Dress appropriately, greet the client by name and present a positive attitude by offering a friendly handshake. Seat the client in a comfortable chair and sit facing them. Sitting at a desk can present an unspoken message of superiority. You want the seating to be comfortable so they can relax. You are there to serve and want to give the client your full attention. Making the client feel special is of utmost importance. This is their time and you are there to support and empower them through the chart reading process.

Here is a true story of what NOT to do at the beginning of a session. Many years ago, a friend told me she had booked an appointment with a well-known astrologer who was living in the area at the time. She was very excited about her appointment and talked about it with joyful anticipation for days. We agreed to meet at the end of her session to discuss her experience. When she arrived she had a disappointed and angry look on her face. She revealed that when she sat down in the office, a video of the astrologer doing a lecture was playing in the background and the astrologer kept looking over her head as he watched himself on camera, completely distracted and not focusing at all on her or her chart. She was so offended and, as the good Scorpio true to her sign, grabbed her things and walked out without a word. The astrologer offered no apology, nor inquired as to the reason for her taking leave. Behavior like that makes the practice of astrology look unprofessional and further perpetuates the myth that astrology is not a serious profession. This is an extreme example of the client feeling neither welcomed nor valued.

After welcoming the client, offer the client water and indicate where the restrooms are. Explain how the session will proceed and let them know if you like to answer questions during the session or at the very end. Verify the birth information of the client, and if you are recording the session, be sure to turn the device on.

The Session Itself

Astrological jargon

Astrology is a language. We think in it, speak in it, and identify everything in our environment with reference to it, but speaking the language to a client who knows little about astrology is unprofessional and even rude. How would you feel if you went to your doctor and he or she began speaking in medical terms about your condition that were over your head? The same holds true in an astrology session. Limit your astrological jargon; if you use any of it, follow it with an explanation of what you mean by certain terms like a *grand trine in water*. Better yet, avoid using astrological language if at all possible. The client has enough information to absorb and needs his or her mind to be uncluttered by unnecessary details.

Listen to the client

Be sure you are listening to the client, not just rendering information. If your client relates something painful or speaks with a lot of emotion, reflect the words back to the client so they know you are compassionate and care about their predicament. While you express compassion and understanding, guide your client forward and avoid getting absorbed in their own reality.

When I was in graduate school getting a degree in psychology we were asked to practice counseling a fellow student while the instructor observed us. When it was my turn, I dialogued with the client for about one minute to see what the issue was and then spouted off about why the client was feeling that way and what I thought could be done about it. I must have gone on for about 5 to 7 minutes when I caught the instructor glaring at me. Later I was told that I talked too much and that a therapy session was about *listening* to the client, not rendering my personal diagnosis or advice for their problem. As an astrologer, we are used to being more proactively engaged in guiding our clients and giving them information. And while we are astrologers and *not* therapists, it is important to develop listening skills. In a session with a client we should provide guidance, but also listen to the client talk and reflect back what they are saying. As astrologers we need to maintain a good balance between giving information and analyzing the birth chart, and between listening and reflecting.

Counseling skills for astrologers

There are organizations and groups that offer counseling skills training for astrologers. Most of these groups include guidelines on ethics and offer peer group work. Some even offer psychological techniques that aid the client. ISAR (International Society for Research and Development), NCGR (National Council for Geocosmic Research), and OPA (The Organization for Professional Astrology) are among those who provide this invaluable training. If you do not have a counseling background, this training is essential and can help you lead more effective astrological sessions.

Why clients are dissatisfied

I have run psychic fairs for many years and we have both astrologers and psychics at these events offering their services. We cheerfully offer refunds if people are dissatisfied with their sessions which usually run 15-20 minutes. The number one reason they ask for a refund is the astrologer talked about themselves during the session. This is a cardinal rule of conducting a professional astrological session. Avoid talking about your personal experiences, even if you feel they could help the client. The session is about the client, not about you. This is their time and the focus should be squarely on them. Do not slip into a comfort zone because you feel friendly with the client and start sharing anecdotes about your life—believe me, they may act interested but they are not.

Ethical considerations

Astrological sessions are confidential, and this confidentiality extends to not allowing anyone access to your files or to the names of your clients. Many astrologers use their clients' charts in the lectures without mentioning names. This is generally acceptable, but most appropriate would be to have the client's permission.

Some astrologers allow a third person in the session, while others find it distracting and inappropriate. Consider that even if the client wants to include the third person they may not open up as much during the session no matter how trusted that friend or partner is. The sessions commonly reveal very delicate and intimate details, so more privacy is recommended.

Another sensitive matter is the reference to a third person's chart during the reading. It is always recommended to have the permission of that third person, and some astrologers will plainly not address a third person's chart who is not present at the reading. Other astrologers will consider addressing charts other than the client who immediately relate to the client's important questions, such as partners or business associates, because looking at these charts does provide essential information. Your client may have to sign an important business deal and need to know if they are compatible with their business partners, and yet not feel confident sharing with them that they are having an astrology reading about it. If you choose to look at third party charts, be sure to only focus on issues pertaining to the questions regarding relevant aspects of their relationship and refrain from gossip or discussing other aspects of the chart. Keep the other chart anonymous and do not ask for last names. The information revealed must serve the best interest of the client and that third person. It is inappropriate to discuss the charts of friends or colleagues if they are not closely linked to important questions of the reading.

Regarding family members, many astrologers will look at the chart of an infant to help the parent understand how to best raise the child. As mentioned earlier, charts of spouses can be referred to in order to help the client understand their relationships and improve their dynamics. These are my personal suggestions, but it is up to your own level of comfort to decide if you feel it necessary to address charts of people close to the client.

Your political and religious views should not enter into an astrological session and the same goes for your personal opinions about sexuality or your stance on recreational drugs. Focus on the reality of your client, for they may reveal things about their lifestyle that are foreign to you. It is important to remain neutral and use the chart to support their process or answer their questions. However, in the unlikely case that the client reveals criminal behavior, you have the right to terminate the session. Generally, refrain from judging your clients and respect diversity—if you are too attached to your own biases, you will not render effective service. Also, use politically correct dialogue and respect your client and their journey.

Refrain from conveying alarming information and deterministic stances, such as "you will never have children" or "your rela-tionships will always bring crises." Emphasize the free will factor. Clients have choices, and these choices determine the direction of their life. Help them make better choices by making them aware of their strengths and weaknesses.

I once knew an astrologer who would not accept a client who was married and having a love affair. He felt this was immoral. He was a very good astrologer but, in my opinion, did a disservice to clients who needed his guidance about their love life. It was his right to refuse clients, and you have the choice to do so if you feel uncomfortable about certain issues. We as astrologers are there to help our clients with intimate issues. My best advice is to leave your judgments behind and enter your sessions with an open mind.

Closing the Session

Questions, closure

Remember to leave time for questions, close the session on time and collect any outstanding fees. You may also give the client a copy of their chart and a recording of the session. Thank the client for coming and let them know your policy for follow up sessions. Be sure to give the client your card and any other pertinent information. If you want to refer the client to a health care professional or other type of professional services, it is advisable, for legal reasons, to provide more than one name so the client can make the choice and not you. In this way, you are not responsible for recommending someone the client may have a bad experience with.

Taking notes

One thing I personally learned from my psychology training was to take client notes after the session. Unless you have a photographic memory, write the notes immediately after the end of the session. This is invaluable if you are going to see the client again. It makes the client feel valued when you remember things about them. Your notes can contain basic information like their marital status, number of children, or significant events in their lives. Also, making astrological notations means you don't have to look them up again for the next session. These notations can be about upcoming progressions, transits or eclipses that will occur in the months and years ahead.

Closing remarks

Astrology is a wonderful profession with many rewards. If astrology is ever to be integrated into the mainstream, it must be held to high standards of ethics and professionalism. Do try to enjoy your astrology practice and your clients. If you can truly help them, you will feel satisfaction and contentment for a job well done. Associating with other professional astrologers in peer group settings or at conferences will help you keep up with the latest astrological research, receive business tips and gain new perspectives on astrological principles. Additionally, you may find social and professional support from your peers. Astrology is a community and you are part of it!

Sandra-Leigh Serio is certified by ISAR, AFA and OPA as a professional astrologer and has written for the Mountain Astrologer, Llewellyn Publications, Horoscope Magazine and StarIQ. She has a M.A. in Psychology and lives in Boulder, Colorado. Since 2003 she has been President of the Rocky Mountain Astrologers (ROMA) in Boulder, Colorado, and serves as a Group Leader and Treasurer for OPA (Organization for Professional Astrology) and a trainer for ISAR's Consulting Skills.
Website: sandraleigh@sandraleigh.com

Chapter 4

The Financial Equation
in the Practice of Astrology
Chris McRae

ISAR.CAP, NCGR.CA, PMAFA

Astrological Evolution of the 20th Century

We can be passionate about astrology's benefits and the insights it unveils to others, but until we can transform it into a legitimate career path with societal acceptance it will be a struggle to be seen as more than a hobby or personal growth process.

I believe that astrology is at a crossroads because it is getting more and more accepted by mainstream society. I started my professional career by teaching and reading charts in 1970 while working in broadcasting and the entertainment industry. I have seen enormous changes in both the way we apply astrological knowledge and the number of practitioners making it a viable profession.

Advanced study in Astrology is now possible through several schools and colleges throughout England, Europe, University of

Wales, Australia, and the United States, including Kepler College and Avalon School. Several organizations offer certification programs in order to elevate the professional status of astrology in the eyes of the general public.

I have also seen an enormous change in my clientele. In addition to my traditional clients I am now seeing doctors, lawyers, and corporate CEO's. It is gratifying to know these people are placing value on the astrological knowledge received about themselves, their families, and the world around them.

In 2015, I am also seeing greater numbers of people in their early 20's coming in for a consultation. These younger clients are attending astrology classes in greater numbers than ever before and many are becoming professional astrologers with new and innovative ways to build an income from a variety of sources, from consulting to internet services.

These younger astrologers are the group born in the early 1990's under the Uranus/Neptune Conjunction in Capricorn that begins a new cycle every 171 years. It was a time of massive change at both government and corporate levels as many senior executives and highly paid employees were given early retirement and buy-out packages. Job loss and personnel replacements were common. The babies born at that time have the consciousness of a new societal thrust built into them. As these young people merge into their adulthood many struggle to find their place in a rapidly changing society. The world is changing and getting ready for them. They will either find their own individual way to participate in the work force, or the world will adapt to their new approach as they begin to mature.

Over the past few decades many astrologers were self-taught. We learned through books written by masters like Alan Leo, Grant Lewi, C.E.O. Carter, Max Heindle, Johndro, Manly P. Hall, Vivian Robson,

William Lilly and more. New insight began emerging through Marc Edmund Jones, Dane Rudhyar, Ivy Goldstein Jacobson, Isabel Hickey, Robert Hand, and others as astrology continued its evolutionary path.

Astrology was a much slower and arduous process in those days because every chart had to be carefully and meticulously calculated by hand and drawn on a blank wheel. While time consuming, it was both a labour of love and a powerful learning tool. Understanding the mathematical structure of a chart allowed us to grasp astrology at a core level.

The microchip age changed all that when computers with sophisticated programs gave us charts and progressions in seconds. We soared throughout the universe as new vistas of astrology were opened up. In order to understand where we are and how to earn a living as an astrologer today, we need to understand the marvel of this transition and the prospects that are opening up for the new generation of astrologers breaking into the dawn of a new era.

A great revolution in thinking that vastly benefited the development of astrology in the modern era began with the advent of the Great Conjunction of Neptune-Pluto cycle of 492 years that began in 1892 in Gemini. It was the time of Zionism, Theosophy and Evangeline Adams, who raised astrology another notch in its possibilities for our modern world.

Another huge milestone in our shifting society exploded with the Uranus/Pluto Conjunction in Virgo in the mid-1960s. It ushered in an enormous societal revolution that changed the way our culture operated. Pluto fuels the need for massive change and Uranus is the revolutionary force that energizes the process. Virgo is how we organize, categorize and systemize data and information. It not only accelerated the evolution of astrology, but energized research in many other fields, including biochemistry and medicine.

Astrology's ascendance was concurrent with the rise in "New Age Consciousness". Interest in astrology exploded as everyone asked each other, "What is your Sun Sign", or "Who am I compatible with?" It could aptly be called "the pops era of astrology" but it elicited curiosity and captivated the imagination of so many.

It was during this upsurge that I started teaching at a local college and developed a semester-long course. The beginners' classes over-flowed with 70 or 80 students but many dropped out when they discovered they had to calculate charts by hand. A dedicated core persisted as we moved forward. This was also when I started doing charts in my spare time, often keeping clients waiting several months for a reading.

Some practitioners felt that if you charged for any type of occult or metaphysical reading, including astrology, you would lose your talent because it was a gift to share freely with others. I was disabused of this faulty premise by author and astrologer Sybil Leek, who told me that if you didn't charge for your services, it would not have any value to the other person.

Astrologers charged fees for readings but few practitioners were able to carry it forward into a full time profession. Early 20th Century Astrologer Evangeline Adams did. Famous newspaper Sun Sign Astrologer Sydney Omarr did, but he confided in me that he was a journalist using his knowledge of astrology to develop a popular newspaper column. Of course, there were others emerging onto the horizon as we astrologers heard our collective calling. It was time to remove the cobwebs and bring astrology out of hiding into the mainstream, ready to brave the inevitable onslaught of scientific criticism. It didn't take long for the mainstream to respond. In 1975 one hundred and eighty-six astronomers, astrophysicists and scientists signed a document condemning astrology as pseudoscience. This announcement flooded the news media worldwide. Undaunted, Astrology soldiered on.

With the invention of the microchip, home computers were emerging onto the consumer marketplace. Along with them came sophisticated astrology programs by such forerunners as Michael Erlewine and Robert Hand in North America. First was the Digicomp DR-70 in 1978 that limited its computations to astrology with 10,000 years of ephemeris. Other systems by Commodore and Apple would offer increasingly sophisticated programs that would spur the growth of computerized chart calculation.

We could now churn out chart after chart, learn faster, see more clients, and generate professional material for conference presentations with much greater speed and efficiency. [The Uranus/Neptune conjunction of early 1990 saw the invasion of home computers into every household in every country around the world.] The interest in astrology was ready for the next step in its evolutionary journey to professional status and acceptability. This changed both the manner in which we generated and interpreted our charts.

The process of upgrading interpretations that had survived astrology's underground era now had to apply to 20th Century living and thinking while preparing to enter the 21st Century. Prediction became more tenuous in a more complex society with more alternatives, initiating the growth of humanistic and psychological astrology by Dane Rudhyar and Marc Edmund Jones.

We next had the task of elevating our professional status beyond the gypsy fortune teller and crystal ball gazer into a legitimate field of study with insight into how our personal journey on planet earth evolves with the cosmic flow. Various astrological organizations began outlining educational requirements. Astrological schools and colleges sprang up throughout Europe, Australia, and North and South America.

Prior to the 1965 New Age Consciousness movement there were very few professionals earning their entire living through astrology. That has changed dramatically in the 21st century. This is certainly due to the speed of generating data, multiple income streams made possible by the internet, and the improvement in educational and certification standards.

Transition into full-time professional

Some students graduating today from schools or colleges of astrology have been able to launch a full-time practice without an interim career. It is possible when one has services that can be offered through the internet and the ability to establish an online platform of services. This diversification is essential for new practitioners in the 21st Century. It is not as necessary for those of us who built our practice before the internet era and have a steady stream of regular clients with new referrals that keep our calendar full.

Many today still learn, practice and develop their astrological skills while enjoying the income from a previously established career. Such was my own transition. We can develop a few clients at a time, build a client base, and gain confidence in our skills as we transition from another career into an astrology practice. Sometimes the transition comes when the other career downshifts or comes to an end. Whatever the reason there are daily living necessities that need to be met.

I would like to quote from a presentation I made a few years ago at an OPA Conference called Astrology at Work:

"You just don't fall into success. Sir Edmund Hillary didn't just stumble around the base of Mt. Everest and one day discover he was at the summit. It took a great deal of planning and preparation. For something to happen, you must set it in motion." Where do you start?

It will be helpful to set two separate financial goals. You need to determine how much money you need to make in order to pay your expected monthly obligations such as rent/mortgage, groceries, car payments, gas (or transportation), insurance payments, supplies, subscriptions, memberships, etc. These figures can help you to know when you are ready to launch a full time practice.

Your second financial goal needs to consider an approximate allotment to personal and professional development such as upgrading your electronic equipment and programs and attending professional seminars and conferences. This assures that you keep abreast of new knowledge and information developing within the profession. This goal can be set as a future plan but it needs due consideration.

Where will you set up your office? If you are seeing a few clients on weekends you will probably work from your home or an office connected with a metaphysical bookstore. You need to provide a quiet, well ventilated area where the client can relax and feel safe. The kitchen table is not particularly professional, nor the living room with children and pets running in and out. The space needs to be private without distractions or even strong odors such as incense that some clients may be allergic to.

When you are ready to go full-time you may rent an office in a commercial building with a profile. If so, make sure the environment and parking area are safe.

Working for oneself is different than getting up every morning, leaving your home at the same time every day and putting in a prescribed number of hours to earn your paycheck. A measure of discipline and routine is essential when you are working for yourself.

I once heard an astrologer say they do not get up until noon if they don't have a morning client. That is a prescription for failure.

Many successful people get up at 5:00 or 6:00 AM. There is email to answer, charts to prepare, newsletters to write, classes to develop, website material to create, and other activities that expand one's personal and professional scope. Set your hours of operation and build a routine. Some people see clients on evenings and weekends but I prefer to keep what I call "professional hours".

Working for oneself requires regulation, discipline and a workable schedule. It is often tempting to sleep in, fritter away business hours with household duties, go on a shopping spree, or spend two or three hours with feet up on the desk sipping coffee and talking to friends. Good work habits breed success. You can schedule a day off periodically to liberate yourself from excessive routine, but your focus must remain fixed on your long-term goals.

Building and Maintaining a Clientele

Sources of income

There are two main market sources. Some astrologers build an entire practice on various internet services, from marketing general reports to emailing personalized forecasts. Others prefer personal consultation in the privacy of their own office including long distance phone or Skype consultations. Some professionals combine both of these modalities.

First of all, determine the services you wish to offer. The following is a potential list:

1. Building a personal consultation practice. This could include:
    - Natal chart analysis and upcoming yearly forecast
    - Relationship analysis

- Family dynamics
- Relocational orientation
- Horary questions and Electional charts

2. Reports

Many astrology software programs offer various types of reports that can be generated for sale to prospective clients. They are popular, inexpensive, and fast. Make sure these reports provide a high quality analysis. You will need to set up a payment link on your website.

3. Teaching

Teaching can be done locally or on the internet through webinars. You need a growing list of contacts in order to generate interest in your teaching programs. Personal contacts and net-working at conferences are excellent methods of generating these lists.

I find many of my clients become students and many students remain clients because they appreciate the professional knowledge gained in both classes and readings. Advertising can be done via the internet, through a local book store, or other community forums.

4. Yearly Transit reports for students of astrology to follow their own trends

An effective way for students to follow their own trends.

5. Writing

This could constitute writing a column for a local newspaper, company newsletter, new age publications, astrology magazine or astrology journals. Many of these do not generate much money directly but they are excellent sources of publicity.

Writing an astrology book rarely generates an income com-mensurate with the time involved unless you write a series that gains momentum over time. However, writing a popular book that becomes a best seller can generate considerable income. Linda Goodman's *Sun Sign* book has been on the market for many years and is still read today. Sydney Omarr made a career in sun sign journalism. I myself wrote a daily syndicated sun sign forecast for eight years. It was both lucrative and enjoyable.

6. Software Design

Astrologers with technical skills have created software programs widely used by their colleagues.

7. Corporate Work explore   Do

It is possible in the very near future that companies will recognize the benefit of having an astrologer in their personnel department. It can assist in vocational orientation, matching aptitudes to departments, and enhancing conflict resolution. Even a cursory knowledge of sun signs can be beneficial in enhancing employee effectiveness.

8. Marketing

Like it or not, you will need to learn self-promotion, if not for your sake, then for the sake of astrology at large. You need to be your own sales team, advertising agent and booking agent unless you are operating on a very large scale with a mass market.

Fees, length of session

As previously discussed, you need to know how much money you require in order to pay your expenses on a weekly and monthly basis. This will help in determining when you are ready to begin your practice or make the transition from another career. How many clients do you need to see in a week as a basic income source from your practice?

The fee you charge for your services comes next. You may already have determined the pace of your consultation. Some astrologers may find they can cover what needs to be said in one hour. That becomes more challenging when we learn that consulting is not just giving information but learning to listen, encourage disclosure, and getting to the heart of the real issue. It has to do with consulting style. The client needs to feel that you are there in the moment with them and that you understand where they are coming from. An effective consultation requires understanding the issue at hand and being able to address it so the client feels validated and can move forward with a deeper understanding.

In setting your fees, you first need to determine the length of your session. In most of North America and Europe, one can set a price of $150.00 per hour or a 90 minute consultation for $200.00. Let us start with a 1.5 hour consultation with a basic fee of $200.00. (For most clients that is reasonable. Otherwise, adjust accordingly.)

Once you arrive at 10 clients per week, your weekly income reaches $2,000.00.

If you work 45 weeks, taking 7 weeks off for vacation or a conference:
-    $2,000 x 45 = $90,000.00

Classes - 3 Semesters per year, minimum of 5 students per semester
-    15 students @ 300.00 each = $ 5,500.00

Reports, articles, appearances: $ 4,500.00

Total: $100,000.00

Ten clients per week would be a comfortable schedule for many astrologers and a reasonable level to aspire to. It is also possible to do a few more without overloading your schedule. These figures can be adjusted to five clients a week with room for expansion and development. Other sources of income may help to reduce the number of clients per week. These figures show the range of possibility.

Fees can be raised 20% once a clientele has been built up and appointments increase in number. It is a question of what your particular market will bear and how well known you become.

Booking appointments

If you are making a transition from part-time to full time astrologer, you may have been seeing clients on evenings, days off, holidays and weekends. As a full time astrologer I only see clients during what I term "professional hours". It elevates the practice of astrology from a hobby to a profession.

When booking a first time client, after I have described how I work, taken down information for my intake sheet, and explained my fee, I then say: "What time suites you best? My professional hours are Monday to Friday from 9:00 AM to 5:00 PM." When someone says they work during the day and cannot come during those hours, I tell them politely that evenings are unavailable. I have never lost a client due to my scheduling constraints. They arrange time to see their dentist, doctor, lawyer, or therapist during regular business hours and learn to make similar adjustments to consult an astrologer. I have three bank managers who are clients. They take an extended noon hour. Others leave work a little early. Many people have saved time off, perhaps from overtime. I have several doctors that I will see on a Saturday morning. I also utilize Saturday morning for out of town clients who come into the city on the weekend.

We need to build a professional reputation or we will remain on the fringes of business for many more years to come. Flexibility is sometimes necessary for international clients, and sometimes we may work overtime or make special allowances for certain situations.

I feel strongly about raising astrological standards to a professional category, which is why I try to keep professional hours. It is also why I advocate astrologers become certified or graduate through a well-rounded program, whether by attending classes or an internet college. Learning must have a structure just as setting up a successful practice needs a structure.

Making a transition from a part-time to full-time astrologer can be a lengthy process. The bottom line is to always do good work and

encourage clients to return yearly for updates and further insight into both personal and global dynamics unfolding in light of astrological developments.

Managing time as an economic consideration:

Set your hours of operation and build a routine for success and dependability. Perhaps some people see clients on evenings and weekends but I prefer professional hours.

Working for oneself requires regulation, discipline and a workable schedule. It is often tempting to be distracted. Good work habits breed success. You can schedule a day off periodically to liberate yourself from excessive routine.

Setting goals and making a business plan is also a good way to manage your time and keep you moving towards professional success. These can be long range on a yearly basis, narrowed to monthly, and fine-tuned for daily activity. At the end of each day, make a list of what you need to do tomorrow and what you would like to accomplish. Anything left unfinished is carried into the next day at the top of your list. You need to look forward to getting up the next day for what it can hold. Otherwise you snuggle back down and snooze until guilt sets in to jolt you out of bed.

Your work space

The work space is exceptionally important for comfort, concentration and ease of client's privacy. Many of my clients are themselves professional people and they do not expect less from me. They will only confide in you if the space is strictly private and confidential. It is sometimes hard enough for some people to explain personal details if the space is not private, particularly some of the older male clients who are not used to sharing their personal thoughts. If they can achieve this, it is very liberating and validating for them.

If you work out of your home, a separate room or office space is essential for your computer, reference books, and seating arrangement for more than one client.

I work at a desk and my computers are at my arms' length but I have a small seating arrangement with a very small low table between us. It eliminates barriers but also provides a small and unobtrusive separation. The chart material is in front of the client which means I work upside down, using color-coded chart material to indicate areas of focus. My clients are aware that the information I am imparting is coming from various parts of the charts we are focusing upon. They seem to like the feeling of cosmic connection and that I am gaining the information from an independent source. My client retains the copy when they leave and I have a copy for my file with notations added later from our visit. I keep track of personal items like names and birthdates of children, names of pet dogs, sports activities, and any information I can utilize to personalize our time together.

You may have an appropriate work space in your home or apartment that is the perfect set up. Or you may set up an office in a professional building with a good atmosphere and safe parking.

I have heard astrologers who do charts professionally on a part-time basis, seeing clients on evenings and weekends, who say they cannot make the transition because it takes them too long to prepare a chart. This needs to be addressed and made more efficient, otherwise you cannot do enough charts on a full time basis to make a living. How many techniques do you need to employ to get to the bottom of the issue? How many ways do you need to progress a chart? How many asteroids, midpoints, Solstice points do you need to add to provide insight into a dilemma or concern of a client you will be with for a limited time? These are wonderful for certain types of in-depth work but not all the time for every chart. Determine the tools you will use to get the most information in the most efficient and effective way. As astrologers our interest and curiosity is so vast that we are constantly adding more to our tool box, but we need to discriminate between what tool to use for a specific job, not unlike a carpenter who knows which tool to use to put a screw into a wall.

Once you get your client preparation time reduced to one hour (or less), add 1-1/2 hours for the consultation, and it means you spend 2-1/2 hours per client. At that rate, in an 8 hour day you could see 2 or maybe 3 clients. Add this to other sources of revenue and it is a reasonable professional income. Perhaps you see only 2 clients per day while collecting income from additional sources such as reports, classes, and journalism. I personally prefer two clients per day with additional time for other creative activity such as writing, preparing lectures, experimenting with new ideas, etc. Occasionally I may have to go into overload to meet client demand.

Finding and adding new clients

The internet, of course, is an obvious way to become known far and wide. Keep adding new material to your website to keep it alive and encourage frequent visits. Traffic helps to increase clients and income.

You may also wish to build a local clientele which is an easy and ready source of new clients. A good consultation often results in the client telling a friend. Many clients like the personal touch of a one-on-one consultation while others find long distance phone calls or Skype satisfactory. Phone or Skype consultations allow you to work with clients from great distances who cannot meet you in person.

Some astrologers have found it useful to advertise among people they know by holding an astrology party where they give 20 minute mini-readings and share a flyer or handout describing other available services. The hostess who invites 5 or 6 guests can have a free consultation or a 50% discount, depending upon your level of generosity, good will and the time factor.

Doing short readings on Saturday afternoon at a local book store is another way to connect with prospective clients.

Sending out periodic newsletters to current clients, prospective clients, friends and associates keeps your name and services in the forefront of peoples' minds. You may also wish to send birthday wishes to current clients.

Always make sure you carry an ample supply of business cards and give them out at every opportunity. You could give one to your bank teller, a local merchant, and anyone who might ask, "What do you do?"

My own clientele has changed somewhat over the years. Along with more professional people as previously mentioned, men over 45 are now more frequent visitors. Many of them are 60 or older, getting ready for retirement and wondering how to keep the next chapter of their lives stimulating and meaningful.

Many of today's maturing clients, both male and female, have been through relationship difficulties since the rise of the career woman in today's society and are hoping for one more chance at personal happiness. Many of these came of age in the 1965 societal revolution as women sought a new identity in today's world.

The newest fad in clientele seems to be a great number of young people in their early to middle twenties who are captivated by the idea of understanding themselves at a deeper level. The younger generation is also gravitating into classes more frequently than in previous years. All of this indicates to me that we need many more highly qualified professional astrologers in the years ahead to meet this new demand.

May you all enjoy this gratifying way to serve humanity and uplift your own evolutionary journey at the same time. We are all fitting into the mosaic of a shifting era.

Chris McRae has been a consultant, teacher, author and international lecturer since 1970. She has lectured at major astrological conferences throughout the world including UAC, NCGR, OPA, AAGB in England, ARGO in South Africa, Balkan Conference in Belgrade, FCA in Australia, etc. She has conducted weekend seminars throughout Canada and the US, as well as in Russia, other parts of Europe, and China. In 1982 she gave up a lucrative broadcasting and television career to become a full-time professional astrologer. Her community service includes current Vice-President ISAR Board, Chair ISAR Certification Program, Chair ISAR Competency Exam, Honorary Life President EAS, previous AFA Board and AFAN Steering Committee. She has authored 3 books, Understanding Interceptions, Geodetic Astrology for Relocation and Mundane, and The Geodetic World Map, as well as contributed to five other texts.
Website: www.astrologychrismcrae.com

Chapter 5

Making your Astrology Practice Financially Viable
Georgia Stathis

We all have dreams about pursuing our astrological practices. However, those dreams are often tempered with judgments regarding our financial viability. Imagination pushes us forward while fear gets in the way. Fearful judgement is our enemy and focused planning is our friend. Both are Saturn qualities representing opposite sides of the coin, or the two faces of Janus. Regardless of whether you choose sales, medicine, or astrology, the potential exists to secure your future security. Unfortunately, a common belief surrounding the profession of astrology is that practitioners cannot make enough money and our lives are fated to limited means in this profession. In reality, this statement reflects practicing without any sort of plan in place.

Consider the concept of financial security or having 'enough' from another perspective. When we pay for rent, food, gasoline, bicycles, medical services, clothing, and other necessities, we owe others money for these goods and services. We really do have to make 'enough' to pay them and still have enough left for our other needs; otherwise we are creating bad karma. We value their services and we must value ours as well.

By placing a value upon our services, getting past our fears and judgments of what we can do based on our early programming or other peoples' opinions of our profession, we can expand our work and security. First we must be willing to move past the 'stuck' place of current beliefs. **If you think you can't, you won't, but if you think you can, you will.** The ruler of the twelfth house and the aspects it creates can offer some insight into how we run our ascendant, and, by extension, our life. By studying that house and its ruler, one gains insight into some of the ideas presented in this chapter.

The complete future is unknown to all of us, but we can use the astrological chart to help plan our future goals by identifying and then prioritizing our values. This is often a second and sometimes eighth house ruler issue. Values are often associated with the planet Venus, and/or the ruler of the second house. Of course, as we move through progressions or solar arcs, those values can alter, but, inevitably they maintain the true essence of the natal position. Knowing our personal values, our value of self and our skills is imperative in the planning for the future.

There are some people who do not want much in life and others who want everything. This is a personal choice, but regardless of wanting a lot or a little, future financial security requires work, a plan, and the ability to implement that plan. The first step is to differentiate our wants from our needs. A good way to start this is at the beginning of every year: 1) Make a two column list 2) Prioritize what is the most important on the list of needs and start from there and 3) Then write down some of the wants, understanding that you don't have to attain those all in one year. It is the hope of this article that some of the ideas presented will capture your imagination so that you can see success annually and have enough of whatever you desire for the year and, ultimately, your life. This is a critical parsing exercise. We want to take that big vacation, but we need a new means of transportation. Which one is the want and which is the need? Does not getting that want now suggest that you can never have that want? Absolutely not!

What is money, really?

Again, depending upon your desired lifestyle and your material needs (and nothing is right or wrong in these choices), your list changes year to year, or, as you mature, from decade to decade. The 'list' also depends upon the other people that depend upon you; families, siblings and even pets. In order to plan one must understand the true value of money – not so much as a thing, but as a means to an end. Though money seems tangible, it is really an intangible asset that, if properly allocated, provides freedom and choice for yourself as well as others. This means that both you and others can benefit if you approach it with a plan. Money is a fluid commodity that must keep moving like a rippling river requiring a good captain to navigate its flow. It doesn't grow when stagnant. It prospers when it is tended, managed and respected.

To have or have not: When you have 'enough' money or security, you may raise your living standard, but may be unable to maintain that standard. This is often due to poor fiscal management. When you don't make a lot, you may not have as wide a range of choices initially, but by managing it, you can expand your options. **In fact, sometimes we are at our most creative when we don't have** *Use* **enough.** The important thing to know is that you can have enough either way by **managing such things as** talent, time, spending, and energy. Learning to set boundaries for what you can or cannot do is also very important.

Some Basics

Most schools don't teach the basics of checkbooks, credit cards, ATMs, or managing savings. Some secondary education schools teach it, but it isn't a course of study one often sees. Without this knowledge, many people head into the world clueless about how to manage their money. The repercussions are vast. They find themselves saddled with credit card and college debt and unable to manage their earnings. It is often assumed that once formal education is completed those debts will be paid off with whatever career we choose. That is not necessarily true; getting a higher education doesn't always insure more income, as we have learned in the current economic climate. Making more income doesn't necessarily mean you know how to manage that income. On the flip side, making less doesn't mean you are unable to prosper.

If you wish to work for yourself as an astrologer, learning these basics, though tedious for some, is the beginning of future stability and a solid financial foundation. **Putting together a business plan** provides you an outline of your vision while you adhere to regular rules and habits of fiscal management. This combined effort is the key to a creative, fulfilling and joyful future. [Dave Grant, a motivational speaker, used to say, "If you have the choice between pleasure and pain, do the pain first, then pleasure is a true reward!" I always felt this was a Saturn/Jupiter statement. Lay down a structure and then you can revel in its benefits.]

Future security starts with defining your values, knowing that they will change throughout your life. This is an important component for planning because if you are either dogmatic about your values or consistently allowing yourself to be easily influenced by others imposing their values upon you, you have already lost the game. What is your attitude towards money? Unfortunately, in much of our esoteric community there **is** a belief that only certain types of people have money and that our industry can never prosper because we aren't 'those type of people'! This is absolute bunk! What is money, anyway? Is it bad? Is it good? If you have it are you really greedy? If you don't, are you entitled to having it? Money is intangible. It is the vehicle that gives us freedom to go or do or be or choose to have whatever we wish. It isn't something that stays long in our hands because it needs to be moving at all times. Just look at economic cycles, markets, costs of goods; they fluctuate up and down. *It doesn't hold us, we hold it* and what we do with it makes the difference. That difference depends on what we value.

Define your value system for right now and then make plans. Gather all pertinent information on your current and potential earnings and the direction you'd like to go, then make a business plan. Business plans are focused but not written in stone because their design allows for flexibility, changes, and addendums. Flexibility allows for growth and learning new skills while staying current with technology. Staying up to date in your field of expertise as well as other fields in which you have an interest gives you the edge to expand in the future and alter some aspects of the plan. Business plans change as you mature.

For example, those in their early fifties and at the last quarter square of transit Saturn to natal Saturn used to prepare for their retirement, but that has changed. People live longer and now study for a new business or vocational direction in these later years, requiring a new business plan for the upcoming second Saturn return (if they wish that).

A Business Plan:

If you are going into business as an astrologer and aspiring to make this your full time work, you have to ask yourself a few key questions, one of which is, 'to whom am I responsible other than myself'? This is important because it factors in choices as you create a plan. The second is to ask yourself if you want to do this part time, full time, or occasionally. Working full time as an astrologer is challenging—it requires patience, endurance, marketing skills, a love of people, and a healthy lifestyle. It also helps to have support from your community, both the community in which you live and your astrological community to which you regularly contribute. Making a business plan starts the process.

After you answer some of the above questions, set the plan in place. A business plan can have a half decade time limit, roughly a sextile between where Saturn is when you begin, and ends at the five-year mark. Since Saturn moves 12° a year, figure, it approaches a sextile (60°) over the course of five years. At 3.5 years from the time you start, it has moved to a semi-square (45°) position, which is a 'hump' period for many businesses, or half way to the seventh year square of Saturn to beginning Saturn. Saturn likes structure and baby steps, like the mountain goat carefully climbing the mountain step by step. Below is one example of a business plan, which contains key elements. These elements may be finessed for your own personal situation. We won't be going through every part of the business plan, but will be discussing specific parts of it. After reviewing this sample template, the discussion explores the idea of earnings and some concepts of investing, and then how or where to spend the net earnings. First let's look at a plan.

Business Plan Suggestion

Part One: Business Overview

- Vision and Mission Statement, for your practice and for the coming year
- Objectives – Primary and Secondary
- Ownership – LLC, Sole Proprietor, or Corporation?
- Location and Facilities

Part Two: Types of Income

- Active
- Passive
- Budgeting the above – expenses and deductibles
- Where will it go: IRA, a SEP, or 401K?

Part Three: Marketing Strategies

- Personal contact – always the best
- Networks and referrals
- Public speaking
- Social Media: Facebook, Twitter, LinkedIn, Instagram
- Snail Mail
- Emails
- Paid ads
- You can fill in your own best form of marketing

Part Four: Regulatory Issues

- Business license for your city – Under professional title "Astrologer" or "Consultant".

- Resale license – State Dept. of Revenue if you sell products. Resale licenses afford you opportunity to purchase something at wholesale and sell at retail.
- Income taxes – Federal. State. Paying quarterly or annually? An accountant should be consulted.
- Intellectual property. Contracts should allow you to be the owner of that property.
- Copyright uses and abuses. When using others' information, make sure they are noted.

Part Five: Structure

- Office or telephone or shared space
- Expertise – bookkeepers, CPAs, database specialists
- Staffing
- In House
- Outside Services

Part VI: Risk

- Your investments for the year. Solidify and expand your practice
- How long a risk in your investment do you wish to continue?
- What's your 'number'? In time, in money, in energy??

Part VII: Implementation Plan – List and Plan your Goals

- Internet site, when do you push the button? When do you upgrade?
- Office, when do you open your doors for practice and take in the first dollar?
- Date to execute your list of goals.
- Balance of expenses and revenues.

Taking ownership?

You now have a plan, so how do you want to own your business? In the United States, you can be a sole proprietor or an LLC (a limited liability company). Since everyone usually starts out fairly small, ownership often begins as a sole proprietor. Think about what you call your type of business on your tax forms. Sole proprietor is a good way to start.

Make sure that any comments you make while consulting or writing are earmarked with such disclaimers as 'my opinion', 'another view might be', or, 'it depends upon one's perspective'. This is a sampling of phrases that are appropriate in a consulting environment, because as a sole proprietor you have more liability. Recording the consulting session also supports your disclaimers as well.

As you grow your business, becoming an LLC, a limited liability company, might be more appropriate. A limited liability company in USA law is a legal form of a business or company offering limited liability to its owners and eventually more tax advantages than a sole proprietor. It is similar to but not the same as a corporation, and is often a more flexible form of ownership that protects assets; in case of bankruptcy, the company is not listed in your name. LLCs can also offer percentages of the partnership to others (who will also have to pay taxes on their percentage of the partnership), and functions as a way of distributing some of the tax ramifications of your business, particularly in estate planning. Usually, regardless of how much a percentage is distributed to partners, the owner (chief partner) has control over the decisions regarding the business even if he or she owns a small percentage. An LLC is not a corporation, however. Corporations are far more complicated entities requiring an inordinate amount of rules, work, and time. There are many types of corporations and unless you develop a large practice where more partners are involved and there are larger numbers, the LLC may be the better bet. Again, consult with a tax attorney and accountant (CPA) for the details of such an idea.

Once you decide whether to be a sole proprietor or an LLC, take a hard look at your spending habits and budgets with a view towards actualizing your dream. With the current Saturn square Neptune (2015), this is a perfect time in which to put form to that dream. But first, a little story from my past. Years ago I had two wonderful clients, a husband and wife team who taught an enlightening course on money. It was the early 1980s. The USA had just come out of a severe recession and interest rates were as high as 20% for home loans. I was married with children and it was a tough time for us. We needed a new perspective. My clients' course was perfect for us. However, in order to attend the class, there was a strict set of rules (Saturn). The first was that if you were a couple who shared finances, both of you needed to attend. Finances is typically one of the biggest issues in a relationship. The course was expensive and in order to facilitate couples attending they offered a substantial discount for spouses with the guarantee that if you didn't make that registration fee back within the course of the eight weeks you got your money back!

The first order of business was to share your earnings figures for the last year with your fellow classmates in the first session! Sharing it was terrifying and embarrassing because we didn't make much. But we did it, because people who wish to become financially viable discuss their issues around money. There were some making $1000 a month and others making far more. Ground rules were laid down before we learned about budgeting and the formula of Earn, Invest and then Spend. **The 'rules' follow:**

- Never use a credit card unless you can pay that charge immediately from either a checking account or savings. This way you avoid accumulation of outrageous interest rates while improving your credit rating for larger future investments. This rule is critical because most people spend over 33% more than what they earn.

- No bartering. Yes, no bartering. This is something often done in our astrological community. The reasoning behind this rule is that barters are not always of equal value in either time or need. It also encourages one to ask for the order and expect that their service is valuable. This does not, however, discount the occasional pro bono work or various professional courtesies.

- Stick to your budget and if you cannot, make an adjustment for income or other costs to insure that the outcome is the same. This is like 'tracking' in *Weightwatchers*! If you don't write it, you 'bite' it!

- Do not be afraid to ask for *reasonable* and *unreasonable* requests. This is a KEY point in the list and bears practicing. It is an art form that gives both parties a win/win outcome.

> A *reasonable* request should be made every day. A reasonable request is something like, "the packaging is missing on this floor model and you don't have any more in stock, so would you discount your model?" It is said calmly and sincerely. It is not delivered as an angry or irritated request. If the merchant says no, then it is no. But there is a fifty percent chance he or she will say yes.

> An *unreasonable* request (and this is how we and others recouped our investment in this course) is asking for something big. This is a bit harder, because

it requires a little bit more creativity and courage. An example is haircuts. That monthly haircut costs you a certain amount each month. You probably go to the same person every month. If you ask that person at the beginning of each year something like, "I see I am spending either $20 or $100/cut and color a month, which is fine. But in figuring it out, that amounts to $240 (or $1200 a year). If I were to give you a check for, say $185 (or $1000) at the beginning of the year, would you consider that full payment for those 12 haircuts? More often than not, they will say yes! You've saved $35 to $200 per year.

This is particularly good for people with whom you do regular monthly business or where you make large purchases or have annual services like a post office box with UPS, who offers limited contracts. What about a longer contract affording a lower per month cost, i.e. a five-year contract? This is something I do with my local UPS store. It is less bookkeeping for them (time, too) and less per month for me. Some people might think this is cheap. I know you are out there, but remember, the un*reasonable* request isn't something meant to intimidate others or take advantage of them. It is just a request. If you really think about it, stores do it all the time. If you bring in a receipt from a competitor and make that request, they often honor it. It's the same thing.

As for your astrological practice, people might ask 'reasonable' requests of you. I am sure they have. You have the option to say no or yes, too.

Making reasonable annual or semi-annual requests of your telephone, cable, and internet services can also lower your numbers and they often comply since there is stiff competition in these industries. The key thing to remember about those reductions is to mark down when that agreement runs out, so you can call again for another negotiation. This saves you between $30 and $40 a month, or, $360-$480 a year.

Budgeting:

Budgeting must become a regular habit if you want to be successful. Once a budget is nailed down you begin the process of implementing your business plan. This is an important step most people avoid, but as an astrologer you are already a keen analyst. You look at figures, distances, and planetary movements every day. If you can wrap your head around the idea that this is just another analytical exercise, you will find it much easier than you expect.

Financial viability is making money work for you rather than you working for money. Remember money is just a vehicle to freedom and knowing where your money goes while being cognizant of spending habits (also assessed by looking at the ruler of the second house and its aspects) is important. Setting an annual plan in place is easy if you work with a pre-made template that has the formulas built into the Excel spreadsheet. There are several available so you don't even have to design one. The one I use is an oldie but goodie and is available by contacting us at www.starcycles.com. It is pre-formulated. If you add income, it shows more at the end of the monthly column and the year. If you add expenses, it subtracts automatically. It is a working template and easy tool.

Remember to include tithing or donations made each month, regardless of how small a contribution is available. The old adage of what goes around comes around is so very true with giving not only of our services, but also of our resources.

There are different ways of **making donations**. From a financial perspective, a dollar amount is deductible from your business expenses. Your service time (value of that time) can also be deducted.

There is also another type of donation—called an 'in kind' donation, which is tangible items; clothing, furniture, software. These can be inventoried, donated, and priced by you. The charity to which you donate them will give you a receipt to present with your taxes at the end of the year. Keeping records of both types of donations is important. It is far more difficult, however, to place the 'in kind' donations into your spreadsheet, because it is not a number, but it may still be deducted from taxes. Non-profit organizations provide you with a receipt with the non-profit account number for the IRS (Internal Revenue Service).

Fixed monthly expenses are easier to place into a spreadsheet than fluctuating figures. Utilities and services often offer a fixed prorated amount based on your annual usage of utilities if you work at home (offices include this in the rent). If your bill is $200 after Christmas but $60 per month in the spring, they can offer you a fixed monthly figure to put into your budget. Automatic payments coming out of your checking or other account are another smart way of balancing your budget so that your rent, water bill or mortgage payments are automatically withdrawn from your account each month and placed into that spreadsheet.

Keeping a separate spreadsheet for your credit card expenses is also a good idea. Most credit card companies offer an online annual summary, but it might be helpful to use a separate template for these costs as well, so you can see where money goes. This can be done for both cash and ATM debits as well, although using a credit card (that you pay off each month) may offer more financial advantages for you if you get airline miles or cash back. You also get to keep your money longer than you do with cash or ATM withdrawals. Cash expenses can be small but mighty, like tolls, parking, supplies, educational expenses, equipment (which is depreciated), services, or even lunches with potential clients. Everything adds up and should be recorded. Keep all receipts.

Housing: If you hold a mortgage and can afford to pay extra on your monthly mortgage principal each month, factor that into your budget as well and see how it looks. Doing that on a regular basis forces savings and accelerates payment on the mortgage. If you reduce the mortgage balance considerably and rates remain low, you can refinance at that lower interest rate, thereby reducing your monthly payment. Even $200 a month helps.

As for budgeting, many people prefer impound accounts (where the real estate taxes and homeowners insurance are included in the house payment). This is a personal choice, but I prefer to pay them separately and use that money to accrue interest even if it is in a very small return. Whether you rent or hold a mortgage, a portion of your home office and home services like heat and electricity can be deductible expenses for your business. If you share your housing with a roommate their rent can be booked as shared expenses rather than income. This was a fairly new change with the IRS a few years ago. In the past, it was considered income but with this change, it is considered shared expense. Check with your state for the rules.

Earn, Invest and then Spend

Now that you have a budget in place, look at earnings and how you distribute those earnings. Earning is one thing, but how you invest or spend is *the key* to future financial viability. The real formula is to earn it first, then invest it, and then spend it.

How will you earn? Do you aspire to be a full or part-time astrologer? Will you hold a separate job while you build your practice? This is an excellent idea because while working the other job you have access to potential clients who know you are building a practice. Building your contacts in a specialized industry in which you work is another advantage to building future earnings. Dual or triple income streams offer assurance for earnings and are easier with advanced technologies. Personally connecting with people is still imperative for building relationships for your business. If you choose to take clients on the phone, this eliminates an office and keeps down costs. However, keep yourself out and about in your community so people get to know you and get a feeling of your personality and integrity.

Separate what you consider active from passive income

Active income is where you actively earn the money in personal consultations, lectures, paid writings, etc. It may come from another job or source. It is alive and viable. If you stop that activity, the income stream stops. Astrologers often focus on building a personal clientele, which is excellent, but they can exhaust themselves unless they expand their other income streams into passive income.

Passive income **makes money when you aren't working.** Passive income can come from a class or a whole course taught and recorded on either MP3 or a WMV file. This is gold! If it is a good class and you want others to experience it, you can put it up for sale on your website or make it available through your newsletter or via marketing materials like a monthly newsletter. Courses, books, e-books, lectures, workshops and seminars require time to assemble (Active time), but if carefully saved, organized, catalogued and distributed, they can provide wonderful *passive income* which makes you money while you sleep. This adds to your income stream. You can also get commissions or income from product development such as selling astrology software. Additionally, if you have high traffic on your website or on YouTube videos, you can earn income from ads.

Non astrological sources for passive income include pensions or annuities (when one retires), income from rentals, shared office spaces, royalties, or income from other jobs. All of these sources should be part of the plan, particularly when starting out. As a professional astrologer, if you think you can build up a solid portfolio for the future by active income alone, you may find yourself tired and exhausted yet still falling short of your financial goals. Conducting session after session every day is tiring, particularly as we age, so thinking ahead and sticking with a plan still allows the best of both possible worlds—seeing clients, but also being able to step back when needed.

Annually or biannually, it is important to examine what you charge for your active services measured against the time you put into those services, including preparation time and consulting time. This is where self-worth issues regarding the value of your services come in. Have you been doing this a long time? Do you have an area of expertise that you are known for? Do you prefer being a specialist or a generalist? Specialists often produce more active earnings. When you look at your preparation time in relationship to your overhead costs and professional experience, do your earnings reflect that?

Do you like group presentations more than one-on-one consultations? Deciding this is important as it provides a basis for your work. If you enjoy presenting and find that you have a good response from your audiences, it may be more strategic to do more of these types of events. You can consult with an individual or speak to an audience of thirty for one hour. It is the same amount of time, but gives different results. The group knows about you and your personal services, lectures or classes. They have friends who may also be interested in your personal consulting services and ongoing lectures. Having books and recorded lectures and courses available for sale at various venues as well as offering special prices for just your 'group' insures a quick return adding to your passive income streams. Creating a balance between individual and group work is a perfect way to supplement your earnings and maintain energy.

Managing your Finances
Suggestions for United States Residents

Investing

Earnings, whether by active or passive means, are the keystones for your future financial security. Painful as it may sometimes feel to save, pay into a pension plan, or invest in a tangible asset like property, it is important for financial viability. If you don't invest a portion of what you earn, you end up spending it all and nothing is left for the future. It is important to explore how you can invest your earnings and develop tax strategies before you have to pay your federal and state taxes, because as the years progress, the taxes will increase exponentially. Always pay yourself first. Following are just some ideas on how to do that.

It is important to work with others who know about different investment vehicles and make educated guesses based on the information gathered. In the United States interest rates are currently at an all-time low, but that will soon change. By the time you pay taxes on the meager interest rates currently offered in traditional savings accounts you may find yourself owing rather than earning. There are, of course, other bank vehicles. Opening a checking account with a credit union that offers a monthly dividend is a simple way to get additional income from dividends if you follow that credit union's rules.

Another avenue of savings is to invest in solid foreign banks like Canadian banks or Australia's Westpac. They typically offer better interest rates and the only requirement by the IRS is that you indicate on tax returns the interest made on those accounts. It is also important when deciding on a foreign bank to see which USA banks they cooperate with (where funds are wired to and from). If they aren't compatible, getting funds in or out can be difficult.

Depending on your circumstances, the issue of senior care as you age is becoming an expensive proposition. One kind of investment that assures you have proper care is Long Term Care Insurance. The younger you are when you purchase it, the lower the price. Some companies allow the paid benefits to go to your spouse if you don't use them. The current cost (depending on where you live in the USA) of a nursing home varies between $5,000 and $8,000 per month, or, between $60,000 and $96,000 a year! That will only go up over time. Having a long term care policy costing $200 a month comes out to $2400 per year. Over the course of ten years that is $24,000, but during the same period the out-of- pocket costs for care at nursing facilities is between $600,000 and $960,000. Which is the better number?

Different types of pensions: SEPS or IRAs

Even if you only have $100 a month to put into an earning vehicle you have begun the process of empowering yourself for future security. As a self-employed astrologer it is important to set up some sort of *Self Employment Pension* (SEP). When tax time comes in the United States, as a self-employed individual you pay a portion of those net earnings to social security. Social security will not pay you what a SEP can pay. When you have a SEP, you pay only a portion to social security and the other portion into your tax deferred SEP, which can include bonds, mutual funds, stocks, equities, muni bonds and other conservative or more aggressive investment vehicles, depending on your age. You typically take more risk when you're young and less as you mature. Check with a tax consultant or an investment specialist at one of the companies like Charles Schwab to assist you in this effort. Annual contributions are based on your net income. After 50 or 55 you can contribute larger annual amounts.

You can also have a *traditional Individual Retirement Account (IRA) or a Roth IRA* as part of your investment package. The primary difference between a traditional IRA and a Roth IRA is the manner in which they're taxed. Contributions to a traditional IRA are tax deductible in the year you contribute; however, you pay taxes on withdrawals made in the future. Upfront tax-deductibility plus tax-deferred growth of earnings are two of the positive aspects of the traditional IRA. The unknown, however, is whether or not taxes will be higher in the future when you withdraw your funds. With a ROTH Ira your contributions are not tax deductible, but any withdrawals you make after age 59 ½, including capital gains, will be totally tax free. Unless you currently have a very high income, the ROTH is probably the better choice. You can withdraw up to the amount you contributed to a Roth IRA anytime without paying tax (because you already paid tax on the money), but you will have to pay a tax penalty for withdrawals prior to 59 ½.

There are choices of what your IRA or SEP contains. They can include stocks and bonds, equities, mutual funds, municipal bonds, tax-free bonds and such things as the new green bonds. As the Pluto/Uranus at 17° Virgo generation of Environmental Anarchists mature and gain more foothold in the marketplace, we will see more investments in solar panels, fuel cells, and geothermal energy. Many of the utilities (which you can explore when looking at bonds) are offering rebates for incorporating these types of improvements into buildings.

Alternate 'retirement' ideas other than traditional pensions are buying land or property, living there for a while and then turning it into a rental unit or selling it. However, if you first live in the property and then convert it into a rental, there is a tax advantage along with passive rental income in the future.

Social Security is not the only option

Many people think that their social security will suffice for their retirement, but with the cost of living constantly increasing, Social Security isn't enough. In the USA, when you retire and enroll in Medicare at age 65 your Medicare benefits are deducted from your Social Security payments. In addition, you are taxed on these same social security benefits. By the time Medicare and taxes are deducted, there isn't much left. Perhaps the laws will change in the future, but for now they remain in place. This is why a pension or retirement plan is essential. Social security alone won't be sufficient to guarantee a comfortable retirement.

At this writing in 2015, the earliest opportunity to collect social security is 62, but your social security benefits will be adjusted upwards of 25% for every year that you wait, which is either 66 or 67 (depending on what year you were born) until 70, the benefit goes up approximately 8%. That seems to be the best choice, but there are many factors in play depending on your financial need at the time as well as your health. Social security is based on how much you earn, so it is important to log your earnings and pay into the system. The key thing that most people don't understand is that social security calculations are based on your average indexed monthly earnings in your 35 highest-earning years after age 21, which gives you a lot of time to think and plan ahead, but means you do have to put in the time! If you work fewer years, it affects your benefits when the government begins tallying at age 62.

Paying others – Taxes

Resale Licenses and Taxes: If you sell any sort of products, you must obtain a resale license and pay taxes to your state's Department of Revenue or Board of Equalization for in-state product sales.

You do not charge tax on personal consultations, however. It is very important to have a resale license if you plan to sell tangible goods like books purchased at wholesale prices. With a resale license, you can purchase those items wholesale without paying tax (which is forwarded on to your customer). You may also sell your personally developed products such as reports, digital recordings, videos, etc., but when you sell those in-state, you charge sales tax. Out of state sales are untaxed. If you are conducting international sales of products, check the new laws with regard to V.A.T. taxes on the internet.

If your products are listed in a shopping cart on the internet, making tax rate changes provided to you by your state in such programs as PayPal requires minimal adjustment. There are several options with PayPal, Square, Apple Pay, and other processing systems. Depending on your state's requirements, you can either pay your resale tax once a year or quarterly. Check with the revenue department to learn the rules and remember to keep careful records for future audits. If you purchase anything tangible for resale, the resale license allows you to purchase it at wholesale prices (you do not pay tax on that) and then pay the tax when you sell it at retail price. Items that have been purchased wholesale are also listed in most sales tax forms and not counted as tax-making entities. However, accounting for those specific records is important in case of audits.

Federal and State Income Tax: Pay taxes on time. Regardless of how much or how little you make, the penalties are severe. Factoring in your quarterly payments for taxes in that budget template is a key for future planning and keeping you on track. Independent contractors usually file quarterly returns, and, as an astrologer, you are an independent contractor. The dates for filing quarterlies are usually April 15, June 15, September 15, January 15, and again in April, when you have two payments—one for what is left of last year's taxes that you owe and the first quarterly payment for the new tax year. Sometimes you cannot get all your figures together and you have to file for an extension. This is fine, but you still have to pay what you owe come April 15.

If you use any outside services for which you pay over $600 per **year** you must send those professionals a *1099 form* by the end of January. Outside services include editors, webmasters, graphic artists, bookkeepers, administrative assistants, etc. However, if you have employees on regular salary, different rules apply. Regular employees require certain costs to be deducted for their W2s like social security, disability, etc.

NOTE on Audits: If you are audited by the IRS, take only what the written letter requests for you to bring to the audit. Many people do not realize that they are not required to bring added information at the request of the interviewer. This is not allowed.

Spending

Once you formulate a plan and stick to it diligently, you can spend the money you've allotted for those 'wants' that were mentioned earlier in this piece. Obviously, in the beginning of any practice, there may not be as much to spend, but if you stick to the principles and do the work, there will be an adequate amount of funds to pay for those things on your bucket list like travel, learning new skills, and other enjoyable activities. As a traveling astrologer, some of those things can be incorporated into your professional life by speaking or working at conferences where some speakers expenses are paid and you can pitch your products. As a volunteer at conferences or a local theater you often have the registration or entrance fees paid on your behalf. If you use the right credit card to travel to the venue (and pay the entire bill off the next month), the credit card can give you miles or points for future extras that fall in the category of your 'wants'.

You can be a professional astrologer and have a financially viable and prosperous future if you stay focused on your plan, change it when your life circumstances change, and remain open minded with regard to finances. Understanding the concept of money as a means to an end that is constantly in flux is another aspect of maintaining financial prosperity. It is like a plant that needs tending, watering and kindness. Discard judgement with regard to money being bad or good; it is merely the vehicle to other places. It is the bus you take to get to your destination. And, folks, there is always another bus and all kinds of destinations!

Georgia Stathis has been a professional astrologer, writer, well-loved lecturer, and investor for over 35 years. She holds an M.B.A. degree from Pepperdine and a B.S. from Northwestern University. She has taught at UAC, NCGR, FAA, ISAR, IAA, and Midwest School of Astrology, is a lifetime member of OPA and currently teaches at Kepler College and other venues, listed on her website www.starcycles.com. In addition to being a founding member of the international Alexandria iBase Library Project for astrologers, she has been a contributing author for numerous publications and is the author of "Business Astrology 101: Weaving the Web Between Business and Myth." She is currently at work on a pair of new books, "Solar Arcs" and "Pushing through Time." She has numerous lectures at her website: www.starcycles.com

Chapter 5
Part II

A Business Plan for Astrologers
Anne C. Ortelee

Whether you've decided to move Astrology from your hobby to your business, hang up a shingle and become a Pro or are already practicing and want to accelerate the growth of your practice, NOW is the time to write your Business Plan!

Why write a Business Plan? A Business Plan seems "so formal"! It is! **Business Plans are an indication that you take your professional course seriously.** If things are written down, they get done!

There are many different kinds of Business Plans. As you begin (or grow) your astrology practice, Business Plans help focus your intent, direct your activities, and make you conscious of where you are developing or failing to act. Business Plans help you become a Professional Astrologer.

Presented below is a Business Plan format which I've used since 1979. It is simple, clear and basic. It helps focus your activities to grow your business. It is called **GOSPA!** Each letter stands for a component of your business. Combining the five letters of GOSPA creates a Business Plan which is vibrant and alive, and can grow and change with you and your astrology practice.

The first 9 years of my career in corporate America, I would sit down and prepare my annual GOSPA. I included all the things I intended to accomplish during the year. I put copies into two binders—one for me and one for my manager. Each month, I would meet with my manager. He'd take my GOSPA binder off the shelf. We'd sit with our GOSPA binders and spend about a half an hour going through it. We'd easily see what had been accomplished, what hadn't been done, note any areas that had fallen off the radar screen, and add new tasks to my GOSPA. We would write in the binders as tasks were completed or add pages for new projects. We used the monthly GOSPA meetings to plan, focus and redirect activity as needed. Since 1979, I have prepared GOSPA for myself and my business. It is a very useful tool to keep track of both business and personal goals. The format is simple. Feel free to adapt GOSPA to your own needs. Prepare a binder, sit down, perhaps once a month, to see where you are. Then, update, change, expand, schedule, and notice what's been left off or not worked on.

GOSPA

G - Goals

O - Objectives

S - Strategies

P - Plans

A – Activities

G is for Goals

Think motherhood and apple pie! The Goal is BIG—this is your vision for your Astrology Practice! Make your Goal juicy, delicious, and motivating. Something you aspire to! Challenge yourself. Dream big! Dream wide! Dream tall!

Remember that you fulfil a special role as an astrologer; you will help your clients realize and live their best possible potential—do not be shy about your vision. You may write as a goal: *"to employ my astrological skills to help people understand their purpose on earth and thrive,"* or *"To create a positive change and stimulate an awakening in people's lives."*

O is for Objectives

This is quantifiable! Objectives have a hard date and a dollar amount tied to it. How will you objectively measure if you reach that Goal of yours? So if your Goal is to be a full time astrologer that means **how much money by when?** If you are transitioning from a corporate job to astrologer, how much money will you need or want to be generating from your astrology practice this year? When I first started my part time reading practice, my Objective was to read two clients a week by a certain date. When I went full time, my Objective was to see six clients a week by a certain date. Now my Objective includes a breakdown of money from consultations, classes & workshops and non-service based revenue (books, mp3s, and webinars). Reset your Objective every year.

Another example for a quantifiable objective with a hard date: *"I want to make $60,000 per year in income as Professional Astrologer by December 31ˢᵗ."* I would suggest using a separate piece of paper to list your Objectives.

S is for Strategy

What are your Strategies to achieve your Objective? Several Strategies can feed their approaches into achieving your Objective.

My three strategies are:

- Revenue Generating
- Outreach
- Credentials/Education

I strategize and detail the Revenue Generating streams from readings, classes, lessons, and workshops.

For Outreach, I strategize and detail how clients will find me, whether through word of mouth, referral, public speaking, internet, podcast, twitter, websites, Yelp! or Facebook.

For Credentials/ Education, I focus on what I need to learn or do to sharpen my skills as an astrologer. We need to continue growing and educating ourselves to help our clients more effectively. Think about what certifications you want, what credentials you have, and what educational or life skills background you bring to your clients.

Each Strategy will generate plans and activities to materialize the GOSPA. Strategies combine to help us reach the Objective and Goals. I recommend starting with three to five Strategies. List your Strategies on a single page.

P is for Plans

These are Plans on how to meet each Strategy. In my binder, I have a tab and a page for each Plan. For example for Revenue Generating, I write how many consultations, or how many private tutoring sessions I would like to generate a week. If you want to start teaching astrology, this is where you will want to write down what your plan is for that: the date you want to start, the fee you will be charging, and the location or platform for the actual classes. I have a separate page for each Plan in my binder.

A is for Activities

List all the Activities that support the accomplishment of each Plan, including all logistics. Activities for the Plan of Teaching Astrology would include the logistical details about finding the space, advertising, enrolling students, preparing the course material, and collecting money.

If you have the idea to teach at a Continuing Education Program at your local college, approach them early so they can advertise and include you in their catalog. The Activities bloom once you start working on your individual Plans—they are the Plan's to-do list.

When you get ready to execute your Plan, MORE Activities will appear to get the Plan accomplished. Additional Activities might include: "schedule classes, create a list of people who are interested in studying astrology, find marketing outlets, developing content, finding an appropriate space, reserving the room, collecting money, prepare the material, enroll the students, hold the class, deliver content to students at and after the class." Think of all the Activities associated with your Plan teaching a class!

The great part about the Activities list supporting your Plan is preparing you for the NEXT TIME. You have your Plan to-do list of Activities already prepared, including knowledge of the things that worked and didn't work so well.

GOSPA helps generate your list of Activities that execute your Plan; Plans complete your Strategy, Strategies achieve your Objectives, and Objectives are how you measure if you ultimately reach your Goal.

Financial tracking

Make sure to include in your GOSPA, a Plan and supportive Activities to support your **Financial Revenue Strategy and Objectives**. Often we get so busy "doing" we don't pay attention to how much we are "making financially with all that activity!" Check your finances regularly! Make sure to include your expenses and "hidden costs"—things that take time which you don't charge for. There are many good financial packages available such as Quicken, Quickbooks, Xero, Microsoft Small Business, Zoho, YNAB, or Freshbooks (as of 2015) to automate your money and practice.

It is very helpful to start computerizing finances when you first collect money for readings. As you watch your income from astrology grow, you can deduct your expenses such as books, classes, webinars, conferences, travel and meals during travel as well as other trainings in similar metaphysical areas. Look at your financial numbers every week to make sure you are staying on track to meet your Objective.

Conclusion

Once your GOSPA is developed, it becomes a living document. Put your GOSPA in a binder. Once a month or so, go through your GOSPA binder to see what has been accomplished, and what hasn't.

As you finish the Plans and Activities in GOSPA, write updates in the binder. If you have new ideas or projects, add them. Sometimes projects will take multiple years and keep appearing in the book year after year. Other projects come in and go out quickly.

Writing your vision down and scheduling it in your calendar makes it happen. Using GOSPA as wide open vision Business Plan allows you to create the astrology practice and life you've dreamed of.

Anne Ortelee *is certified by the three major astrology organizations; the National Council for Geocosmic Research (NCGR) as a Level 3 Astrologer, the American Federation of Astrologers (AFA) as a AMAFA, and the International Society for Astrological Research as an ISAR-CAP. Anne has volunteered as an Associate for the NYC Chapter of the NCGR since May 1995 and been a frequent lecturer at conferences since December 1998.*

In 1995 Anne organized a monthly Astrology Discussion Group and an astrologically-based stock investment club in 2000, achieving excellent annual returns. Anne's articles appear in various publications: The Ingress, Gaia, and The NCGR Member Letter. Anne was the Recording Secretary for the Uranian Astrologers Special Interest Group for seven years. She currently serves as a director for the C. Jung Foundation in NYC.

Website: www.anneortelee.com

4 Articles

Chapter 6

Legal Issues in the Practice of Astrology
Robert Woodliff and Leisa Schaim

Additional edits by Pat Dumas, Frank Piechoski, and Laura Tadd

---

As astrologers we look back at planetary cycles and use them to describe future events. Knowing the history of our fight for legal legitimacy is important for the future of the astrological community. AFAN has been involved in astrological legal issues since its inception, and is dedicated to fighting discrimination against astrologers as one of its primary missions. As a practicing astrologer, it is important for you to be aware of the legal context that exists where you live, and if necessary, we can help you to challenge any laws on the books that astrology may fall under.

Most of AFAN's legal history up to this point has involved legal challenges to astrologers in the United States. Since the nature of the law is very place-specific in terms of legal principles and precedents, some of the legal guidelines contained in this chapter may be extrapolated for use outside the United States, while other more specific information may not be as applicable. If you live in another country, we'd love to hear from you about any laws governing astrology where you are.

History

V. Imp.

The Association for Astrological Networking (AFAN) is a service organization that exists for the well-being of the entire astrological community, and has since the very beginning worked to counter legal injustices involving astrologers. Begun in the early 1980s, numerous legal issues almost immediately cropped up and became one of the primary focuses of this new organization. In early 1983, two legal issues arose almost simultaneously that initially directed this focus on astrology and the law. The first was a 'psychic fair' at the Mercury Limited Bookstore in West Allis, Wisconsin that was targeted by religious fundamentalists and closed by the police. A local ordinance was subsequently proposed to ban 'fortune telling' in the city.

Around the same time in the spring of 1983, a practicing astrologer in San Jose, California named Shirley Sunderbruch was arrested while in the midst of a consultation. As Jim Lewis recounted in his article on the history of AFAN, "Forty minutes into the reading, a loud knock was heard at Shirley's door. When she opened it, she was forced against the wall by four uniformed police officers with holster guards opened. Shirley was handcuffed and told she was 'under arrest for fortune-telling'. Her astrological books, tape recorder, and even prepared readings were confiscated, and she only escaped being taken away to jail through the efforts of her husband, who was able to convince the brave upholders of the law that Shirley suffered from heart problems...To add insult to injury, the manager of her retirement community evicted her and her husband."

Other instances of legal harassment were heard from in Mobile, Alabama; Pleasanton, California; and Long Island, New York; Milwaukee and Los Angeles were added to the list by January 1984. AFAN raised money from astrologers and astrology businesses for Shirley Sunderbruch's legal defense and coordinated a national letter writing campaign to counter the West Allis proposed ordinance, directed towards local officials and media. AFAN would work on Sunderbruch's case for the next two years until she was exonerated by a higher court ruling; the West Allis proposed ordinance was defeated when the national letter writing and coordination of local community members to speak at the city council meeting helped sway the ordinance vote.

A letter written by the Assistant City Attorney at the time, Gregory Bihn, concerning the advisability of the city adopting such an ordinance also recommended against it. While noting that court opinions on these topics in both Wisconsin and across the country presented a very mixed picture, Bihn particularly pointed out that large newspapers and bookstores profit from astrological forecasting through sun-sign columns and selling astrology books, and so a local law against astrologers themselves would violate equal enforcement clauses—if you're going to prosecute the individual practicing astrologer, you'll be equally obliged to sue all the newspapers and bookstores as well.

Another major drawback Bihn pointed out was the unlikely enforceability if fortune telling was done under the auspices of a religious organization, since it would be protected through freedom of religion. Finally, he pointed out that legislation seeking to define fortune telling as inherently fraudulent seemed to be contradicted by the fact that these activities and businesses had been already operating for some time locally with no consumer complaints of fraud. These several ideas would repeat in the defense of astrology for other legal work that came after this in the 1980s and1990s.

California Supreme Court case

The landmark case *Spiritual Psychic Church v City of Azusa*, 39 Cal. 3d50 (1985) rose through appeals to finally be heard by the California Supreme Court in 1985. This case essentially declared that the free speech Constitutional protections win out against a legislative body deciding on behalf of its constituents that fortune telling is always inherently fraudulent. It also noted that many other people besides fortune tellers forecast the future without penalty, such as economists, investment advisers, religious clergy, and sportswriters predicting athletic event results. This decision also declared that the attempt by a city to outlaw fortune telling as a purely commercial regulation did not get to supersede free speech rights—in other words, the fact that someone is charging money for predicting the future doesn't suddenly grant a city the ability to outlaw it under business regulations.

This was a major legal precedent that was used to help overturn numerous discriminatory ordinances all over the United States. The fact that this case rose to the level of a state Supreme Court doesn't make it foolproof that every other state would decide in the same way, but does make it a lot easier to prevail based on first amendment rights in other cases involving astrology.

Legality based on location

Astrology has come a long way legally in the United States. Around the world, there is much variation in the legal status of astrology. For instance, in February 2011, the Bombay High Court in India declared astrology to be a science, against a challenge by those who wanted it banned under a law against false advertising. In contrast, in Saudi

Arabia astrological or psychic predictions have landed practitioners with a death sentence under anti-witchcraft sentiment. The legal status of professional astrology can and does vary in the United States and around the world not only from country to country and state to state, but even between different counties and cities. When in doubt, seek out information about local ordinances to be sure.

Within the U.S., the United States Supreme Court has not yet ruled on an explicitly astrology-oriented case, so if one needs to defend oneself in an anti-fortune telling case, it would be necessary to use a possible combination of the U.S. or state Constitution, state case precedent, and argument based on local laws. Higher up court decisions from another state, such as the California Azusa case, will not be legally binding if you do not live in that state, but they can still be used in the mix as persuasive case precedent. The same applies if you are getting close to legal trouble and need to communicate with local officials and/or legislators about how this has been viewed in other places.

Definitions and Unique Local Laws

The definition of an astrologer in the U.S. Department of Labor's Dictionary of Occupational Titles is a surprisingly correct description of what astrologers actually do. The job description is as follows:

ASTROLOGER (159.207-010): Prepares and analyzes horoscopes to advise clients regarding future trends and events: prepares horoscopes by computing positions of planets, their relationship to each other and to zodiacal signs, based on factors, such as time and place the subject was born. Analyzes horoscope chart to advise clients, such as person or company, regarding conditions which lie ahead, course of action to follow, and probability of success or failure of that action.

However, it is best not to make too much of that, as "Astrologer" is still unfortunately catalogued under the heading 159, which is the category for Amusement and Recreation occupations.

Another legal definition came from astrologer David Railey and fellow Georgia astrologers in response to Atlanta and Georgia statutes. This offers a concise, clear definition of astrology that has existed since 1970. It is as follows:

> For the purpose of this ordinance "Astrology" is defined as the interpretation of human experience based upon an examination and correlation to celestial activity for fee, gift, or donation. Article C of the Atlanta City Code - Section 14 - 5091.

The City of Atlanta has a unique situation that requires applicants for a business license for the purpose of practicing astrology to pass one of two seven-hour written examinations, either a city exam designed by a Board of Astrology Examiners or the professional exam offered by the American Federation of Astrologers (AFA).

Some cities, upon lobbying by astrologers, have adopted specific definitions for astrologers to set them apart from generic anti-fortune telling laws. Alternately, some others have amended their fortune telling laws to only specifically target those people who claim to be able to change a client's fortune through supernatural means. The intent behind this is to go after the stereotypical defrauding of someone saying s/he can lift a curse in exchange for ten thousand dollars, etc. It does seem in theory that a minority of U.S. astrologers could have the potential to get caught in these kinds of laws, such as if one were recommending gemstones or the like for remediation, but in practice we have not yet heard of anything like this happening.

Sample Examples of Legal Cases and Contexts

In some jurisdictions, certain practices such as palmistry and astrology have been determined not to be "fortune telling." [*People ex rel Priess v. Adams*}, 32 NY Crim 326 (1914); **People v. Malcolm**, 90 Misc 517, 154 NYS 919 (1915); **Pellman v. Valentine**, 185 Misc 873, 57 NYS 2d 617 (1945) (1983 West Allis). This, however, has sometimes depended on either a judge's feelings about the particular case, or been based on a distinction that an astrologer can legally provide character analysis or give general advice, but not give any specific predictions about the future.

Still other jurisdictions permit the practice of fortune telling under license. Certain states prohibit only fraudulent fortune telling, with courts having held that the belief in the practice of certain fortune telling practices did not, per se, constitute fraud (1983 West Allis City).

1983 Oregon Court of Appeals, Marks v. City of Roseburg 670 P.2d 201 (1983) declared unconstitutional a city ordinance prohibiting fortune telling, on the basis of rights of free expression in the Oregon Constitution, regardless of receiving money for it. The court opinion states, "The fact that the ordinance prohibits communication only if it is offered for 'hire or profit' does not insulate it from scrutiny under Article I, section 8, which forecloses the enactment of laws 'restraining' free expression and 'restricting' the right to speak and write, not just laws flatly prohibiting those rights. Obviously, a law prohibiting a speaker or writer from accepting a fee for his communication constitutes a restriction on his right to speak or write."

1991 proposed Los Angeles ordinance was dropped after AFAN communication. The ordinance would have required background checks, fingerprinting, and excessive license fees for astrologers. This combination of requirements has been fairly typical for proposed anti-fortune telling ordinances in many cities.

1995-96 Albany, California AFAN filed a legal brief against the city of Albany, CA after an astrologer would have been required to do a background check and pay unreasonable licensing fees. (1995 and 1996 Albany). The city repealed the ordinance and enacted AFAN-drafted 'Alternative Consultants' business license ordinance.

AFAN has come to the aid of astrologers in California, Michigan, Pennsylvania, Florida, New Jersey, New York, Massachusetts, Oregon, Georgia, Ohio, Washington, Texas, Wisconsin, Maryland, Missouri, and Illinois, among others. The First Amendment states that speech, opinion, philosophy, and belief systems have the legal right to be both expressed and made available to any citizen who desires to make use of them. It is unlawful to regulate free speech through bias and/or prejudice. The use of this defense as one of the main arguments has increasingly been a winning strategy against anti-astrology ordinances and laws.

Current day discrimination issues

The legal situation in the U.S. for astrologers is markedly better than just a few decades ago. However, discrimination does still exist. Aside from isolated legal issues, we have found that discrimination more commonly comes in two forms now: social and financial. While social discrimination can be unpleasant, it is not something that astrologers can deal with through legal means. Social bias has caused many astrologers to put 'counselor', 'advisor', or some other term as their professional title. Even those practitioners who are prominent and greatly respected within the astrological community sometimes report feeling odd telling people that they are astrologers. However, the situation may be looking up, as Americans who think astrology is "not at all scientific" declined from nearly two-thirds in 2010 to slightly more than half in 2012 (the last year for which data is available). The NSF (National Science Foundation) reports that this is the lowest percentage responding this way since 1983.

The other category of discrimination is financial discrimination. This would include issues such as credit card processors denying or cancelling an astrologer's account, astrologers not being able to get business loans, or otherwise being denied equal consideration financially. The most common complaint that AFAN has been made aware of in this category during the past several years involves credit card processors cancelling accounts under the auspices of 'occult' exclusions. At the current moment, there are options such as Paypal that do not list any sort of exclusions for metaphysical services. There are other credit card processors, Square being a prominent one, that have long lists of exclusions including 'occult services', which they consider astrology to fall under.

One of AFAN's members recently had their account cancelled with Square after being an account holder in good standing. In response, AFAN wrote asking them to change their procedure for astrological services. The company proved to be less than transparent and vague in their reply, as well as hard to contact. We have also heard of other less well-known credit card processors that had similar exclusions in their terms used to cancel astrologers' accounts. It's not impossible, but harder, to challenge these companies' policies since they are private entities, so it is best to read the fine print of excluded products and services before signing up with a credit card processor if you will be using it to process payments for astrology services. It is recommended to simply use a company that doesn't have such exclusions; alternately, some astrologers have reported no problems using processors that do have exclusions if it is under their own name rather than an obviously astrological company name. But if your account is not already established, it seems best to vote with your money for companies who do not discriminate in this way.

AFAN has not yet heard of cases of outright rejection for business loans or credit solely due to being an astrologer. The potential is there for lenders to be sued for discrimination if this happened; on the other hand, this type of discrimination would be subtle and potentially hard to spot, and harder still to prove.

Setting Up an Astrology Business

This next section is about personal and legal protection and the procedure to set up a business. We have found these steps to be fairly standard and are as follows:

First, check the state statutes/regulations barring astrologers. The best resource is a state legal library. Some terms to look for: Astrology, Astrologer, Divination, Fortune Telling, or Occult Services. Then do the same check for city ordinances that place any restrictions on astrology (or the above terms).

Second, if you are looking for a physical location then you will want to search for private contractor restrictions, which for the most part will be zoning restrictions to keep private housing zones free of additional business traffic.

Next, decide if you will have a localized shop to do your astrology in or if you want to focus on only doing remote consultations via phone or Skype. If a local business is desired then you should get business license. It is debatable whether one needs a business license to conduct mostly remote consultations, but one could get one to be on the safe side. A business license is also often

INVEStigate

needed if you want to do readings at large events such as fairs. Do let AFAN know if a business license in your city as an astrologer would cost you inordinately more than other types of business licenses.

Finally, you may want to legally incorporate if you have a lot of clients. This protects you and your personal assets, such as your house or car, from being taken if your business goes under, or if a client decided to sue you.

Miscellaneous legal considerations

After you start your practice, you may want to be cautious in some of the wording that you use in making predictions, while still representing your interpretations accurately, in order to help avoid any future legal issues with clients. Recording your sessions may provide some protection along these lines as well, since sometimes clients can hear something in a certain light that can be different than how the astrologer puts it into words.

Be particularly cautious in making health or illness-related statements in the United States, as there are some pretty clear laws on the books regarding practicing medicine without a license that you could potentially run into. It is most ideal if you are going to practice medical astrology or even make astrologically based health recommendations of any sort such as herbs, etc. that you concurrently hold some sort of health practitioner license, such as that of a TCM practitioner (Traditional Chinese Medicine) or ND (Naturopathic Doctor), so that you would be more legally covered in making such statements. Otherwise, it may be best to stick to more general statements regarding health, if any. AFAN has not had dealings so far with astrologers getting into trouble with these kinds of laws, but it is a risk that exists.

Finally, some astrologers in certain locations where there are anti-fortune telling laws still on the books such as New York, choose to write a disclaimer statement on their websites or other business materials that for legal purposes, their services are for the purpose of entertainment only. Other astrologers bristle at making such a statement since it feels denigrating to the real purpose of what they are doing, even if it would seem to provide more legal protection.

Do This

The Legal Future

Looking towards the future, AFAN would like to work in conjunction with the entire astrological community for the repeal of any remaining anti-astrology laws and ordinances. We have to work together in order to do this, because the nature of the law is that there needs to be a local constituent who is personally affected. So look up your state and local laws, let us know if there is an anti-astrology law where you live that you would like help in challenging, and we can provide the support, advice, and some background case law to help you do it. Hopefully one day legal discrimination involving astrology will be just history, but until that day AFAN and our community will continue to fight against astrological discrimination. You can contact AFAN via the website: www.afan.org

Ask
NCGR

Bibliography:

"Astrology And Its Problems: Popper, Kuhn and Feyerabend." *The Kindly Ones*. N.p., 2011. Web. 18 Aug. 2015. <http://thekindlyones.org/2011/02/14/astrology-and-its-problems-popper-kuhn-and-feyerabend>.

"Astrology is a Time-Tested Science: High Court Rules" February 5, 2011. Examiner.com Entertainment | AXS Network | © 2006-2015 AXS Digital Group LLC d/b/a Examiner.com. Web. 08/2015. Visited 08/10/2015. <http://www.examiner.com/article/astrology-is-a-time-tested-science-high-court-rules>.

Bihn, G.H. "1983 West Allis City." AFAN Legal File Documents. If one needs or wants to see it, they can email AFAN at democratic@afan.org.

Lewis, Jim. "History of AFAN." All contents copyright © AFAN. Web. 08/2015. Visited 08/10/2015. <http://www.afan.org/inside/about/afan-history>.

Jacobs, Jayj. "1991 Los Angeles ordinance letter." AFAN Legal File Documents. If one needs or wants to see it, they can email AFAN at democratic@afan.org.

Jacobs, Jayj. "1994 Astrology: Its Place in, and Contribution to, Western Civilization." AFAN Legal File Documents. If one needs or wants to see it, they can email AFAN at democratic@afan.org.

Marks v. City of Roseburg. 670 P.2d 201. Oregon Court of Appeals, 12 Oct. 1983.

Oja, Dorothy "1995 Albany CA letter." AFAN Legal File Documents. If one needs or wants to see it, they can email AFAN at democratic@afan.org.

Oja, Dorothy "1996 Albany CA letter 2." AFAN Legal File Documents. If one needs or wants to see it, they can email AFAN at democratic@afan.org.

"Science and Engineering Indicators 2014." *National Science Foundation*. Web. Visited 9/4/2015. <http://www.nsf.gov/statistics/seind14/index.cfm/chapter-7/c7h.htm>.

Robby Woodliff *is a Salt Lake City, Utah-based astrologer with a particular interest in astrological research and astrological history. He focuses on Western modern astrology with a touch of traditional flavor. He has a degree in Philosophy with a teaching history minor from the University of Utah. He plans to get a masters in education from the University of Utah to become a high school history teacher. He has studied under Christopher Renstrom (rulingplanets.com) for four years, while writing a weekly horoscope blog for two years privately at whereisrobby.com. He is serving under the legal chair and mentoring chair of the Association for Astrological networking (AFAN). Email: whereisrobby333@gmail.com*

Leisa Schaim *is a Denver, Colorado-based astrologer with a particular interest in combining the best of modern and traditional astrological approaches. She has a BA in Interdisciplinary Social Sciences from Antioch College and did graduate work in Religious Studies at the University of Colorado. She is the current presiding officer of the Association for Astrological Networking (AFAN) and served as its legal chair prior to that, and is co-organizer of the Denver Astrology Group. She offers consultations and writes articles at LeisaSchaim.com and SaturnReturnStories.com.*

Chapter 7

The Times are a-Changin'

A Contemporary Approach to Astrology Practice

Wendy Stacey

Astrological consultations have been valued for centuries—from the time our ancestors' survival was dependent upon their knowledge of the land, sea and the sky. The practice of astrology continues to survive and develop in various forms around the globe and has the potential to thrive in our ever-changing society.

We are currently living through a technological revolution, entering a virtual world and digital age where social barriers are dissolving and new generations have different needs. We astrologers must find new approaches and techniques to address these needs. How might we adapt to the changes and challenges that present themselves? How can we continue to improve and extend our services? One thing is certain: developing our astrological practices is essential if we are going to meet the diverse needs of our clients.

The aim of this chapter is to offer some insight into the modern practice of astrology and how we as consultants may feel the need to accommodate contemporary issues and future trends. I have split this chapter into four different sections:

1. Incorporating roaming consultations into our practices
2. Cycles and change: how these reflect your clientele
3. The role of Astrologers within a profession, culture and community
4. Beyond 2020...

Incorporating Roaming Consultations into our Practices

In our fast paced era people are accustomed to finding solutions at the click of a button. Booking an appointment three to six weeks (or months) in advance becomes impractical. There is a demand for an immediate response as people are pressed to make quicker decisions in their lives. As consultants, we might need to adapt (within reason) to the demands of a much busier lifestyle. In this fast-paced society many clients may expect a consultation right after booking it, so we need to decide how available we will be. Are we available on weekdays, evenings and weekends? The more flexible we are, the more accessible and rapid our response will be. Some of us with busy practices may have long waiting lists, so setting aside spare slots for emergency sessions can be the sensible thing to do—and there often are emergencies!

As astrologers we need to be willing and able to respond to these changing demands. This means the traditional consultation space may change from a room to a roaming location which accommodates both the astrologer and the client's lifestyles.

Over the past decade, astrological consulting has grown to include different session formats. Beyond the standard one-and-a-half-hour session in an office or home, many astrologers now conduct consultations through a laptop, tablet or mobile device from anywhere in the world. There has been an increase in the popularity of brief *micro-consultations* conducted via remote distance.

We are not dependent on our local community for our clientele anymore; we can now extend the scope of our practice to reach clients from anywhere in the world. It can be helpful to do our own astrocartography to find where our practice might thrive in different regions.

Astrological consultancy is now available to a global market and instead of being dependent on word of mouth we now have to be proactive in reaching a wider audience. We have the opportunity, but also the challenge, of recruiting our clientele from anywhere in the world. We can travel through Brazil yet give a client from Paris a consultation over the web. How we manage our time and our practice requires consideration of practicalities and the technology options at our disposal.

In my experience, clients who want quick consultations are not necessarily looking for shortcuts; they are in fact looking to get to the heart of a matter more rapidly. As consultants, we can think about including this format when appropriate for ourselves and our clients. We must consider that people no longer have the luxury of time as they once did. They are expected to make decisions, both in business and their personal lives, much quicker than a decade ago. Since then, technology has taught us to engage with each other on different levels and has reshaped the way we communicate and operate professionally. The changes in society and the next generation of clients will require us to continually rethink how we consult.

Another advantage of virtual consultations is that they can be instant. If a client wishes to talk there and then, and we are available, we can talk to each other quickly and easily. Discussion via a virtual meeting still offers face-to-face contact when a stable internet connection is available. As astrologers we understand the need for dialogue throughout a consultation and the virtual meeting allows for this. It offers the ability to share in a more interactive way.

An additional advantage is that we do not need to invest in an office or allocate space in our home. The disadvantage is that we lose in-person contact, which is always valuable when working with a client. Clients are more likely to engage in a dialogue when present in the same room as us—many clients still want an astrologer they can physically visit. Continue to be available for these: they are rewarding and a lot of good work can be done. The same holds true for written analyses, if you wish to offer these.

The more options we can offer, the more likely we are to attract new and returning clients. As astrologers, we need to think about how we want to offer astrological consultations right now, and we must also anticipate how we might want to conduct them in the future as technology progresses.

Beyond the consultation format, we might want to give some thought to *how the cycles of the planets might influence our astrological practices in the future*—not only assessing how and where we may practice, but also what our clients will be asking of us and the type of clientele we might attract.

Cycles and Change: How these Reflect your Clientele

The clients we attract will usually be a reflection of the transits at that particular point in time as well as the placements in our own natal chart.

When transiting planets change signs we understand certain shifts are taking place and these will trigger events around the world as well as the natal charts of our clients. Often during these times our client work increases. For example, when Pluto and Uranus moved into cardinal signs between 2008 and 2011, my own consultancy and that of others saw an increase in clients, and most were seeking guidance on how to deal with unexpected change. Many of these clients had planets or angles that resided in the early degrees of cardinal signs and needed assistance understanding the cardinal-type challenges and crises they were confronted with. As these transiting planets continue their journey through these signs, it will not be surprising to find that our clientele (particularly new clients) have planets at the same degrees in cardinal signs in their own natal chart.

Similarly, when Neptune ingressed into Pisces in 2011 and 2012, many clients who have planets (particularly the luminaries) and angles at the early degrees of Pisces (or the mutable signs) were struggling in their lives. When Neptune in Pisces triggers natal points it is understandable that people can feel lost, and sometimes the despair and helplessness can be felt very deeply and impact all areas of their lives. These clients need to feel empowered and transmute the energy of the transit. In the case of Neptune, we can help them understand the pain within and around themselves and know that it is OK to start believing in and once again seeking the beauty of the world around them.

On a larger societal scale, the Neptune transit will bring issues of reality versus fantasy, spiritual attachments, a change in perception and an interest in the creative, the magical and the unknown. This period will also give rise to issues of dependency and service and will spotlight the ailing sectors of society. These matters will also manifest on an individual level and we will see this within our astrological practice and the subjects that arise in clients' lives during this time.

Certain transits (for instance, Pluto on the natal Ascendant) will only occur in *some* of the population's charts and, for those who are

affected, they will happen just once in a lifetime. Understanding
what these outer planetary cycles might mean can aid us in adjusting
our perception, our perspective and our practice to help us be of
better service to our clients.

To make sense of the complexities within our clients' natal charts,
it is important to consider what was going on around the world
when they were born. It is not just the current astrological
significators (such as transits) that can tell us about the client's
present experiences, but also those placements that the client was
born with, placements which paint a larger picture of how the
planetary cycles will unfold and how they are lived out on an
individual level.

For instance, the Uranus–Pluto in Virgo generation born in the
1960s has much to do with recent changes in the nature of work and
us becoming more process-driven. This is the generation who has
contributed to how much we overwork and to making modern life
'busier'. We have seen Virgoan changes in our society in how we
work, along with such areas as our concept of our bodies, the way in
which we conduct our daily lives, organize our homes and families,
our interests and leisure pursuits, and what and how we eat. This
generation is interested in self-improvement and analysis, and will
require a deeper exploration of their problems with their astrologers
rather than simple band-aid solutions. Those born in the 1960s are at
the time of writing in their forties and fifties and will represent part
of our client base.

Another sector of our client base can also be considered. Due to
the elliptical orbit of Pluto's journey (making it travel faster through
some parts of the zodiac than others), we have an older generation
who are experiencing Pluto half-returns—i.e. transiting Pluto opposite its natal placement. Many of those born with Pluto in Cancer
(1912 to 1939) will have Pluto in Capricorn opposing their own natal

Pluto. On a mundane level we can see the issue of an aging society unfolding, and this will be felt on an individual level as well. Issues of food (or shortage thereof), family, the home, population and respect for one's elders will be addressed as Pluto opposes those with Pluto in Cancer during the 2010s.

Tracking the outer planets through the signs helps us understand the different needs of each generation astrologically. Those with Pluto in Libra will have an emphasis on relationships, fairness, and a need to have balance in their lives. Those with Pluto in Scorpio will need to feel vividly alive, which may compel them to enter situations that test their survival. Sex, death and taboos belong to this astrological signature for a reason. Pluto in Sagittarius will seek answers. In their pursuit of the Holy Grail this generation will want to explore new frontiers intellectually and physically, so they will be interested in new forms of knowledge and power.

Now we are entering an era where the Uranus and Neptune in Capricorn generation (born in the late 1980s and early 1990s, some with Saturn in Capricorn too) will be leading the way for the next few decades and form another section of our client base. What might this mean for the future of astrological consultancy? I can envision that they will be intent on cleaning up the mess the Uranus-Pluto in Virgo generation has made. They are the generation that can turn fantasy into reality (Saturn–Neptune in Capricorn), particularly during the sextile between Neptune in Pisces and Pluto in Capricorn. They might slow things down for a period, put more emphasis on getting it right, and hopefully understand the levels of risk that changes in society bring. This generation will be focused on vocation and likely want to know more about business astrology. Pluto will be transiting Capricorn throughout the 2010s and early 2020s, triggering those born with these planets in Capricorn, and here we might see clients being slightly risk-averse and feeling the need to consolidate before taking further action or large leaps forward. This group will do this before handing over the reins of society to the next generations, including those born during the recent Uranus–Pluto squares.

Astrologers Relocated in Profession, Culture, Community and Education

With the development of psychology in the early twentieth century, the focus of astrology in the western world shifted from a less deterministic view centered around prediction to a more free-will approach. Much of the development of this work can be mainly attributed to the brilliant works of Alan Leo, Dane Rudhyar and Liz Greene. In 1915, Alan Leo was responsible for founding one of the oldest astrological organizations in the world, The Astrological Lodge of London, where astrologers still meet every Monday evening for talks, meetings and classes.

The growing interest in psychology paved the way for astrological consultancy to develop in a way never seen before. In the latter part of the century it produced the foundations for client work that are integral to the practice of astrology today. With this shift, astrologers formed associations, organizations and learning institutions, and different schools of thought grew in and out of favor as various branches of astrology were studied and new theories were explored. The 1970s saw a focus on science and many astrologers came together to explain astrology in a scientific manner. In the late 1980s the astrological community was arguably at its height. Astrologers were busy, astrology schools were full, and the number of events and conferences increased. Several new official bodies were formed to cater to the growing interest in the field. The development of astrological software amplified astrological research and revolutionized the speed at which charts could be calculated for consultations.

Support and supervision became available for professional astrologers and with the entrance of Saturn (followed by Uranus and Neptune) into Capricorn in the late 1980s, an emphasis on improving the quality of service, ethics and professionalism became priorities in the astrological community.

While the practise of astrology was not legitimized, recognized or respected in comparison to the more mainstream professions such as counseling or psychotherapy, there was a growth of the number of astrological communities concerned with quality research, education and professional practice which led to the development of self-regulating bodies. This is not dissimilar to what homeopaths, chiropractors and acupuncturists went through before entering the mainstream.

Self-regulation between groups or organizations of astrologers is a positive thing. For example, what does a client do if they wish to make a complaint? Both the client and the astrologer should have an avenue for resolution. Appropriate measures need to be in place for both clients and astrologers to be safeguarded. This could include a support network, registration with professional bodies and a clear set of ethical guidelines for professional practice regarding confidentiality, limitations on predicting events, transparency on what astrology can and can't tell us, and so forth.

In recent decades, astrological organizations have brought astrologers together and worked for the good of astrology around the world. In the US the National Council for Geocosmic Research (NCGR), the International Society for Astrological Research (ISAR), the AFA/AFAN, and OPA have all labored to raise standards in astrological education, research, or ethical guidelines to assist astrological consultants and their clients.

43
63

In the UK, the Astrological Association was formed in 1958 to support the profession of astrology. The birth of The Advisory Panel on Astrological Education (APAE) in 1980 had a remit to assess standards of astrological education. The Association of Professional Astrologers International (APAI – originally named the Association of Professional Astrologers) was formed in 1990, and students who held a diploma from a recognized school were eligible to become members. The APAI advertises its members' services and offers a group insurance policy, which is difficult for astrology practitioners to obtain independently. The group policy covers all astrologers registered with this organization in Professional Indemnity and Public Liability.

The growth of these organizations across the globe has been instrumental in defining where astrologers should be educated and how astrology should be practiced. Through this work ethics and professionalism have become an essential focus for astrology consultants. With globalization and technological advancement we have seen in a relatively short space of time these local, regional and national communities and organizations knit together and form networks of astrologers who share ideas and experiences to strengthen the profession as a whole.

It is probable that the development of professionalization will be high on the agenda for astrological consultancy in the near future, particularly with (at the time of writing) Pluto travelling through Capricorn and the Capricorn stellium generation (born in the 90's) coming of age to lead the way in the astrological community. Although there may be debate on the pros and cons of fostering public recognition and respectability, there will be a need, an indisputable need, for responsibility within our own community to enhance self-regulation and create support systems and learning environments to insure quality education and premium service to clients. Organizations such as quality schools and regulatory bodies which offer further training, supervision, and ethical and professional standards will be beneficial in achieving this.

On a more personal level, individual astrologers may need to think about how and where they wish to study—what they want to specialize in. In recent decades education in general has changed, particularly in terms of demand, quality and access. Astrological consultancy has also changed and, similar to other professions, any evidence of learning, such as a diploma or a degree, is increasingly a necessity, especially in regards to counseling skills. We have a responsibility to our clients who are seeking guidance, many of whom are vulnerable, and it is beneficial to have some sort of training in this area.

Beyond 2020…the Jupiter/Saturn Conjunction in Aquarius and its Effect on Astrology Practise

Jupiter and Saturn will begin an unbroken sequence of conjunctions in the Air element in 2020 when they conjoin at 0° Aquarius, and we will witness a shift from the focus on ownership and material resources (represented by the Earth element of the previous Jupiter Saturn conjunction in Taurus in the year 2000) to a more cerebral one, where intellectual property and the increased exchange of information, ideas and physical mobility will occupy the forefront of our economy and dominate our lives—and those of our clients. This may portend a shift in focus for the next generation. The future generation might not be interested in mortgages, owning their own homes (or owning anything), as they are likely to be attracted to pushing the boundaries in technology, focusing on innovations that provide stimuli and finding new ways of interacting. We will no longer be anchored by the denseness that the Earth element brings each minute, hour and day and in every aspect of our lives (such as how we sleep, eat and work), but instead be inspired and interested in ways to develop human capabilities and link with each other and the environment we operate within.

There will likely be a change in awareness and observation, and therefore perspective, on life and our place within it. People will identify themselves with what they know and understand. Networks of a different kind will grow and the nuclear family may be replaced with like-minded or like-abled groups. When Jupiter–Saturn conjoined in Libra in 1980, we saw the growth and acceptance of divorces which led to families being fragmented. As a result, family structures became more complex, many featuring step-parents and step or half-siblings, and it became normal to have several parents or grandparents because of this new family structure. This will be reflected in our clients' lives and experiences and the changing questions they will bring to consultations.

The Jupiter–Saturn conjunctions would normally take some time to take effect, but what will follow from this conjunction is the arrival of **Pluto into Aquarius in 2024.** This will undoubtedly spearhead us into an exciting intellectual cyber world where our clients' needs will change again from being concerned with material needs to understanding their place in the larger scheme of life (and the Universe) and the needs of the planet. *WORK for it*

yes!

Throughout history, humans have always faced challenges in their lives, whether in matters of survival, love, or relationships with friends, family and colleagues, and these will no doubt continue. People will still want to know what is around the corner and how they can best be prepared for it. These situations will always be brought into the astrological consultation. However, the *nature* of all of these issues is changing and will be reflected in the needs of our clients as Jupiter, Saturn, and Pluto enter Aquarius and then again when the generation born of it reach adulthood.

Our roles as astrologers are transforming gradually from counsellor and analyst to consultant and mentor, and I personally believe that some of the ways we currently practice will become redundant in the next few decades. We will have to be well-rounded and trained in all areas, but we must also highlight the areas in which we specialize, as the sign of Aquarius is concerned with originality and uniqueness. Future clients will know exactly what they want from a consultation as they will be more informed, embrace freedom of thought and be intent on making independent decisions. Thus, there will be a growth in educating the public about what our astrology services encompass—which go beyond the current media sun sign columns.

Astrology may be faced again with challenges concerning the concepts of fate and free-will—that is, to what extent the client has choice and to what extent life is predestined. This might raise debate or discussion between different branches of astrology such as Natal and Psychological, which promote free-will and individual autonomy, as opposed to the Vedic or Traditional, which take a more predetermined approach. There is still much uncertainty about how astrology actually works, so renewed theorizing might become common. If research is unable to come up with coherent theories and explanations astrology may suffer a loss of popularity in some places.

Summary

It is important to be adaptable and open to cultural changes while having faith in your abilities as a modern astrology consultant. Astrology can be an exciting profession with many rewards when we keep ourselves open to various formats of consultancy and adapt to the changing demands of clients in the fast-moving technological society we live in.

I believe the art of a good astrologer is knowing people. However, people and the society in which we live are different than they were two decades ago. Younger generations interact in a way never seen before in human history—conducting multiple conversations simultaneously via electronic devices. These generations will bring new challenges to the astrological consultancy.

However these changes might manifest, look at your own chart and explore what sort of astrologer you are, where your skills lie and what the best service you can offer is. Study your chart to see what sort of clients you might attract and what practice you would like to build for the future. Above all else, be true to yourself so you can be true to your clients.

Wendy Stacey, B.A, M.A, Dip LSA is the principal of the international Mayo School of Astrology and tutor for the London School of Astrology. She is the Chairperson for the Astrological Association UK (since 2002), has written over 50 articles for students in the Astrological Journal and is the author of Consulting With Astrology and Uranus Square Pluto. Her book Unaspected Planets is due for release 2016. In 2014 Wendy was the recipient of the British Charles Harvey award for 'Exceptional Service to Astrology'.
Website: www.wendystacey.com

Chapter 8

Building a Feedback Loop into your Professional Practice
Monica Dimino

All businesses incorporate client feedback into their practices. Airlines, hotels, and hospitals have all made this part of their daily procedure. Businesses recognize that getting to know the people they work for is the best way to provide client satisfaction. Professional astrologers can develop structures in their practices to achieve the same rewards.

Businesses accomplish this with their ubiquitous questionnaires. Fly anywhere these days and the airline will e-mail a request for feedback before you get home. Ditto for health services, hospitals, and other major service providers.

Bombarding our clients with questionnaires would add stress to both astrologer and client. Consequently, we have to find ways to obtain the feedback without burdening those we aim to help. Each astrologer can develop their own tools to achieve this. In this writing we will explore the methods this professional astrologer has used to keep abreast of clients and their needs.

It started over 50 years ago while I was still learning astrology. It seemed essential to connect this information to real people in order to supplement the formal learning. Applying theories to people was the next step. Anyone who had birth data was invited to attend a free reading. It was important to see and hear from real people. How did the individual's life correlate to the template of the birth chart? Careful listening and note-taking created new dimensions for studying astrology. The readings/consultations were also a font of deeper understanding of astrological mechanics. Learning thrived with each chart.

There were surprises along the way. Not all the aspects in the natal chart created the same picture that was expected from the classroom descriptions. Taking note of these variations led to creating tallies and sidebars for further study. My volunteer "clients" helped define some of these contrasts. Bit by bit, these notes turned into teaching guides for later years.

Later it was time to add transits and progressions to the learning process. Trying them out meant connecting this information with the subjects of earlier studies, the individuals who had already received free mini readings. Once again, these volunteers were invited to continue with what was labeled "a learning process." An interesting discovery occurred. Most of these volunteers did not know there was something in astrology besides the natal chart. Occasionally someone would ask about Solar Returns, but that was the only reference to any ongoing awareness of the continual movement of the heavens, that there may be more to astrology than the birth chart alone

My telling **everyone** about my astrological studies was inevitable. Who doesn't remember the emotional highs when our paths first crossed with astrology? Everyone in that world was trapped into a barrage of questions: when were you born? Where?

Do you know what time? Would you like to hear about your chart? Appointments were scheduled and those friendly volunteers asked questions. Promising nothing, we speculated on the charts' promise and possibilities. Animated conversations led to enduring curiosity for both of us.

In the beginning it was necessary to pursue these cases, offering additional readings to follow up on developments since the initial study. This, however, opened the door to unexpected benefits. Not only was the learning of astrology enhanced, but participants were educated as well. While these volunteers were not official clients, they became interested consumers of astrological services. Astrology was no longer a simple column in a daily newspaper. It could go beyond warning us about things that merely added up to a bad hair day.

Another feature of these follow up sessions was to make me aware of the ongoing need for tracking astrology beyond the simple reading of the natal chart. Time and again, it became clear that the average person has no idea about the possibilities offered by astrology. Our very ability to provide value for our work is undermined by popular beliefs that ours is a tool to tell the future, or that all is fixed in a chart without past or future celestial influences. Too often it is seen as a dead end street, or at best, a structure that harbors inevitability.

Establishing a feedback loop in client work radiates out into a number of areas for development and a broader understanding of what our profession needs to make it a viable career. We are dealing with a public that is well conditioned to labeling our work as quackery, or at best, simple entertainment. Who or what may turn the tide? Practicing astrologers skilled in their wise handling of their craft. The public needs better information about what our work really is. Perhaps we could start by showing how interesting even the simplest facets of astrology can be.

An example of an experience I had almost a decade ago will illustrate this point. I was invited to do a two week stint at a Spa which wanted me to do weekly lectures about astrology every evening followed up by scheduled readings for anyone in the audience who might be interested. I was told that no one in the Spa was savvy in astrology so the talks would have to be basic and essentially promotional to sell the follow up readings. I'd never addressed an audience of non-astrologers before so I hardly knew where to begin. I decided to approach the task as I had in the very beginning of my astrological studies. I was "hooked" by astrology via the excitement I felt learning about a new world that was unknown to me. That would have to be the approach with this group!

My first lecture was to describe astrology's base as one more calendar in our lives. Just as we use calendars to track the Sun and Moon throughout the year, astrology has additional calendars which track the movement of the remaining planets in the Solar System. That planets have seasons and phases just as the sun and moon. That reading a horoscope was essentially viewing the phases of the other bodies moving around the sun. Each planet relates to a facet of life just as the seasons relate to the Sun and the tides to the Moon. It was a 90 minute talk, open to questions at the end. The Spa had a capacity for 75 guests. Less than 10 turned up for the free lecture. Half of them signed up for a reading of their horoscope. I was booked for two days.

The following evening I lectured on another topic and the room with a capacity for 25-30 was almost full. (Yes, word of mouth works.) This, too, led to more signing up for chart readings. And so it went for the first week. Each day the attendance increased and by the end of that week the evening sessions had standing room only.

The second week provided more of the same. My bookings for chart readings were filled for the duration and, as there was not enough room for so many requests, many booked for phone consultations upon their return home.

How does this happen? It's not related to my media world, fame, or advertising skills; I have none of the above. It's Astrology, one of the most interesting subjects in the universe, with evolving stages that never end. Here's a sample of the feedback that I received: "I would never have consulted an astrologer until I attended your lecture. I'm not interested in predictions, but that's not what it's really about. It's so interesting." Or, "Why isn't this information about seasons and cycles available to non-astrologers?" I think we struggle to promote astrology without knowing what people want, nor which facets of astrology might be important for the great variety of interests in potential consumers. Providing a feedback loop is the best tool to achieve this.

A lot was learned in this fortnight with an audience which was not at the spa for astrology. It shows that the average astrologer has numerous opportunities to establish a following by word of mouth as long as he or she keeps it simple and interesting.

This brings me back to our need to create a feedback loop in our consulting practice. It's the only way to address the needs of our clients. We can make assumptions about them in studying their horoscopes, but how often do we miss the point? We often hear that when a client comes to an astrologer, it's to solve a problem or deal with a crisis. In those cases, our task is whittled down to finding the malefic and calculating the duration of the transit/progression. Consultations based on crisis identification and duration can be mechanical and perhaps boring for both client and astrologer. Sure, there may be the initial relief to know that the trouble has an identifiable cause. End of story.

On the other hand, input from a healthy feedback loop leads us to any number of healing opportunities that neither client nor astrologer may discover on his or her own. Let's say you've done an initial reading with a client. In the process you may have successfully picked up the sore spots in the horoscope. In your dialogue with the client a few additional comments might suggest that if there is any lack of clarity or need to review what was said a free, brief phone follow-up is available for additional information. That assurance alone can relax the client, perhaps enhancing the ability to hear or process information.

Another benefit of a follow-up call has been to discover that the initial reading brought up issues that weren't addressed in the first session. The astrologer can handle this by leaving the door open for further dialog. There can often be discoveries after a full session and the client should be able to share that via a brief free phone follow-up. The client needs to be validated in this self-discovery that was awakened via the initial reading. It creates a chain reaction that leads to multiple opportunities for our clients to grow via astrology.

Eventually, this process leads to a number of positives for us dedicated to building and growing a profession that has virtually unlimited benefits for everyone. New clients are better connected to our services. It's a teaching opportunity where explanations of cycles and sessions make sense of what often seems like chronic chaos. It leads clients to understand the connected nature of so many life events.

To us, the practicing astrologers, the feedback process lends itself to unforeseen growth in our ability to help our clients. Their stories can be correlated to chart patterns, aspects, or, eventually, to progressions. We get to see how T-squares manifest over time: are they always active? Does their behavior contradict a major theme? We learn how to weigh the apparently contradictory elements in clients' charts. We begin to move away from the tenets of our early education as observations in real life suggest that there are better ways to understand the chart's complexities.

I have been practicing as a full time professional astrologer since 1970. Now I have clients that I've known for several Saturn cycles, progressed new moons, and most of the heavy transits. I've learned from these client histories that the same themes turn up again and again. It's up to the astrologer to connect the dots. This is where the art of astrology takes root. A dynamic flow of celestial data meets the real world, tended to by the astrologer who is able to stay in touch with this real world via observations and feedback.

Methods to Create a Feedback Loop

It was not so easy to do this in the beginning. Perhaps the same will be true for many who are actively beginning to practice professionally. It goes along with the questions we all tend to have when we start: "How long should the sessions be?" "What should we cover in a session?" "Can one session be enough to cover all I have to say?" Whatever your doubts may be, it might be useful to think about your early consulting as you would if you were launching any project.
- Visualize what you want your consulting practice to look like.
- Develop an intake process, explaining your services.
- Define time, place, fees.

As you explain your services, you might add that brief, optional follow-up sessions are included. The client may be puzzled. Simply explain that this means clarity can be added in a follow-up conversation should there be any questions or details that call for further explanation.

If this is not part of your intake procedure, it can easily be added to the closing of the session. A client may benefit from hearing that additional insights may surface in the days or weeks ahead when they listen to the recording. They can be reminded that a free follow-up can be scheduled to look at those issues.

I always tell clients that astrologers learn from feedback. Then I ask them to contribute by getting back to me via a phone conversation, if for no other reason than to tell me how things are going. Some don't, but those that do provide information for their file. Most of those become regular clients.

Keeping records

Setting up **files for each client** is a good way to manage the Feedback Loop. That's the way virtually all professionals handle their client work. The first entry should include data of the initial session: who referred the client, what is the primary problem or need, a brief note regarding themes addressed, etc. A basic natal chart is an essential part of every client's file. Additional printouts can also be added with transit spreads or progressions highlighted to show which areas of the astrological consultation were featured in the reading. The cost of the session may also be added to these notes.

Follow-up dates should be listed as well as any additional input from subsequent conversations. Was it just a simple call back, or were there new matters to add to the file? All these steps create the framework for an active learning process with a vital feedback loop. Too much to keep track of? Cognitive science show that creating connections in all learning secures the information and paves strong synaptic pathways to retain the bigger pictures of a client's world.

How can we handle all these files? It takes time to keep files and they should be dealt with immediately after a session. I have always kept files in filing cabinets on real paper. I am a native of the pre-computer days when there were no other options. Today we have numerous filing systems available to us via the computer. This should make the record keeping process easy for everyone.

Scheduling the work day to include phone follow-ups

Deciding to become a full time professional astrologer is a big step. How prepared are you to keep regular office hours? Perhaps the best way to develop an active practice in the beginning is to be available. Think of this practice as your day job. When do you want to start? How many hours a day do you want to work? Do you offer readings on weekends? How about evenings? Circumstances are different for each of us, but to start your practice, visualizing your day's work is helpful.

I know many of you would resist the idea of having a practice that included a 9-5 office schedule. Before you reject it, think of the benefits of that arrangement. It provides time for routines that will facilitate your work. You will be available for phone calls and able to handle your office tasks, such as mailings or writing blogs and newsletters.

Consider prep time. By the time you are ready to have a full time professional practice, the prep time should be fairly definable. I find that over the years my preparation is longer, but that's because I'm always adding bits and pieces of new research to my data base with each client. There is no set amount of preparation; it depends on your comfort zone. Often we are told that if we spend more than X minutes/hours preparing for a client, it's overkill. However, the prep process isn't like herding sheep. Somewhere along the way you will feel that "you've got it". Trust that feeling. You can always modify if the feedback loop tells you you've missed too much.

Duration and number of sessions in a day, or in a week.

How long do you want your sessions to be? In the beginning, an hour seems right. That's because our early formula for a reading can be limited to the client's issues without the need to explore all aspects of the chart. This pattern will eventually expand as we add more teaching to our sessions. Input from our feedback loop will show us the way to expand the time.

We all know there are astrologers who will fill their days with back-to-back readings. God bless them! I know many of them do a fine job with clients. Developing a practice with a full-bodied feedback loop, however, does not work that way. Let's consider the goals of one's consulting strategies. Quick one-timers are useful to many. The development of a sustainable professional practice, however, calls for a different approach.

It necessitates building confidence in astrology itself. Training in consulting skills plays a major role. These practices include mindful listening. The astrologer refrains from intervening until he or she hears the client to determine their needs. With this approach, we soon realize that the *whole* chart does not have to be a part of the consultation. Instead, we can see where the fault lines in the chart relate to the client's concerns. With training and experience, the professional astrologer becomes proficient in identifying patterns. This enables us to establish ourselves as reliable servants providing guidance to those who consult us.

As we progress in our practices we will learn that longer sessions will lead to better opportunities to teach clients. This is a facet that should never be overlooked. So many of our clients are ill prepared to work with us. It's not necessary to present all our study notes to serve them. It would help if each astrologer knew how to teach some of the basics, as I did with the non-astrological crowd that I lectured to at the Spa.

Once again, the feedback loop provides much of the structure for our teaching. It enables us to see if this particular client is sensitive to Saturn cycles or Mars action. We soon see that the Pluto stuff is hardly noticed for some, while it is the big bomb for others. The feedback loop offers input that allows us to be more discerning when applying chart information to a client's reading.

Once these strategies are incorporated into planning our professional practice the organization of the daily practice will come naturally. Be aware of the pitfalls of stringently following the lessons learned in our studies. In the past, learned astrologers dedicated a lot of time to "judging" a nativity. We don't think that way now, so we have to do our own rewrites. The feedback loop provides us with answers that build confidence in our work.

The client has all the answers

That statement may surprise you and perhaps raise your ire, but think about it for a moment. As we connect the dots of a client's story, it invariably leads us to the deeper areas of pain that tend to rattle an individual's life over and over again. Sometimes I think there's only one story that keeps playing itself out in a variety of scenarios. Eventually the astrologer will identify the recurring stories. In doing so, we can begin to connect the details to the theme of existing trauma.

Not all of our consulting has to deal with crisis or trauma. Too often I hear people say they aren't interested in an astrological consultation because they don't know what to ask. That's why we need to work on creating better information about astrology. What does it do? What can it tell us?

When I first encountered astrology via that great French astrologer, Andre Barbault, it was only from reading a very basic book he'd written in 1958. The interesting tomes he wrote at the time catapulted me into studying astrology. I wanted everyone to know about this incredible stuff! I didn't even know that astrology was used for other reasons. I just wanted to do charts to show people how interesting charts are. In time I succeeded in persuading many others to join me in this world of discovery. By the time I began my professional practice, after a great deal of prodding from those who enjoyed the discoveries with me, I already had enough people to have a full time schedule from Day One.

Details of learning and discoveries acquired via the feedback loop

Let's start with the rewards. The benefits extend to clients, astrologers, and the profession of astrology itself.

Using the language tools derived from consulting skills programs

This opens the dialog and introduces the possibility for hearing and listening. It changes the dynamic, as the client is no longer the recipient of unquestioned information. Agreements and disagreements can be expressed easily. The follow-up session gives the client time to think about the initial consultation. What is remembered? Were there issues that confused the client? Are there areas calling for additional attention, possibly with another consultation?

The client has an opportunity to better connect with the astrologer. He or she will cite topics that had the greatest meaning for them. Sometimes the follow-up will highlight areas that the astrologer may have downplayed in the original consultation. This input can be added to the client's file.

Cataloging exceptions that differ from classic text book rules

Sometimes this is the area where astrology itself benefits the most. How long has it been since an upgraded astrology text book hit the market? Any professional dedicated to writing would have tomes to illustrate this. Simply tallying our findings from client to client enables us to trim and shape book learning into more relevant interpretations. Doing this from my earliest years revealed that Aries is not the leader suggested in most texts, Cancer is not the sign yearning for motherhood, Virgo is not the clean-clean guy in the Zodiac, and Capricorn is not always hard working and successful. You may think that these are the exceptions that prove the rule. I, however, see these as invitations to dig deeper into the meaning of signs, getting to their essence via client experiences which often provide a better understanding of the core issues.

The same holds true when applying transits or progressions to a client's world. Does every little flicker mean something significant? If so, where does that fit into the larger life cycles that are often more important for the individual. When are events life-changing?

Growth in our profession depends on these adjustments

Just as other professions grow as new experiences bring insights and deeper understanding, so should it be for us in astrology. Practicing astrologers can bring this growth to our profession, perhaps as much as research or greater complexity in our computer programs has already done. How much does time affect the classic interpretation? Do we think astrologically as we did in the 19th Century? In the 20th? As we apply astrology to our 21st Century world, one which is dramatically changed by computerized programs and globalization, we will have to revise our purpose and the way our profession can best serve our clients. Incorporating a Feedback Loop into our regular work will be a fundamental step in achieving this.

Monica Hable Dimino *is a practicing Professional Astrologer from Watertown, MA. She works internationally with clients around the world. Her career as an astrological consultant, teacher and trainer spans 55 years. She holds a professional diploma from the AFA, has a level IV certificate from NCGR, and is an ISAR CAP. She was a charter member of OPA when it was founded in 1989 (as ProSig) and served two terms as president in the 1990's. Email: Mhabled@aol.com*

Chapter 9

Counseling Techniques for the Consulting Astrologer
Jacqueline L. Janes

"Each person is a unique individual. Hence, psychotherapy should be formulated to meet the uniqueness of the individual's needs, rather than tailoring the person to fit the Procrustean bed of a hypothetical theory of human behavior."

Milton H. Erickson, M.D.

"Each person is a unique individual. Hence, the astrological consultation should be formulated to meet the uniqueness of the individual's needs, rather than tailoring the person to fit what the astrologer has to say about the natal chart."

Jacqueline L. Janes

For the past thirty years I have been combining psychotherapy and astrology in my work with clients. I would like to share my experiences, successes, and challenges as a consulting astrologer. I want to give future astrologers tools to use in their practices and ideas to consider in forming their own unique consulting techniques.

It took many years before I found my profession. At twelve I swam on my back in an Indiana lake, fittingly named Crooked Lake, and decided that, if I was not going to be a musician and music teacher, I wanted to be an astronomer. At sixteen, while attending a music conservatory in Chicago, I came to the realization that playing and teaching music was not going to give form or satisfaction to my life. I was searching for a way to be of service in the world and music wasn't the answer.

Later, as a professional astrologer, I discovered that Saturn, retrograde in the twelfth house of my natal chart, went direct in my seventeenth year. That summer in Chicago I was working on the issue I call "standing upright in the world," Saturn's task. I was considering how to give form to myself.

In college I discovered theoretical economics. I loved studying cycles and economic charts, analyzing trends, and conducting research. Within the field of economics I was intrigued by consumer issues. Amidst the abstractions, I was still a people person. Economics became my major.

After graduating I used my college skills in a number of jobs, but I still felt that I had not yet given form to myself. I was lost.

Giving birth to my daughter and taking time to be a mother and adjust to a different, non-driven flow of life began to open up other avenues of interest—spirituality, metaphysics, and educational philosophy (Saturn rules my eighth house and co-rules the ninth and tenth houses). I had never explored these disciplines because they had not been part of my early environment. They were missing from my fundamentalist education and experiences.

Between twenty-six and thirty years of age, in this new life flow, I started practicing the piano again, lived in an intentional community and nurtured others. During that time I read Marcia Moores' *Astrology, The Divine Science.* Marcia Moores' astrological descriptions invited me into the possibility that an individual's natal chart was one way to see a person's divine energy, energy formed from Above and lived Below. I was intrigued.

At my Saturn return, my partner and I brought a new life from Asia into our family and then I became pregnant with our third child. Two children within nine months was a challenge. At the same time I recall saying to myself, "Astrology would be a wonderful tool for parents to use in raising children since each person has a unique energy system." Watch what you say! The gods are listening. My third child's natal chart is a challenging chart to interpret, and she has had a demanding physical journey. My adopted son does not have an exact birth date so I have learned to note important dates in his life. My first daughter's chart formed a SeeSaw Pattern with energies evenly divided between two hemispheres, a simple pattern with its own complexities. I have had my very own laboratory to work out the truth of that excited utterance about astrology's value to parents.

By the time Saturn, moving forward in the twelfth house, returned to the exact birth degree in my natal chart I was slogging my way through the National Council for Geocosmic Research (NCGR) proficiency tests. I was also a year away from graduating with a Masters in Counseling.

I tell this story with the hope that you will understand that what I write comes from a journey of exploration: music, economics, mothering, caring, astrology, and counseling. I gave form to myself by becoming a **psychotherapist** who uses astrological information in responding to my clients while becoming a **consulting astrologer** who delivers astrological information attuned to professional counseling practices.

As a consulting astrologer I analyze a chart with the idea that I am looking at an individual's energy potentials, the divine tasks ✓. *lnp.* within. It is only when I am actually in the presence of the client that I discover how those potentials have manifested, given other factors like environment, physical DNA, personal relationships and choices. The client's Will to Be is a major determining factor in how the energies have been formed.

I view the consultation as an opportunity to join the client's life journey for a brief time. In my hand is the natal chart; not a fixed account of what's necessarily going to happen, but rather a map offering clues of the life journey, now and in the months ahead.

My job is to act as a translator, decoding the symbolic language of the chart into information and tools that will aid the client in making good choices on the journey. This is where my own tool box, filled with skills and information taken from my journey, is important, as it provides me with the images and words that will be helpful in translating from the symbolic to the substantive.

Analogies

A counseling skill called *therapeutic self-disclosure* is used to make a connection, a bond, with the client. Self-disclosure means saying something personal about yourself. This is a skill that must be used with care. For example, I do not give the client my astrological information, even when asked. The danger is that in doing so the client, who might have an elementary understanding of astrology, becomes focused on the consultant rather than the session, which is, after all, for their benefit.

However, therapeutic self-disclosure can be subtly used in a consulting session, utilizing the experiences you have had on your life journey as material translated into wonderful analogies, pictures, and metaphors to heighten the understanding of the astrological knowledge you wish to convey. In this way you are disclosing an image or language that the client might use in referencing their own experiences. Think of all the fields of study you have engaged in on your own journey as support for understanding and translating the symbolic language of astrology.

For example, I had a business client who had challenging aspects to Jupiter that manifested as extreme overwork, causing physical problems and relationship issues with his family. In my tool box of experiences was the language of economic theory, so I used the *theory of diminishing returns* to explain that at some point more production or work (Jupiter) did not glean greater profits or quality of life. The client got it.

I believe his connection with astrology was strengthened because I used vocabulary he understood to make the analogy between the symbolic language and his real life experience.

In another instance I had a client who had three major conjunctions of planets in different signs. Thus, in two instances a planet in a fire sign was closely conjunct a planet in an earth sign; the third example was a planet in an earth sign conjunct a planet in an air sign. He had a fourth conjunction of two planets, both in water signs. Working with the differing sign energies was challenging because the promise of the blending, like the possible aesthetic harmony with a Mercury/Venus conjunction, had a slight out-of-step feel or dissonance to it. Incorporating my study of music, I suggested the dissonance was like a Bela Bartok orchestral piece in which there might be a sense of dis-ease until the harmonic resolution was accomplished. Harmony had to be worked for because it was not elementally structured, and, thus, not accomplished easily. The client, who had studied music in college, understood immediately. What we bring to the study of astrology from our life experience is fodder for the translation of the symbolic language of our craft. In both of the examples above, I did give a subtle self-disclosure revealing the breadth of my knowledge.

And then there is the body of astrological language itself. A thorough study of the language and its nuances is paramount to becoming a consultant, particularly in how the language applies to the consultant's life.

Know yourself astrologically

A psychotherapist should have had therapy (and even continue in therapy or supervision) before sitting opposite a client; a consulting astrologer should likewise know her own natal chart thoroughly and have had consultations with other astrologers. When we walk into the consulting room our energies interact with the energies of the client. We need to consider what our effect on the client might be. We can't know it unless we ourselves have sat in the client's chair at some point in our lives and tried to thoroughly understand our own natal charts.

For example, if a consulting astrologer has mutable energy by sign and house and a fixed energy client walks into the consulting room, be prepared to slow down the pace of the session and be thorough in your explanations.

If the consulting astrologer has cardinal energy by sign and house, a fixed/mutable energy client, who might need to think about a project for a long time and plan thoroughly before launching, may seem tedious to the astrological consultant who doesn't understand why the client can't "just do it." Calculating several start dates and explaining the various natures of the energies for each date might be an advisable preparation for this client.

The Organization of Professional Astrologer's (OPA) Peer Group Supervision is a wonderful experience set in a caring environment where astrologers can gain personal knowledge about their own natal charts from other practitioners and also get feedback on their professional performance. Objective criteria, wherein we can judge our competence and our ability to serve a client, are vital.

We can't know all there is to discover in the body of astrological knowledge, but we can certainly obtain a foundation of basic terms and meanings. If you are considering becoming a professional astrological consultant, I'm assuming you have this knowledge. If you have the knowledge base, then **the challenge is in knowing how to communicate your wisdom to the client.** A critical lesson is developing the art of listening.

Listening

Listening begins with the initial contact with the client. The consultant asks the client, "What are you seeking from an astrological consultation?" A specific question is being asked. The psycho-therapist would call this *determining the presenting problem*. However, as a consulting astrologer we do not consider our clients or their charts as evidence of a problem, but rather the map of a journey, their life path. The consulting astrologer is the tour guide and interpreter of this unique path.

For the consulting astrologer, the client's answer to the initial question will give form to the preparation for the session. This goes back to my rewording of Erickson's statement as applied to the consulting astrologer. The consultation should be formulated to meet the uniqueness of the individual's needs. Astrology has a wealth of wisdom to impart. What specifically does the client wish to glean from the session? We need to hear the client's answer to that initial question before beginning our analysis of the chart.

Moon Zlotnick, in her column "Enhancing Your Astrology Practice" (OPA Career Astrology, Autumn and Winter 2014, Spring 2015) speaks to the importance of that initial question. She suggests

that writing down the client's response can be utilized during the consultation to make sure the client's concerns were met and as a seamless way to bring the session to a conclusion within the allotted time frame.

The International Society of Astrology Research's (ISAR) Consulting Skills Training speaks about **empathic listening,** which is taken from the counseling skills model of **active listening**. The consultation is formed from the astrological consultant's ability to listen deeply. In fact, listening can sometimes be more important than speaking. This is opposite from how we usually think about astrological consultations. Generally, we think that we are giving out, speaking, more than taking in, listening.

Achieving a balance between listening and then speaking is what works best in a consultation. Our words have no meaning for the client, no matter how profound they are astrologically, if they are not addressing the client's needs in a comprehensible fashion. That is where deep listening creates a bond with the client, furrowing a path for our words to be heard.

I've been pleased to teach at the Midwest School of Astrology in Cincinnati, Ohio and one of the phrases I give to the students is, "The client is speaking their chart. All the astrologer has to do is listen." To hear the client speak their chart **you must listen** and **then apply what you hear to what you know in the natal chart.** This is an inner/outer process occurring throughout the consultation. We take it for granted that we are listening to the client when we, in fact, may be forming our next statement rather than responding to what is being said.

Deep listening gives the astrological consultant information about what experiences the client has had and how they interpret them. The client's degree of consciousness can be determined if one listens well. For example, does the client feel victimized or empowered during a Pluto transit? Is the client conscious enough to embrace change, or do they seek to maintain control in every situation? Their responses inform us on which approach to take to guide them effectively through the Pluto transit. This is important because the level of interpretation, the astrological words and patterns being called forth from the astrological consultant's knowledge of the natal chart, is determined by the clients own choice of words.

Another example would be if a client talks about being stuck and unable to move forward with their exciting plans for fame and fortune. The client wants the consultant to determine the best time to initiate a project in the next year. Before proceeding you might want to pause. I had this happen in a session many years ago. The client had mutable energy in cardinal houses with an emphasis on the fire element. *Move it, move it, move it* was the desire! She was ready to step out on the world stage, or so she thought.

I looked to where Saturn was natally—fifth house in the Sign of Libra—and then by progression and transit. The words "stuck" and "plan" had told me that Saturn was involved. Having really listened to the client I could then ask important questions regarding how she was "feeling stuck," and what might be hindering the forward movement of the project. With Saturn involved, I thought it might mean that the stuck feeling was because the plan was not well formulated (Saturn is a forming agent.) The client exhibited impatient energy, just wanting to go now, but foundations needed to be laid first (Transiting Saturn in the fourth house). The client left the session with a time table and more work to do laying the foundation for the fame and fortune that was going to come her way, which it did eventually as the result of good preparation during that part of her Saturn Cycle.

Listening deeply to what the client says can also reveal their personal examples of how the natal energy in the chart has worked for them. Using the client's own language and life examples in your interpretations or explanations create a bond with the client. The consultant mirrors the client. The client feels seen and heard- significant factors in forming the relationship in the session. An effective bond keeps the client engaged with the astrological consultant when new decisions emerge that need a geocosmic perspective.

Mark Jones in his OPA lecture, "An Introduction to Therapeutic Astrology" (Free Monthly Talk for Members, January 2015) suggests the astrological consultation should be considered a *collaborative affair* where the consultant marries the client's being with the natal chart. That imagery succinctly speaks to deep listening joined with astrological knowledge to create dialogue and, thus, a meaningful consultation.

Monica Dimino in her OPA lecture, "Counseling Skills: Working With the Best Teachers We Have" (Free Monthly Talk for Members, March 2015) speaks of the client's life descriptions as providing the *connecting threads* to the natal chart needed by the consulting astrologer to form relevant interpretation. Monica also notes that our clients become our astrology teachers if we listen with care.

The following counseling techniques are additional ways to help make the consulting session relevant and enhance connection with the client.

Closed questions and open-ended questions

The purpose of a **closed question** is to glean specific information, such as the example for the initial contact: "What are you seeking from an astrological consultation?" Short, succinct answers are elicited.

Closed questions also are a wonderful technique to use for the client who gets lost during the session telling his story. The closed question is an intervention that gives the consultant an entry point into the monologue so that a collaborative dialog can be established.

The astrological consultant can ask a specific question, i.e. the age the event being related occurred, thus giving an entry for astrological interpretation. Using a Solar Arc over an angle or a planet, a secondary moon aspect, a Transit to a specific planet or planetary configuration as a possible explanation for the nature of the client's event can heighten the client's understanding of their story.

I always ask closed questions when working with the Huber Age Point or the Saturn Cycle issues. Asking a client what was going on in her life at specific Saturn points in the cycle gives information about how Saturn evolved in the past and how the Saturnian energy played out in their life. The consultant doesn't have to guess how Saturn energy was defined for the client. By asking the question about Saturn before you convey information from the chart, the client begins to think that there may be connections between the energy (Planets) and the occurrences (Events) in their life. Your skill is in knowing what period in the client's life to ask about.

You can take the client's answers and weave them into the scenario playing out in present time. The Saturn Cycle ceases being a theoretical phenomenon and is now seen as having real life, present time meaning for the client. The evolution of greater consciousness becomes a life defining event for the client.

Specific questions are critical when the client is seeking timing to begin a project. It is important to ask the client, "Do you have parameters for when this project needs to be launched?" When I haven't asked that important question, I have calculated an ideal time to launch a project, only to discover that the client had other criteria that he had not related to me. Now I ask.

Asking specific questions is also important for that client who is seeking a consultation because it was given as a gift. These are sometimes challenging sessions because the client often has no idea how to use the reading. That is when giving specific information about what is possible to glean from the natal chart and asking specific questions about where the client might be in their life journey is very important in order to make the consultation relevant.

Another specific question which Moon Zlotnick (OPA Career Astrology, Spring 2015) says is essential to ask before the session ends is: "Is this what you were hoping to get out of our time together?" I believe it's also helpful to ask check-in questions throughout the session: "Does my explanation of the energy in your life make sense?"

Near the close of the session I try to do a brief summary of the relevant questions covered during the consultation and ask if the client has any additional questions.

An **open-ended question** could be described as a "thoughtful inquiry." The question has no correct answer, but rather is meant to further the dialogue between the consultant and the client. The question and the answer tend to be longer and more involved. For the astrological consultant the open-ended question can be a beautiful technique to test what you know from the chart and how it may apply to the client.

For example, I might say to the client, "Your natal chart suggests a pattern of questioning and questing behavior. (Aspect patterns involving quincunxes and/or semi-sextiles). Sometimes this energy physically feels like an inner niggling, a nervousness that doesn't surface as a body expression, but rather as an internally felt experience. I wonder if you can relate to what I've said or have a sense of that questioning/questing drive?"

Remember, I said that in order to use these techniques you must have a solid base of astrological information and how it is translated in real life. When asking an open-ended question, remember the protocol of the injunction to a lawyer; "In a trial, never ask a question of someone unless you are relatively certain of the answer." Similarly, you want to have some sense of what the client's answer might be. Experience gives the astrological consultant that skill. In the example I used above, I have never had a client deny the "niggling feeling" no matter how calm they present themselves. In fact, clients are generally thrilled that they finally have a name for that inner felt experience.

Another example occurred during a session when a client mentioned that he felt that he often had a hard time speaking up for himself. I gave him information based on his natal chart, but in the form of a gentle inquiry: "Energetically I wonder if you don't stand up more for the rights of others than you stand up for yourself. For instance, do you have any experiences being an advocate for individuals who might be called the underdog?" He had Mars in Pisces in the 12th house, which was the ruler of his chart with Aries Rising.

What my open-ended question to this client did was give him another way to view himself. Eventually a discussion about energy patterns connected to the Mars placement ensued. By listening deeply, I discerned from the client a hint that he stands up for causes or others. Rather than seeing himself as having a problem, he could understand where the focus of his assertive energy tended to be directed and make choices to use the energy to advocate for himself.

In another instance a client was nervously preparing a workshop presentation with a friend who kept talking about "just winging it" (possibly mutable energy). My client had a fixed T-Square involving the Sun, Jupiter/Pluto, and Mars in cardinal houses. I asked the client if she might feel better if there was a plan for the presentation with the content divided between her and her friend. This sounds simple and is a more *direct* open-ended question, but the wording was based on the energy of the natal chart and led into a discussion allowing the client to express how she functioned best. From previous sessions with her, I knew that her tendency was to be accommodating rather than advocate for her needs. In this case the open-ended question was meant to be supportive and empowering in light of my knowledge of her natal chart. Her nervousness was relieved when given a purpose (cardinal energy) in forming the presentation (Saturn and Jupiter/Pluto), a translation of fixed energy in cardinal houses.

The client called me back saying that the presentation went well because she had insisted on planning out how the information was to be delivered jointly with her friend. Then, during the presentation she felt able to follow her workshop partner when she "spread her wings."

Reflective one or two word prompts

Reflective one or two word prompts are stated in such a way as to be considered a type of inquiry of the client. This technique subtly solicits more information from the client when it might be needed to make the connection to the natal chart information. These reflective prompts also let the client know you are paying attention to what they are saying; you are attending to their words through deep listening.

For example, the client might be describing childhood experiences as "confusing and chaotic." Merely repeating the words, "confusing and chaotic" with a questioning tone invites more detail. These details from the client allow the astrological consultant to better define and localize these descriptions in the chart, which may be coming from the fourth, tenth, or even the third house. Knowing wherein the experience of "confusing and chaotic" occurred can help the astrological consultant provide appropriate translation and guidance.

I advise using this technique occasionally. In my experience it can sound forced if the consultant is not comfortable with the intervention. When used with skill, it can be a gentle nudge for the client to say more.

Longer reflective responses

A longer reflective response is meant to confirm what you have heard, especially if there is some confusion, and to elicit a fuller understanding of the client's issues and thoughts. This technique reflects back to the client what you heard them say in order to clarify your understanding and perhaps encourage more elaboration of the issues brought to the consultation. The longer reflective response is sometimes referred to as **paraphrasing the client's content** to assure the client that the consultant is listening and "has it right."

The reflection should not be long-winded and should only address what the client has said. For example, in responding to the client's thoughts on frustrating, unsatisfying relationships, the astrological consultant might say, "I hear your concern that relationships haven't seemed to meet your needs." This response invites the client to elaborate on what specific needs are not getting addressed in relationships.

In my experience, knowing where the client is focused on an issue and how dissatisfaction is defined, i.e. not being respected in a relationship (possibly found in a Capricorn or Leo seventh house cusp or Sun placement in the seventh house), gives me specifics to relate back to my analysis. By knowing the lens through which they view the issue I can give the client an interpretation that may broaden their understanding and awareness.

Reflective responses should not be overused in a session. Constantly repeating a phrase like "I sense that..." or "you're saying that..." can get tedious for the client.

Reflective response also can be used to intervene in a client monologue. Briefly paraphrasing the points of a client's monologue and making reference to astrological symbolism pertinent to the issue puts the astrological consultant back into the session. The client feels heard and hopefully is now ready to listen to the astrological consultant's information.

Reflective responses should not be used when the client is expecting definite information. If the client asks for specific information, you give it. My client who was giving the workshop presentation asked what the energies for the day of the presentation were like. It would have been inappropriate to say, "I sense you are nervous that the energies of that day will not be beneficial to giving a presentation?" Such a response would have run the risk of refocusing her on her nervousness about the presentation. Instead, I gave her specific information about the energy of the day, citing possible times (void of course moon) of low attention which would be an excellent time for a break. My information supported her ability to control the presentation.

Reframing

I love exploring the possibilities of the reframing technique. I wrote an OPA pamphlet, "Reframing, A Counseling Tool for the Consulting Astrologer," because I believe reframing is the perfect tool for consulting astrologers. Astrologers have a body of astrological symbolism and vocabulary that is perfect to use with this technique.

Reframing is not a word one can find in the dictionary. I looked in three. An Internet source described reframing as "renew," and I also got the word "reform" as a substitute. Reframing is not is reform. Reform is defined as making or becoming better by the removal of faults and errors. Reforming is a corrective measure. Reframing may come closer to the word, "renew" since during the process one may be uplifted and learn to see in a more positive light.

Reframing is found in the therapeutic lexicon. Reframing was used by Milton H. Erickson as part of the toolbox developed for therapists learning Erickson Therapy. In reframing the essence of an event a concept, idea, or description is maintained, but stated in a different way so that new information, understanding, or consciousness can occur. We don't remove a fault, but rather try to embrace the essence of a concept or situation with a new perspective thus expanding the client's frame of reference.

For example, a client calls the astrological consultant saying that his company is downsizing and he is afraid that he will be next on the list to go. At the onset one of the things that reframing can do is give a *different context* to the client's situation. In the Chinese language the word "crisis" is made up of two characters: the first character implies "danger," the second character implies "opportunity." The astrological consultant can reframe his client's situation with a welcome, "Come on in. Let's explore the energies around this possible event and perhaps the opportunities also inherent in this situation."

This reframing recommendation suggests that the astrological consultant will not just be gazing into a crystal ball giving good or bad news. Reframing the meaning of the "danger" in the initial contact moves the reading out of the realm of a forecast into the arena of a professional consultation addressing all the factors involved in the issue of downsizing for the client.

Yes, the loss of employment is a possibility. This fact may bring up basic survival issues for the client. However, by reframing the situation from the onset as a time to explore possible options, the session takes on a different context. One might think of reframing as one step in a symbolic alchemical process of turning lead into gold, inviting greater awareness and possibility into any life event.

In the actual consultation, reframing can involve expanding the experience (houses) to be addressed. The very nature of the word "downsizing" suggests a possible change in profession or employment, a tenth house experience, which can conjure up fear of losing status. Dealing with this possibility directly, I often reframe tenth house matters with the question, "How do you want to stand upright in the world?" Our skeleton structure helps support us standing upright; Saturn rules the skeleton structure as well as the tenth house. This question is meant to evoke second and sixth house issues as well—self-worth, skill set, defining work routines, relationship with fellow employees—which contribute to our ability to stand upright within a profession or career or simply as a responsible citizen in the world.

Within a broader context the client may explore whether his present employment is adequately using his skill set. On deeper reflection he may decide that he is being underutilized in his present position. He may even begin to consider whether he and his work output are valued in the ways he needs or wishes them to be.

On the other hand, if he considers his present employment his ideal job, a reframe may help him consider other factors, perhaps even deeper spiritual reasons, for a potential outcome bringing change into his work life. I worked with a client who made an employment decision based on her commute time in order to bring more simplicity and less frenetic highway energy into her daily existence, allowing her time for personal exploration and spiritual study.

The "downsized" reframe actually allowed me to experience what a wonderful tool astrological symbolism was in enlarging the perspective for the client. In this specific case the consultation was reframed from the onset and continued to expand as the perimeters of the issue were broadened.

Astrological sign descriptions can be powerful tools for a reframe. Inherent within the astrological lexicon for signs are many words and images collected and researched over time. Often I cringe when I hear Scorpios described only as dark and sexy and Geminis depicted only as flakey and flighty. These two signs are more than these simple adjectives and images. Shallow descriptive words do not do justice to these or any other astrological sign. There is a level of consciousness attached to the words we use. Being aware of that fact, the astrological consultant can be measured and careful in their choice of descriptive language.

For example, I was invited to attend a motivational talk sponsored by the local business association for women. Upon discovering that I was an astrological consultant, a woman announced that she was a Taurus and was always being told how stubborn she was. I responded by saying that she might be very persistent or loyal to a particular point of view she valued. Further, I stated that often Taureans were very enduring, staying with an idea or project until the very end. This kind of 'stubbornness' could be very valuable in getting a project brought to completion.

At the end of the evening, the woman returned and said the best motivation she had received from the evening were my words about Taurus characteristics. She was going home with a different, more positive view of herself that she was certain would be helpful in her profession.

Are Taureans stubborn? Yes, and they could even be described as bull-headed sometimes. But stubborn and bull-headed have negative connotations, suggesting, among other traits, possible unreasonableness. If instead we say that a person is persistent, forbearing, staunch, and prevailing, we get the image of someone who is strong and/or trustworthy. Changing the adjective can reframe the tone, aura, or personality possibilities for an individual.

Positive reframes are always the best approach. In the example above changing the descriptive words that apply to the image of a Taurus reframed an individual's image of herself and perhaps opened the possibility for seeing her interactions with her fellow employees in a different light. There is always the hope with the reframe technique that greater consciousness and awareness will bring a better quality of life.

What else can we learn from the counseling profession?

For the more experienced astrological consultant, learning specific techniques from a given disciplined, such as Gestalt Therapy (Susan Falk, "Integrating Gestalt Therapy into Astrological Counseling," OPA Career Astrologer, Winter 2014) or Astro Drama, the acting out of astrological symbolism via zodiac signs and planetary energies, adds depth and innovation to the consultant's skill set. These practices take the client further in understanding the astrological symbolism unfolding in their life.

There is even simpler information from the counseling profession that is valuable to the consulting astrologer:

- Therapists and astrological consultants should be warm and understanding with a positive outlook on life. Research has shown that a positive outlook tends to produce positive therapy results.

- Clients respond to the therapist or the astrological consultant's words when there is a feeling of genuine respect and regard for the client. If you don't feel liked or respected, why would you place value on the astrological consultant's words, no matter how wise they might appear to be?

- Clients respond positively when they feel attended to. Deep listening is the connector between the client and the therapist or astrological consultant. When the client feels heard, he listens.

- Clients sense and respond to a therapist or astrological consultant's congruence and evidence of self-knowledge. We all are on a journey. Being real, not perfect, indicates that you know what it is like to walk the path of self-knowledge. The client then feels "She has done this; I can do it too."

- Clients respond favorably to a therapist or astrological consultant admitting to not being right all the time. I've been confronted by my clients about what I've said or how I've said it. If I can genuinely listen to the client's point of view with an openness to learn, then there is space for revelation to occur for both of us.

- The consultation room needs to be comfortable and appropriate. An appropriate space is tidy and clean with a minimum of distractions, i.e. perplexing art work or statues. The client's chair should not be too hard or too soft. I always have fresh flowers; it has become my signature touch and regular clients look forward to seeing what the floral arrangement for the day is.

These are notions that a practitioner learns from experience over time, researched by those dedicated to proving what works in therapy. These concepts serve the astrological consultant as well as the traditional therapist.

Here's a radical thought: perhaps it isn't critical that the information you impart is spot-on all the time. Yes, it is helpful to be well educated in the craft, but along with proficiency it's equally important that the client feel the astrological consultant is a good person with whom to be in a consultative relationship. When this is established, what you have to say is heard and used. You may become part of the client's journey, a resource to their inner map for a number of years wherein a significant relationship for both the client and consultant is formed.

More important than any astrological tome, the astrological consultant is fortunate to have the client's life journey to learn from and to witness astrological symbolism coming alive.

May it be so.

References

Monica Dimino, "Counseling Skills: Working With the Best Teachers We Have," OPA Free Monthly Talk for Members, March 2015.

Susan Falk, "Integrating Gestalt Therapy into Astrological Counseling," OPA Career Astrologer, Winter 2014.

Jacqueline L. Janes, "Reframing, A Counseling Tool for the Consulting Asrologer," OPA, 2007.

Jacqueline L. Janes, "Counseling Tips for Astrologers," Lecture for Rocky Mountain Astrologers, Boulder, Colorado, May 2014.

Mark Jones, "An Introduction to Therapeutic Astrology," OPA Free Monthly Talk for Members, January 2015.

Carl R. Rogers, On Becoming a Person, Boston and New York, Houghton Mifflin Company, 1961.

Jeffrey K. Zeig and Stephen R. Lanklton, Developing Ericksonian Therapy, New York, NY: Brunner/Mazel, Inc. 1988.

Moon Zlotnick, "Enhancing Your Astrology Practice," OPA Career Astrology, Autumn and Winter 2014, Spring 2015.

www.astrologyy-and-science.com, "Using Astrology as a Counselling Tool, Strategies that work."

www.analytictech.com/mb119/reflecti.htm, Dalmar Fisher, "Active Listening," drawn from Communication in Organization.

dspace.mit.edu/bitstream/handle/1721.1/55898/15-281, JoAnne Yates, "Active Listening and Reflective Responses," MIT Sloan Com. Program.

Jacqueline L. Janes, *MA, LPC is a Certified Counseling Astrologer, NCGR IV as well as a licensed professional counselor in Connecticut. In 2000 she was recognized by I.S.A.R. as a Certified Astrological Professional. In 1993, she opened her present psychotherapy and astrological consultation practice, Jacqueline has combined astrological consultation with psychotherapy, developing a unique counseling relationship for those seeking greater consciousness. She has lectured at SOTA, ROMA, OPA, NCGR, ISAR, UAC and her home community, the Astrological Society of Connecticut. Email: jacquelinejanes@yahoo.com*

Chapter 10

Writing and Astrology
Arlan Wise

This chapter heading might be puzzling at first glance. Writing and astrology are separate crafts and many astrologers might avow that if they'd wanted to be writers they would have chosen that career path instead. On closer examination, however, we see that writing is an essential skill in the development of a successful astrological career. Through refining our writing abilities we can develop three key areas of our practice: **Promotion, Education, and Articulation.**

Promotion is essential in nurturing a practice. Writing in a forum, whether it be a local newspaper or a national astrology publication, puts your name in the public sphere and establishes your credibility as a legitimate professional. It's the best form of free publicity and allows a depth of detail that's impossible in a standard advertisement. As more people become aware of your skills, you establish yourself as a resource for prospective clients and colleagues. When people read your words they get a sense of what they will hear in a reading.

Educating the public on the value of astrology is an ongoing challenge. Despite the gains made in recent decades, wide swaths of the public still see astrology as funny pages content, somewhere between Garfield and the crossword puzzle. Skillful writing helps astrologers dispel this misconception and create the perception of astrology as a credible, detailed information system with rigorous training and methodology.

Developing your writing skills goes hand-in-hand with enhancing your ability to articulate astrological concepts for clients. Analyzing an astrological chart is a technical skill, yet it's only part of the reading process. Translating this information into comprehensible language for the layman is a separate discipline that ultimately defines the client's experience. The more one practices crystallizing abstract thoughts into clear, comprehensible language, the more the client will gain from the reading.

Some professional writing is private, like the notes you take after a consultation or the lesson plans you write out for your classes. The process helps you create your own images and explanations; think of it as mental doodling.

Private writing includes journals and diaries where you record your personal thoughts, experiences, and feelings about astrology, clients, and colleagues. Because these are things that no one will read you can be brutally honest.

Some astrologers keep a transit diary by watching the planets as they move through the signs making aspects to the chart. By recording what happens, both on the inner and outer level, they learn astrology and build a body of written work to use later on. This can be a valuable tool for learning and teaching that deepens your understanding of planetary transits. You can look back in later years and see what happened when Pluto approached your Moon or other critical events. The transit diary will instruct you when your memories have gotten hazy.

There is also the writing you do for correspondence courses. This is still relatively private, as you are only revealing your thoughts to a teacher. If the course is centered on you and astrology rather than just astrology, you can document your transformation as you write about yourself and have that to look back on. Years ago I did The Chiron Project correspondence course with the late, great Dennis Elwell, and I still find those writings to be immensely valuable. If you are doing an online correspondence course with a teacher, be sure to print out all the back-and-forth documents and put them in a folder for safe keeping.

Writing for the public takes more care but is well worth the effort. Take advantage of as many opportunities as possible to let the public read your words. OPA offers the Question of the Month, the dialogues on the forum, and the Career Astrologer. You can think up, write, and submit articles for other astrology journals. You can also write letters to the editors of these publications. Write a daily forecast and news articles for your website. Contribute to your local newspaper or for health/fitness newsletters that love featuring astrology. Don't worry about getting paid; it's the writing that is important. The money will follow.

The advantage of having a forum to publish in, whether it a newspaper, newsletter, or magazine, is that it imposes external discipline in the form of a deadline. Without this, writing can easily become like exercise, diet, or that stack of books we always intend to read but never seem to get to. Our moods, whims and distractions can pull us off task. However, when a publication is holding space for you and expecting a quality product by a fixed time, it imposes a rigor and discipline on you that will focus the mind and insure you put in the necessary hours to develop your skills. Monthly or weekly submissions will keep you focused in a way that journals and diaries rarely achieve.

If you have the urge to write a book, remember that it doesn't have to be an astrology book, per se; it can be a book with astrology in it. Look at *The Luminaries* by Eleanor Catton, which won the Booker Prize in 2013. It's an old fashioned mystery that is formed around an astrological matrix. There are many mysteries where the protagonist used astrology to solve the crime. Steven Forrest wrote a good one—*Anubis Rising*. If you like to cook, create an astrology cookbook. Write children's books with astrological characters.

You can even write the astrology book that comes from your life and from your own loves and interests. Don't be afraid to put anything out there as long as it is well written.

There is another category of public writing, communicating with peers. These days it is done by emails, texting, and posting on social media and online forums, but it used to be written by hand and mailed. There was *The Mercury Hour*, a collection of letters written by astrologers to astrologers and compiled each month by Edie Custer. Edie saw the value of sharing thoughts and knowledge on various astrological topics (Edie had Mercury in Aquarius on her Midheaven). Anyone could write for it and it was a jumping in place for new astrologers to make themselves heard. Just as we never imagined back then the speed and ease of setting up our own websites, we can't image how we will write to each other in the future.

The Astrology to Consider

Mercury wants to write this section; he is the god to bring to mind when we think about writing. Mercury is slim and beautiful, young and lithe. His Sanskrit name is Budhi, which means wisdom. The

ancient Vedic scholars thought that he was the son of the Moon (who is masculine in Vedic mythology.) He is the guide between the worlds, the lord of commerce, the patron of travelers, and the conductor of dreams. He is also the writer's friend. He finds words for your thoughts. He shows you, and those who look at your chart, how you communicate, where you communicate best, and what help you receive from the other planets.

Examine your Mercury. Have a dialogue with him and see what he has to say to you. Look at his sign, his house placement, and aspects to and from other planets. Examine the *third house* and note the sign on the cusp, which planets are living there, how many and if they are in different signs, and then see which houses they rule. You also want to look at the ruler of the third house and aspects to and from that planet. *The dispositor of Mercury* gives you a lot of information. *Saturn* is a key player in assessing stamina and ability to focus. Saturn's connections to Mercury give you the ability to persist and finish what you start. *Jupiter* connections help the words flow. Take a look at the *Moon*; think of her as Mercury's mother and how that influences their relationship. She is also an indicator of memories and imagination. When you examine your chart in this way you get a deeper understanding of your personal relationship to writing, what you want to say, and how you say it.

Take the charts of your favorite authors and look at them while funneling them through this prism.

Here are some examples:

Dane Rudhyar

Future generations of astrologers will know him only through his writing now that he has passed on. He was a pioneer who opened the minds of many with his innovative concepts about astrology. His Mercury is in dreamy Pisces. Rudhyar used that Piscean influence in his avant-garde, atonal musical compositions and his spiritual novels. It is not easy to read his writing but well worth the effort. Mercury is in the third house, a common place for Mercury in a writer's chart.

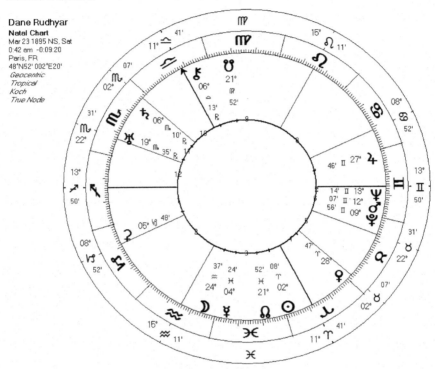

Chart 1 – Dane Rudhyar

The Sun, the Moon, and the Moon's North Node accompany Mercury. They are in three different signs to indicate Rudhyar's different modes of communication. Mercury receives a square from the Pluto-Mars-Neptune combination in Mercury's sign of Gemini. This drove Rudhyar to express himself in words as well as music.

Saturn sends a trine to give him the focus and concentration to compose the music and essays, the astrology books and novels for which we are very grateful. Mercury is his own final dispositor, which brings the emphasis back to the 3rd house.

Agatha Christie

She was born five years before Dane Rudhyar, and shares his Neptune/Pluto in Gemini conjunction (although Rudhyar's conjunction has Mars to keep him in motion and multi-tasking). Her

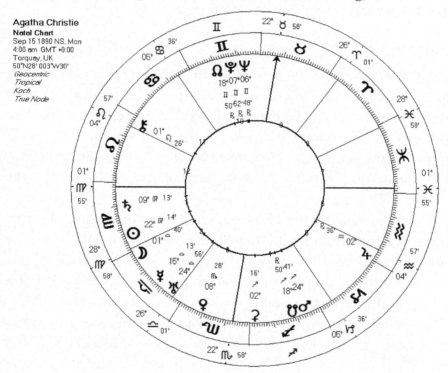

Chart 2 – Agatha Christie

Mercury is in Libra and sits close to Uranus. This would have helped her invent the sudden surprise endings to her stories. Mercury's fashionable Libran outfit is a bit disheveled as Uranus keeps him alert yet adds genius and originality to Agatha's thinking. Mercury and Uranus must have had great fun writing thrillers that have a twist at the end. Mercury is in the 2nd house, indicating that Agatha used him to help her make money.

Venus is in the house she rules, the 3rd house. There are a string of dispositors, ending up with Mercury as his own dispositor. Agatha has a Mercury-ruled ascendant as well as Saturn and the Sun in Virgo in the first. She was born to work, and this was channeled into her writing career. She wrote 91 books.

Salman Rushdie

Salman was born on the new Moon in Mercury ruled Gemini. His Mercury is in Cancer and sits on the IC, a fitting placement for a man who won the most distinguished writing prize, the Booker of Bookers, for *Midnight's Children*, a novel about the birth of India. He writes of his homeland, setting his books in both Pakistan and India. He calls up deep family memories, retelling the stories he was told in his childhood.

Mercury rules his third house and is its own dispositor. Mercury receives a trine from Jupiter to help the words flow. Mercury has a sextile from Mars in Taurus to help him write and continue on through difficult circumstances. Saturn rules his MC and sits in the fourth house of home, family, country and is in conjunction with Pluto. He spent many years of his life in exile after receiving a life threatening fatwa for his supposed insults about Mohammed in his novel *The Satanic Verses*. The Moon deposes his Mercury. She is conjunct Uranus and urges him to be daring in his writing.

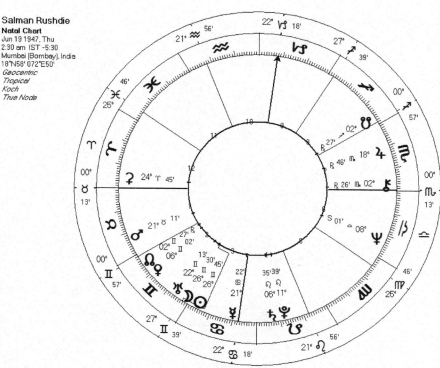

Chart 3 - Salman Rushdie

Robert Blaschke

Robert was a beloved astrologer, teacher, lecturer, and author of *Astrology: A Language of Life,* a series of five books. He also republished a number of out-of-print astrology books. His Mercury is in Scorpio in the third house and sits next to his Sun. His work came from the depths of his being. Mercury is retrograde, showing that he looked within for his information. Mercury receives stimulation from Jupiter, Uranus, and Pluto. He rules the Virgo Ascendant and the Gemini Midheaven.

Robert's Mercury is trine the South Node, giving voice to wisdom carried through from the past. A peregrine Mars in Libra deposes Mercury.

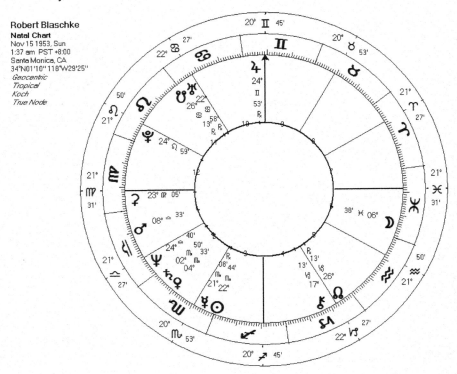

Chart 4 – Robert Blaschke

How to Write

There are hundreds of how-to books about writing and an endless stream of workshops and courses. Those disinclined to sift through this mountain of information can benefit by adopting some of the basic pointers outlined below. Just as thousands of diet books can be boiled down to the maxim "eat better, eat less, exercise more," the tips that follow distill the basics outlined in these books. If you still wish to refer to a text, read Stephen King's *On Writing* and Strunk and White's *The Elements of Style*. These slim, easy-to-read texts are goldmines.

Think of how many times you started to read an article in a magazine or newsletter and stopped halfway because it was poorly written, rambled on, and didn't say much of substance. You want people to read your writing, not skim through it. Writing is a talent that some have in greater or lesser amounts, but everyone can write. It is a process that is learnt through practicing. Start by deleting from your memory all those incidents when you received a low grade on a term paper or essay. Wipe those times out of your mind and just remember when you got praised or complimented on what you wrote. Once you feel good about writing, you will do more of it and it will become a pleasure rather than a chore.

You need to write every day. Do it for yourself in a journal or diary, or do it for the public in a blog or website forecast. Keep something in mind that you want to write. Mercury in earth and air signs will make lists and plan out what you need to write and when. Mercury in water and fire signs will feel inspiration in the moment and just let the words come. The important thing is to do it every day until it becomes a meditation and you create a channel for Neptune to download creative inspiration from his realm to your fingertips.

Deadlines are essential. They organize you and keep the pressure on. If you don't have an external deadline imposed on you, make one. Those with grand trines in air can get the assignment finished the night before it's due, but for the rest of us, schedules and deadlines are a big help.

In *On Writing*, Steven King talks about the need for a dedicated writing space. He suggests a place where you can shut the door to tell the world, and by extension yourself, that you mean business. As King says:

"Like your bedroom, your writing room should be private, a place where you go to dream. Your schedule – in about the same time every day, out when you have achieved your goal - exists in order to habituate yourself, to make you ready to dream just as you make yourself ready to sleep by going to bed at roughly the same time every night and following the same ritual as you go."

Find your place, set your goal, and sit down and begin. Focus on writing and block out distractions. Find the best time of day for you to concentrate and dedicate it to writing alone. On those days when life intervenes and there isn't time for a long session, do 5 or 10 minutes of free form writing. Just let the words come with no censoring.

How do you write? Some people like to use pen and paper. Some need to type. There are people who need to talk it out and can make use of the new software that turns spoken words into print. Find what works best for you. If you prefer to type, find a keyboard that fits your fingers.

There is a difference in writing for a book or journal and writing online. You still need to follow the basic rules of grammar but **online writing is shorter, sharper, has more bullet points and shorter sentences.** You need to get to the point quickly, as readers have less patience when browsing online material. You can practice by making statements on social media forums.

Writing is a singular activity but there is great benefit in sharing your work and receiving encouragement from others who are also writing. Take writing workshops whenever you can. Attend workshops that are both astrological and non-astrological in order to experience other forms of writing. These classes will give you tools to use and boost your confidence as you emerge with a body of written work. A weekend spent learning to write poetry will be of use to you even though you many never write another poem again.

The best thing is to find, or create, an ongoing writing group modeled on OPA's peer groups. If you meet on a regular basis with the same people, you will learn to trust each other and be able to be helpful and be helped. There are online writing groups you can seek out if you can't form one in your local area. Membership in a writing group gives you an obligation to produce a certain amount of work for each meeting.

The basic rules of writing to keep in mind:

1. Be specific
2. Less is more
3. Edit with a scalpel, then edit again
4. Avoid the passive voice

Nouns name and describe things, people, and places. *Pronouns* stand in for nouns. Instead of "we went out to eat," say: "Jay and I went to the Indian restaurant for dinner." Which gives more information? Being specific does. Always reread and see where you can put in the noun rather than the pronoun. You want to think in *good* generalities and write in specifics. *Example*

Here is what the masters of grammar, Strunk and White, have to say about the virtue of brevity:

"*Vigorous writing is concise. A sentence should contain no unnecessary words, a paragraph no unnecessary sentences, for the same reasons that a drawing should have no unnecessary lines and a machine no unnecessary parts. This requires not that the writer make all his sentences short, or that he avoid all detail and treat his subjects only in outline, but that every word tell.*"

This includes cutting back on your use of adverbs. Too many adverbs are a sign of sloppy writing. In writing, less is more.

The classic phrase about editing is "Kill your darlings". Stephen King recommends that you cut your first draft by 10% when you rewrite. It's always easy to add words if you go short, but deadly to have too many words and anesthetize the reader. There are many self-published books on the market today and it's easy to spot which ones needed the eyes of a professional editor; excessive wordiness is the dead giveaway.

It's important to have someone else read your work before you submit it. Have the other person read it aloud to you so you can hear what flows and what doesn't work. Be warned that there is a cottage industry of sub-par editors hawking their services. They will take your money and degrade your manuscript. Since there is no licensing for editors, you need to get a recommendation for someone who does quality work. You may pay more up front but it will be worth it. If you use a hack, you will end up paying twice, once to them and once to a pro to correct the damage.

Write in active voice

The planet does something, the eclipse did a number on him, everyone had a good time. Avoid using the passive voice—it was done by the planet, he was hammered by the eclipse, a good time was had by all. The active voice moves the reader forward. The reader is slowed down by the passive voice.

Listen to your clients. They often express the perfect explanation of a transit or aspect that explains astrology in clear, precise English. They will give you metaphors taken from their life experience, as in the former white river rafting guide who described her Pluto transit in terms of riding the river. Those are the words people will understand when you write astrology for the mainstream.

Think before you write. Jot down ideas and let them marinate inside your mind for a while. Write, then reread and edit. Cut 10-20%. Reread and cut some more. In the words of Elmore Leonard, "Try to leave out the part that readers tend to skip." Check and see if you have used the same word too many times. Use a thesaurus to find an alternate word. Cut out clichés and create your own metaphors, similes, and comparisons. Check your facts, tenses, and your spelling. Think of your readers and be kind to them.

Books to read

These books want to be on your bookshelf:

The Elements of Style	William Strunk, Jr. & E.B.White
On Writing	Stephen King
The Synonym Finder	J. I. Rodale
Advice to Writers	Jon Winokur
Writing from the Heart	Nancy Aronie
The Rulership Book	Rex E. Bills
Astrological Keywords	Manly P. Hall
The Book of Rulerships	Lee Lehman, PhD.
Word Watcher's Handbook	Phyllis Martin

Exercise for practice and fun

Write with abandon and enjoyment!

Articles

- Why Saturn is my friend
- What I didn't say…
- A dialogue between two planets in your chart
- Here and now I am….
- Explain retrograde Mercury to a fundamentalist (of any religion)
- When I first became aware of astrology
- The first time I went to an astrologer   *funny Donna t "shotgun" story*
- The first time I went to an astrology conference

Donna + Jent story

PL Reg Linda P, story

In conclusion

Once you move beyond the fundamentals, there's no substitute for sitting down and writing regularly. Writing is a skill, and like all skills it improves with practice and dedicated effort. In time your own unique style and voice will emerge. For now, the most important thing is to get started and write regularly. Stephen King's advice boils down to a few words: "Read a lot. Write a lot." Maureen Dowd echoes this sentiment, saying: "I never presume to give advice on writing. I think the best way to learn to write is to read good books and stories by good writers. It's a hard thing to preach about. As Thelonius Monk once said about his field, "Talking about music is like dancing about architecture."

Arlan Wise, *C.A.P., is a professional consulting astrologer who has been in practice since 1979. She teaches students at all levels. She wrote the astrology column for the Martha's Vineyard Times for 17 years. She is a frequent contributor to the Career Astrologer, OPA's magazine. Arlan has spoken at Prosig and OPA, and MAC conferences. Arlan has been on the Board of OPA since 1996, serving as President for a four year term, as the Newsletter Editor, Membership Secretary, and is currently as the Director of Publications.*
Website: www.arlanwise.com

Chapter 11

In Print

A Practical Guide for Writers of Astrology

Frank C. Clifford

In this chapter I'll be discussing the various ways in which astrologers can get their work published—whether it's a book, article, blog, or Sun sign column—and offering advice about approaching magazines and publishers. I'll also provide some tips on how to start the writing process and discover your niche as a writer.

This is a vast subject and there are plenty of websites and books dedicated to writing and getting published. I'd like to focus on what I've learned on my journey as a writer and publisher in the area of astrology. I'd like to thank my astrologer friends Jane Struthers and Diana McMahon-Collis, both of whom have much experience in publishing and were generous in sharing their ideas for this chapter.

Know Your Strengths

There are so many astrology blogs and how-to websites, not to mention the array of astrology books already out there. If I need a reminder, I just take a look at how many read (and unread) books I have on my bookshelves! You and I are blessed to be in a field where there are so many bright, intelligent professionals teaching and writing, hence the many high quality astrology books in print. So, before going any further, it's worth asking whether you feel you *really* have something to write that will make people sit up and pay attention. What will you add that is new or innovative to the canon? Once you've pinpointed your strengths as an astrologer, can you write something that's fresh, original and stimulating ... something that hasn't already been done—and done better—by others?

The first step is to take an honest look at what you're able to do. If you have important ideas to share but writing is not your forte, you can invest in a writing course to practise and hone ways to communicate your astrological knowledge. While you're building your confidence as a writer, you can always present your material through recordings or transcriptions of your seminars and talks.

Write what you know

Like most people who publish, I simply love books: their feel, shape, smell, and design. In May 1997, soon after turning twenty-four, I self-published my first book. I'd been studying astrology for eight years and knew that any attempt to compete with what was already on the market would be foolish. But I felt I could contribute something new, so I decided to write about what I knew best and what interested me most at the time. I published a book of celebrity data and biographies called *British Entertainers: The Astrological Profiles*. With each set of data I provided some biography, key life dates and astrological commentary about a given performer.

I already knew the area well. I had begun working with Lois Rodden, who led the field in cataloguing accurate astrological data, and was aware that there was a small but interested market out there. In 1996, I contacted hundreds of British celebrities for their data, skimmed through thousands of newspaper interviews I'd been filing away, and bought lots of biographies (this was before the internet was The Internet). Over the next six months, I proceeded to write the 700 short profiles that comprised the book.

By early 1997, I had bought a couple of self-publishing how-to books and got myself an ISBN number and barcode. I laid out the book myself using **QuarkXPress** and I sought out friends to help me with three essential tasks: copy editing (spotting mistakes and making revisions), proof-reading (checking the finished product before print), and cover design. I then approached a printer, which led to a first print run of around 800 copies arriving at my door in late May. All of a sudden, I was a publisher! The book was never going to be a mass-market best seller, but it sold steadily over the next few years, thanks to specialist bookshops and advertising through *The Astrological Journal*. (Had I had the courage to lecture at this point, I imagine I would have shifted these copies faster.)

As a young, enthusiastic Aries, I now rushed forward and began publishing other astrologers' books, but I didn't feel ready to write my own "astrological magnum opus." I wrote two books on palmistry (modern hand analysis) for mainstream publishers in 2002 and 2003, and some small self-published volumes on astrology, but the idea that I could write a full-length book that would be placed on bookshelves next to those of the great astrologers … well, that seemed like a long way off. It took me fifteen years from my first self-publication to write and publish a full-length textbook on astrology

(*Getting to the Heart of Your Chart*). I stayed away until I had found my own voice through lecturing, teaching, consulting, and writing articles for various magazines. And, of course, until I had learned more as an astrologer.

Be curious

Some astrologers proudly proclaim, "I haven't read an astrology book in years." To me, this comes across as arrogant or ignorant (or both). They sound as though they've stopped learning. I think it's imperative that we read others' work and stay open to different approaches and the latest developments. Keeping curious and interested are the keys to being a good astrologer and writer.

Other astrologers say, "I don't read other people's work because I don't want to be derivative." In fact, I believe that exploring the subject as fully as possible stops you from ending up that way! I continue to attend lectures on subjects that interest me — and subjects I'd like to write about. But if I see someone doing a better job than I potentially could, I think, "I'll buy *their* book — or offer to publish it when they're ready."

So, I suggest you read books, blogs and articles on your favourite subjects and by the authors you admire. Devour as much as you can. Your writing will be a reflection of the work that's shaped you, and at best you will take these ideas into new realms. Keep reading, keep learning, keep adding to your knowledge. Stay interested and involved.

"You gotta get a gimmick"

In showbiz circles, it's always been good to have a skill or specialty that attracts interest and publicity. It's important to stand out from the crowd if you want to be noticed. But it's easy to be typecast, and we astrologers are as guilty of this as anyone else: "Oh, you're the

Chiron lady," or, "You're the guy that's into Eris." But if you're trying to sell and promote your ideas and to become familiar to others in the community, then it's better to be known for *something* than have people ask, "What *is* it you do, again?"

That data kid

For the longest time, because of my research into birth times, my first data book and the Clifford Data Compendium I compiled for the Solar Fire software, I was for many people "the data guy" — the one they would call for a celebrity's birth data or confirmation of an accurate birth time. In recent years the immediate association has been for my work on Solar Arc Directions, chart synthesis and easy ways to spot patterns in the horoscope. These areas interest me and I enjoy lecturing on them. I've felt that I have had something new to say, so I've run with it!   *ARTICLES*

So, give this some thought. What is it that people already know you for? What interests you most now? And if you have the time to write a book, article, or blog, which subject would take priority?

Think small and specific

Some of you may wish to make your first writing project your magnum opus or, as inspiration flows, expand an initial idea into something more substantial. Over the years, though, I've noticed that some writers find completing such a mammoth task too great a hurdle—it can take too long to write, and the pressure to complete it becomes immense. Often, it ends up half-written. This is particularly true if the writer wants to create a definitive textbook of astrology and along the way realises how many established astrology writers have already done so. So, some of you may wish to consider a less daunting project as a first writing assignment, while others will indeed pursue a larger project from the outset. Do what's best for you, your workload and time-frame.

My advice would be to find a specialized area of astrology, lecture on it, and explore fresh ways of communicating it to an audience. Then, write your first article on this subject and seek feedback from colleagues you respect. The next stage would be to create a small volume (to self-publish or offer to a publisher) on this subject. If a book (or booklet) is done well and the subject attracts attention, you may be invited to talk on the subject for various astrology groups and, as your audience grows, they'll await further publications from you.

I began writing 40-page booklets (in full colour and professionally printed) about five years ago. I find them easier to write, edit and lay out, and they are designed to give readers instant access to an area of astrology. My first booklet was on the predictive method of Solar Arc Directions. As an Aries, I saw it as a challenge to communicate the essentials of this powerful tool succinctly and effectively in 40 pages. The booklets have gone down a storm because they are inexpensive, quick to read, and accessible. From the feedback I've had, readers grab one of my booklets off their shelves, place it in a bag to read on a journey, and devour it in one sitting. It's also short enough to read cover-to-cover over again.

Starting to Write

The art of writing is the art of applying the seat of one's pants to the seat of one's chair — Mary Heaton Vorse

There are many websites offering writing tips and techniques – check these out. But most importantly: Get started, and stay on task.

Begin with setting boundaries. Commonly, friends and family think that because you're writing and working from home, you're available for chats at any time of day. Let them know you're working. You need to find a quiet place to write where you won't be disturbed. Close your email program, keep the Internet on (for research!), or go to the library and check the accuracy of facts and references.

Dedicate at least a couple of hours during a day to brainstorming and mind-mapping sections, and getting key ideas down on paper. Start with the essentials – the meaty bit of the article/book – and then gradually build around these. (It's often helpful to leave the introduction to the end until the rest of the text has taken shape – and keep this introduction short.) Organize work into chapters and sub-sections, and remember to back up your files!

Get up and walk around, take some breaks for the ideas to percolate, but return later and continue writing. Keep writing, even if it's coming out back to front! You can return to it and re-arrange, expand, cut, edit, and fine-tune later. There'll be a nugget or two there, even if it seems hopeless as you're writing. Churn it out and thrash it out!

It's been said that if you want to write a good article, write 500 because *no one can write 500 bad ones*. At first, the quality doesn't matter—it's about finding your voice and practising your craft.

If you're stuck on a section, leave it—print it out and read it later. But *keep the process going* by beginning work on another section. Move on—you'll have plenty of time to fine-tune everything later as you wade through a number of drafts. On the other hand, if thoughts are running away with themselves, record them into a dictaphone or mind-map them to help put these spontaneous ideas into a framework. Keep a notebook and pen for when you're away from the computer.

Enjoy the process

If you haven't already read Julia Cameron's *The Artist's Way*, check it out—it's designed to help you gain confidence in your talents and skills. Make writing a *joy*—enjoy the process of discovery and the connections you make. So many people turn the process into a hard slog, becoming too self-conscious in the process. The very thought of "writing a book" turns eloquent lecturers into writers of long, convoluted sentences who lose their voice while trying to be authoritative or to justify their opinion. Say it simply; imagine you're writing to a friend. Often astrologers write as though they're handing out abbreviated lecture notes or make the assumption that readers already know what they mean. When astrology writers get stuck in this way, my advice for those who lecture is to go back and listen to their classes and talks and see how freely they've expressed themselves there. I recommend they transcribe these or use them as the basis of the first draft. It's worthwhile capturing this easy, more colloquial approach on paper and then shaping it to fit the intended style of the article or chapter. Those who lecture and write often find it a great compliment to hear a student or reader say, "When I read your book, I can hear you speak."

Writing is a discipline. The professional writers I know treat it as a regular job, taking a cup of coffee to the desk and writing in the morning, breaking for lunch, and continuing to write in the afternoon. Even with that vital routine established, I don't know many "natural" writers for whom the genius flows from page to page—the rest of us need to work hard to make it look easy.

Don't worry too much about what other writers do. Some will produce 3000 words a day before lunchtime, four to five days a week. Others will write nothing for weeks then blaze through 500 or 1000 words a day for an intense few weeks (usually prompted by something called "the deadline"). There's no one way or right way, only your way. Most astrologers have to balance their day job, client work, and teaching with time for writing, but if you want to produce something, you'll have to make time in your schedule every week to write and hone your craft.

Rewrites

Writing the book or article is only the first stage. Be prepared to go back and edit—over and over again. Keep a thesaurus by your desk (or open on your computer). Check your work (spelling, grammar, punctuation, syntax) scrupulously. Print out your text (choose an unusual font so it *looks different*) and read it aloud to yourself. Or read it to someone else—that way you'll spot mistakes and realize that some of your explanations don't make sense to your listener or might be presumptuous. Keep polishing the text without losing its rhythm or your own voice. Improve your English by reading cleverly crafted newspaper views, reviews, and interviews. All writers learn their craft by practising—by doing it.

Speaking of editing, a few years ago I commissioned a number of astrology articles for a magazine. I knew that all of the contributors were great astrologers but some were not natural writers. I spent much time reworking one article in particular – in fact, I rewrote it completely. The writer took a look and was so impressed with what he'd thought he'd written—it sounded just like what he'd imagined in his own head that he later emailed wanting the finished version for his new book. If he'd taken the time to see what had been improved upon and compared it to his original version, it may have helped his future writings.

Writing—the discipline, the craft, the application—can be a mix of blood, sweat, and tears. However much we write, it's still hard work, but the process does become easier and over time we learn to trust that something decent will emerge from the effort.

Writing blogs

Blogs are your chance to be on an equal footing with other writers, and to have free rein to produce what you want. The way to distinguish yourself from the 1001 other blogs and bloggers is to develop your own authentic voice and specialism. The Internet has thousands of astrology blogs, and *often "free content" is content-free.* You'll encounter blogs with interpretations that defy belief ("Venus–Saturn aspects mean you'll *never* have financial security and will *never* be loved"), so start by looking at some ethical, well written blogs online: Donna Cunningham's Sky Writer is comprehensive and student-geared (with a section of great advice on how to write), Penny Thornton's Astrolutely offers insights into mundane (world) events, and Barry Goddard's Astrotabletalk is fun, no-nonsense, and opinionated. There are many more to discover.

If you want to write a blog, ensure that you have a warm, accessible "About Me" section on your site. It needs a conversational tone, and it's usually the first section people go to. Readers want to know who you are, and they want to know they can trust and respect your words. In short, they're looking to make a connection (as a reader or potential client). And don't forget to have it proof-read by someone who knows what they're doing – you and your blog will look amateurish if it's riddled with bad spelling and grammar.

Before writing a blog you might want to contribute to various forums (Deborah Houlding's Skyscript is a great website for those interested in traditional astrology) or to join various astrology groups on Facebook. The problem is that you may encounter some arrogant, condescending trolls who "know it all" — the type who turn simple discussions about the meanings of planetary placements into all-out war. You'll need a tough skin if you get involved in forums, but they can be useful in finding out who's doing what in our community.

Do people actually read blogs? Well, I'm told that commissioning
agents hunt around for new authors, books, and ideas by checking
out blogs. They are also more inclined to pursue a writer who has a
large following on their blog or on Twitter (see below in Getting
Published).

Writing for magazines

If you're interested in having an article published there are several
high quality astrological publications to choose from, and some
reach a large number of astrologers and students. The best way to
start is to look at the magazines you admire most, or to consider those
that publish articles in your specialism. For instance, if your area of
interest and expertise is the history of astrology, then the UK-based
academic journal *Culture and Cosmos* may be the first place to start. If
it's academic research, then perhaps *Correlation*. You might want to
write Sun sign pieces for tabloid newspapers or non-astrology
magazines. In these cases, competition is tough and there may
already be an in-house astrologer or new age writer. You'll need a
"hook" and an immediate, accessible writing style that is in line with
the publication you're pursuing. When I've been featured in tabloids
and broadsheets, it's usually been in the form of an interview or
profile of my work, or reporting on the "accuracy" of a reading I've
done for the publication's freelance journalist.

Some Astrology Magazines

Member-led organizations such as the NCGR (National Council for
Geocosmic Research), the AAGB (Astrological Association of Great
Britain), and ISAR (International Society for Astrological Research)
have their own well produced publications. NCGR has the *Geocosmic
Journal*, the AA has its prestigious *Astrological Journal*, and ISAR
produces *International Astrologer*. Most won't pay authors for articles,

but they can offer good publicity for your work (or a place to advertise your own publications and blogs). All three of the above provide space for articles and letters/discussions in email newsletters (*E-News* and *Member letter* from NCGR, *In the Loop* from AAGB, and *E-Zine* from ISAR). The Federation of Australian Astrologers has its *FAA Journal*, and there are numerous newsletters (such as *Horizons* and *Mercury Messenger*) from local Australian groups featuring articles and adverts for their upcoming events and speakers. The Astrological Lodge of London has its *Quarterly*, now published sporadically. There are also some non-English publications that will translate and publish your articles (I was recently introduced to *AstroLogos* in Finland and recall a Serbian publication with the same name).

Dell Horoscope (a UK version was published for many years simply as *Horoscope*) offers a mix of articles for the "pop" end of the astrology market, as do *Soul & Spirit* (in the UK) and *Horoscope Guide* (originally *American Astrology*). In Australia, *WellBeing* magazine produces its own glossy *Wellbeing Astrology* guide each year under the editorship of Kelly Surtees and offers an eclectic, well-chosen range of "going further" articles, rather than just The Year Ahead for the twelve Sun signs. And in the UK, there are also Mind, Body, Spirit (MBS) titles such as *Kindred Spirit*.

The Mountain Astrologer

I've been fortunate enough to have had some involvement with almost all of the above publications and many others, but I want to single out *The Mountain Astrologer* magazine. It stands tall in our field because of the range and quality of its articles and authors, the care taken (and given) during the editing process, and its openness to new writers of all levels and from every astrological discipline. It also has the widest readership for a magazine of its kind. It can be bought in stores, so advertising can be effective, and its thoughtful book reviews can help promote your product. And to top it all, authors get paid for articles!

TMA's online site has a blog and an article index (by subject, author, and chart wheel), which is very useful given how important it can be to know what's already been published and by whom. It took me a while to submit a piece to *TMA* because I wanted to offer something that hadn't been written about before and, to be frank, I was afraid of having my work rejected. I wanted my first submission to be good enough for them to want more! I finally submitted a piece in mid-2008 (on *Shadow Transits*), then they approached me to write a cover piece on the newly-elected President Obama, and I've been contributing ever since.

I say more about the editing process elsewhere in this chapter, but I'm a writer who loves being edited and having my work improved — and it makes a huge difference knowing that an editor cares as much about the finished product as you do. *TMA* is the only magazine I've regularly written for where the team comes back to me with numerous questions and edits to ensure the article is as cogent and clearly expressed as it can be. Such attention to detail can, surprisingly, infuriate some writers, who take any edits or suggestions as professional slight. But the goal is to produce a piece of work that presents the writer's research and thoughts in a clear, accessible, and intelligent way. It's a sobering thought that most editing teams (in any area of publishing) don't have the time or expertise to focus on this stage of the process. My advice: Pursue and write for the ones that do!

For any magazine, it's always worthwhile finding out the current editor's email and getting in touch directly. But first, check the magazine's website for writing and submission guidelines. *The Mountain Astrologer* appears to have the strictest guidelines, perhaps because of the volume of submissions they receive. On its website, *TMA* asks that writers send query letters that are:

> One to three pages maximum — and be very specific about the proposed topic, estimated length (in words or characters-plus-spaces, *not* pages), and charts or illustrations to be included. The article outline should include the main points you wish to cover and sample paragraphs from various parts of the article, not just the introduction. Please provide biographical information about yourself and your work and interests, as well as how readers may contact you; your bio should be 100 words maximum, including contact information.

Unlike most other astrology magazines, *TMA* rarely accepts articles that have appeared elsewhere nor does it pre-accept any article simply based on a query letter or proposal. If *TMA* does accept your proposal, you'll be encouraged to submit the completed article, which the editors will then review. *TMA* was one of the first magazines to insist that authors present birth data with reliable, verified sources (rated by accuracy), which also appealed to me.

Sun sign work

If you're looking for a paid Sun sign writing job with a magazine, these positions are rare and usually come via existing contacts in publishing. Publishers have "friends who know someone interested in astrology," or are acquainted with someone who just wants to write! There are many cases over the years where copy has been written by someone who knows nothing about the actual planetary movements. After three years of my being at one magazine, the editor asked if I could focus more on "predicting" sex for readers. When I avoided doing so, I was replaced by a friend of the editor who had dabbled in tarot.

I did Sun sign monthlies and weeklies (dailies would have driven me mad) for thirteen years. Over the years, the columns provided a steady income and, although it was good practice thinking of new ways to describe ingresses and aspects, the workload was heavy (especially when writing and recording forecasts for their phonelines were part of the deal). I saw my columns as a chance to give a bit of "rough and ready" electional advice so that readers could plan weekly activities in tune with the cosmos. I also found an opportunity, at times, to reflect on the bigger picture (and wider transits). These columns were the only places where I felt free to be more directive with my astrology. In consultations I steer clear of telling clients *what to do* (not easy for a Sun in Aries), but in Sun sign columns it was necessary to give some advice and instruction: "This month, pay attention to…" and "This month, it's time to put X into action."

Nowadays, it's rare to earn a living from these types of columns. The Sun sign market has been in decline for years because publishers feel less inclined to pay high salaries and instead are more willing to give percentage shares of revenue from phonelines, for which the astrologers are also expected to write. Some of the big-name Sun sign astrologers have phoneline deals already set up with service providers and have so many syndicated columns that they can offer these for free and instead take a good portion of the phoneline revenue.

Nowadays, the choice you'll have is to write your own Sun sign forecasts for your own blog or write them for someone's site for no money (or for a paltry sum, a percentage of close to zero income, or in exchange for free advertising space). Then you might attract paid advertising to your own site (again, rare), or someone may see your blog and may want you to contribute to their magazine or project (ditto).

I have respect for those who write good, astrology-based Sun sign columns—there's an art to them—but it's slave labour for many and I wouldn't advise students to write them unless they love doing Sun signs, want to hone their writing skills, or have a unique communication style.

Your Book is Your Ambassador

It is said that we all have "a book in us" and astrology is no different—everyone seems to be writing a book or promising to do so. There's no question that having a book published lends prestige and authority to an astrologer, particularly in the eyes of the general public. The public likes to elevate all experts, even if astrology is given a bad rap from many quarters. Once a book is published, an astrologer's credibility increases. Marketing experts tell us that having a book published acts as a powerful and personal way of branding yourself and that writing and launching a book is one of the fastest ways to position yourself as an expert in your field. A book becomes your ambassador.

It's the age we're in and a result of the huge promotional impact of Oprah's Book Club in the last decade and the range of experts who appear on TV—everyone's promoting something they've written. Of course, astrology *has* been big publishing business (think back to 1968 when *Linda Goodman's Sun Signs* was an international bestseller, or in the late 1980s/early 1990s when Aquarian Press and Arkana put out a series of books by noted astrologers). But astrology is currently in a lull—even for books that only focus on the popular, Sun sign end of the market. Many major publishers have a MBS (Mind, Body, Spirit) list of titles and the market has been saturated with "pop" Sun sign titles for years. Almost every possibility of using personal birth dates to say something about you has been published (think of the immensely popular *The Secret Language of Birthdays*).

Publishers are always interested in motivational and inspirational "self-help" titles that can enhance their readers' lives. The paranormal and New Age are still popular but we astrologers have sat back for years and watched mass-market volumes on teenage witches, feng shui, cosmic ordering/the law of attraction, and any magic book linked to the *Harry Potter* and *Twilight* films take up our space in bookstores! Astrology has been around the block forever. Luckily for us, it's not a fad—it's enduring but is rarely the "in" thing anymore.

Book publishers

Perhaps the days when astrology books were bestsellers are long gone, but although the market is small, it is deep—and students and teachers (if not major publishers) are always on the lookout for well researched and well explained books on various areas of the subject.

Check out the publishers who have put out books that have shaped your ideas, published the authors you admire, and have covers and layouts that appeal to you. These might be mainstream publishers (who usually stick to producing Sun sign books or volumes that don't require readers to know more than the basics) or small publishing houses that specialise in astrology, MBS or esoteric titles.

One of the most helpful books I read when starting out was the late Michael Legat's *An Author's Guide to Publishing*. I'd still recommend this book, as it covers so many aspects of publishing with candour and common sense. I'd also recommend the thorough and practical DIY book *How to ... Publish a Book* by Robert Spicer, particularly if you decide to go down the self-publishing route (discussed later in this chapter).

Who decides which book to publish? Usually the sales team makes many of the decisions. The bottom line is money, of course. Firstly, publishers don't want to take on books that cost a great deal of money to produce. Secondly, they are looking for authors who can help sell books: writers with their own following, their own popular Twitter accounts or blogs, or who are credible authorities who already lecture and promote their own work, what publishers refer to as "having a platform." To attract a publisher, it helps to have an international following, to speak various languages, and to have lectured abroad. Most publishers won't know the astrology field — they'll need you to be the expert who has the contacts, and will want to see an author's willingness to get behind their own work.

It helps to have an agent if you want to go with a mainstream publisher (and these publishers will be able to sell foreign rights more easily and have your book in the few bookstores remaining on high streets). An agent will check the contract for you and probably want you to write a similar book again and again for other publishers. But the growth of online book purchases means that the smaller imprints can reach the market too, so you might consider going with an astrology publisher who knows the field and has contacts with the main outlets and international astrology conferences. If you approach one of these, they'll have a better understanding of the market but they will still be primarily concerned with the business side, and you must be prepared to receive a paltry advance (or none at all) and to take on any promotional efforts yourself.

Book proposals

When contacting a publisher, you'll need to write a brief letter or email, attach a proposal summarizing your ideas, and include a sample chapter. Some people wait to finish a book before they contact a publisher, but it's worth getting feedback (if it's forthcoming) from the publisher before you write the whole manuscript. Don't expect to hear back for a number of weeks or even a few months. If your subject is current, bear in mind that most publishers have at least a nine- to twelve-month lead-in time before publication.

In a two to three-page book proposal, you'll need to prove to a publisher that you can research, organize, and write. As Michael Larsen in *How to Write a Book Proposal* states, "It will require a fundamental shift in your thinking from that of a writer with something to say, to that of an author with something to sell." I recommend buying Larsen's book, but here are some main points to keep in mind:

- Your proposal's introduction: this has to be irresistible! It has to show that the book will succeed in a small but competitive marketplace, and that you're an authority who has a solid, marketable idea. Provide the "hook" (e.g. "[The title] will be the first book to ..."), which must be the single most compelling idea that you can write about your book. (All of the text for the introduction may end up forming much of the back-page blurb, so read a number of these before you start. Creating this text early and keeping it on your desk is useful during the writing process itself—things can change but it'll keep you focused on the goal.)

- Estimate the number of words and number of illustrations.

- Note any other features (from your writing style to any exercises/checklists to be included).

- Describe the potential market and subsidiary rights possibilities (e.g. if you have a following in China); and how you will help promote the book.

V. imp.

- Include a short biography of your experience.
- Include any past reviews or future endorsements from noted people in the field.

Along with the proposal, include one sample chapter—the strongest of the book to show it at its best. Publishers also like some information about competing titles so they can see if there is a gap in the market for the proposed book or if the market is already overcrowded. The information should include the title, author, publisher and date of publication, plus a couple of sentences about the book itself.

Publishers reject proposals because:

- They already have something similar on their list.
- The work is too specialized.
- It's badly written/presented.

As a publisher, when I've received a shoddy or lazily edited proposal, it puts me off working with the writer. Another no-go is encountering a writer who's so fixed on how everything should look visually that there's no room in their minds for improvement. I remember someone collaring me at a party and selling their book proposal on "astronomy for astrologers" only to say that they wanted nothing changed and the diagrams had to be laid out exactly their way. I suggested that he self-publish. And then there are times when the author's sense of self-importance is so great that the project has "an unnecessary hassle" written all over it. One pompous writer's email warned, "I am not accustomed to taking direction … It will be of a stylistic quality that does not really require editing … [so] I do not expect to be told what to do." If I'd had the time, I might have looked further and pinpointed some deep-rooted insecurity but, once the ego has landed, ignore attempts at psychoanalysis and run for cover. Luckily, most writers are sincere and keen to let publishers and editors do what they do best. One writer's book that I published some years ago was originally a collection of interviews. The author was open to crafting these into chapters around particular themes, which made all the difference to the final product.

Publishing contracts

If a publisher accepts your work, you'll be asked to sign a contract. There may be lots of clauses therein, but here are the most important. Publishers will usually want the following exclusive rights for the full legal term of copyright: to publish your book worldwide and in ebook format, and to act on your behalf to sell subsidiary rights, including foreign language (translation) rights.

As the author, you'll be contracted to deliver an "acceptable manuscript," one that is professionally written and presented, where you own the copyright to the work and it's free from libelous or inflammatory statements. You'll be contracted to deliver on a date agreed in a particular format (Microsoft Word, double-spaced, etc.) and of a specified length (e.g. 50,000 words). Publishers are usually quite flexible with first-time authors when it comes to missing a deadline by a few weeks, but they will be infuriated by an author who goes into hiding and refuses to answer the phone as the eleventh hour approaches. Always keep them updated with news of your progress! The book has a production schedule and, if that starts to drift, it can cause problems for all concerned, not least the writer, who is unlikely to be contracted again.

Once delivered, you'll be given a time frame to correct, revise, and return the publishers' proofs (usually 21 days, as stated in the contract). At this point, only minor changes will usually be accepted, so ensure that the manuscript you deliver at the deadline is everything you wish to have in the final book.

If the publisher expects you to provide any necessary illustrations, the contract will state this. If you're needing photographs of people or places, most publishers have access to photo library services, but these can prove expensive. You'll be encouraged to keep to a minimum all illustrations that require a fee, so stick with charts and computer-generated forms or lists. If you need copyright (for song lyrics or other material owned by a third party), then you'll be required to seek out permission and spend your own money paying the copyright holders for usage. Usually, authors are responsible for compiling an index, but it's worth investing in a professional indexer if you have no experience. Most books benefit from having a thorough index.

In most contracts you'll retain the copyright. When this is not the case, it's usually because the publishers want the freedom to use your text again later in a different volume (often under someone else's name). They will offer a flat fee for your writing and take the copyright from under you, so only sign if this is agreeable to you.

The publishers will be contracted to publish your book within a time frame (usually 12 or 18 months), they will display your name prominently on the cover, and you'll be sent a handful of author copies (and the right to buy additional ones at a 50% discount, usually postage-free). They may want you to sign an option clause giving them first refusal on your next book and to ensure that you won't write a work that competes directly with the contracted publication until a specified time scale has elapsed. You're a working author who should have the freedom to write elsewhere or to write on the subject again at a later date, so you may wish to dispute either or both stipulations.

Most books are now published POD (print on demand), meaning that publishers print copies when they've received orders from bookshops, wholesalers or distributors. This saves 2000 copies of a book sitting in a warehouse gathering dust and turning brown! But if there is overstock and the book ends up being remaindered (i.e. sold off cheaply), ask for a clause in the contract that gives you first option to buy the remaindered books at the same, substantial discount that would be offered to remainder buyers for bargain bookshops. When a book goes out of print, the rights will revert back to you, but you may have to contact the publisher for official confirmation.

(Money)

Do expect to get paid for your work. If you are not offered a flat fee, you should be offered an advance on future royalties—even a few hundred dollars. It's a sign that the publisher is willing to invest in you. Too many astrologers "just want their book published" and let some small publishers get away with paying nothing for an advance. Advances are usually paid in three stages: on signature of contract, on delivery of the manuscript, and finally upon publication of the book.

Publishers will pay you royalties every six months (once the money paid to you as an advance has been recouped through book sales). Royalties will usually be around 7.5% of the *net receipts*. It used to be the same percentage of the *published price* of a book, but nowadays with every bookstore (particularly online shops) offering discounts on any title that shows promise, publishers won't offer you that. If a book is $10, then in the past an author would have been entitled to 75¢ a copy (7.5%), but now retailers (and distributors) expect anything from a 40% to 55% discount, so an author will get 7.5% of what the publisher receives (their net receipts). If they've sold the $20 book for a 55% discount, the author will get 7.5% of the $9 a publisher has received, amounting to roughly 68¢ a copy. If you thought you'd make big money on your year-long writing investment, think again. Having a book published usually turns out to be more about prestige than profit. The only way the books make money for astrologers nowadays is if the title is sold to foreign markets, or if the author self-publishes and sells many books directly through their website or at lectures – more of this later.

Designs

If you sign with a publisher, you probably won't have much say in the design, layout, and cover. It's rare that a publisher involves an author in the stylistic decision-making process. You may not get to keep your title, either, but hopefully you'll be included in discussions. Even if most general publishers don't know the astrology field, they do know what sells, so it's worth listening to their ideas. You're both investing in each other.

Small astrological publishing houses are notorious for either bland covers or crudely designed covers with ugly fonts and glaring colours. (Walk around any astrology conference bookstall if you doubt my words.) I almost signed with one publisher and made the mistake of saying I hoped for a better cover than a recent title she'd released. Her daughter had designed the atrocity! She proceeded to give me a stern lecture on how much she knew about publishing and her audience. I then checked out her other covers (as I should have done earlier). After that, I knew I couldn't go forward with the woman or her daughter's designs. Lesson learned. Approach people whose work you respect and whose artistic ethos complements your own.

A (Select) Bit About You

Publishers will ask for biographical information and possible publicity leads, contacts, and ideas. Yes, it's important to build yourself up a little when writing a biography (and readers do like to think they're learning from an authority), but steer clear of promoting yourself to an embarrassing level. A quote, a review, an endorsement, a website address, and some facts go further in proclaiming one's genius than a sentence of hyperbole in a biography that looks self-composed.

In truth, the author is often not the best person to write the biography or to consider how a book should look inside and out. But a happy author is a happy author, and one who will proudly promote their book. I've played difficult author a couple of times; my first palmistry book was badly edited to the extent that the proof reader managed to *add* a few hundred errors while she was working her way through it. Knowing that, in the reader's mind, the buck stops with the author, I didn't want my first book to look unprofessional. So, I did the work of the editor, helped with the layout, was anxious about the final result (which still had some errors), and came out of the experience knowing that I should self-publish.

Self-publishing

Self-publishing is easier than ever, but it still takes the same amount of time, energy, and devotion to make a good product *before* it goes to print. In the era of Amazon's online domination of the book market and the folding of most main street bookshops, self-publishing can put us on a near, even keel with big-name publishers.

There are now a number of companies that will help you self-publish. Amazon has its own version, *Create Space*, that's worth looking at. I have used *Lightning Source* for some time and helped other astrologers get started with it.

As you're writing and editing, hire a professional designer to work on the cover and a skilled copy editor to get the text right. I'd also recommend hiring someone to do the layout of the book if you have no previous experience; they will choose the right font and think of myriad essential things to ensure it looks good inside. Choose a good title and ensure it's clear on the cover so it can be seen when reduced on a webpage. Decide on the size of your book and ensure the printer can print to those specifications.

Get a few **ISBNs** and a **barcode** for the books.

- For UK publications, see:
  http://www.isbn.nielsenbook.co.uk

- For USA publications, see:
  https://www.myidentifiers.com/self_publisher

Do some research on prices of comparable books, and whether you wish to include Sterling, Dollar and Euro prices on your back cover. Check a number of books to see what's included on their back covers (barcode with ISBN, author info, pricing) as well as copyright notices inside their first few pages. (As astrology is often defined as "for entertainment purposes only" and the world is becoming lawsuit-loopy, you might wish to add a disclaimer that *"the information in this book is not intended to be taken as a replacement for professional advice."*)

You'll be asked (by Lightning Source or whichever firm you choose) to upload the text and cover files to their website, decide on the price of the book, and to state the discount you're willing to offer retailers. A discount of 25% is reasonable for our kind of market (if you deal with Amazon directly, you'll be expected to pay for postage and they'll demand 55% of the cover price). You'll be given an option to pay for extras (e.g. to be included in catalogues and promotions).

About a week after uploading the files, Lightning Source will send a PDF proof (or hard copy, if requested) and you'll be asked to check and approve it.

The process begins

V, Imp.

If you decide to work with Lightning Source, they will handle all steps from hereon. It has step-by-step instructions online, so it's easy to get onboard. The company deals with distributing information and supplying/shipping copies to Amazon and fulfilling other direct orders. It then accounts to you at the end of each month. (You'll need to keep the book market interested to stimulate and maintain sales, of course.) In the report, you'll receive details of quantities sold, net sales, the print charge, and your own publisher compensation. If you wish to place any orders yourself, you can go online and order copies, pay for these immediately and have these sent to any address. If I'm lecturing abroad, I often order copies a few weeks before I'm due to travel, and have Lightning Source send these to the conference venue or my hotel.

V, Imp.

Once your book is for sale online, encourage friends to post glowing, five-star reviews of the title. If you're not selling it online yourself, then ensure you have links from your website to these online bookstores (some offer a referral fee—a percentage of the book price). Contact library agencies to see if they'll sell copies of your book to libraries, and if so join PLR UK (in the UK) or your country's equivalent. Every time someone borrows your book from a library that carries it in the UK and Ireland, PLR recovers money for its authors. Depending on the number of libraries stocking a book, this can amount to a small but nice, extra sum that you're entitled to each year. While you're at it, join the Society of Authors (or a non-UK equivalent). By law, you'll be required to send a few copies of your book to the relevant "legal deposit" address in your country.

Above is a quick guide to self-publishing but what isn't advisable is "vanity publishing," where you pay a company a high price to put together and print your book. You'll see their adverts in many magazines: "Authors Wanted." You'll be expected to pay for everything and the publisher won't promote, sell, or distribute your book (most won't edit it, either). You're better off going down the self-publishing route described above. Then, you're only paying to print copies and you can order as many as you like. You're also free to update the book online at any time without having hundreds of printed copies in stock.

An A.I. sheet

If you're self-publishing and want to generate interest from bookstores or attract foreign publishers, you'll need to create an A.I. (Advance Information) sheet with the cover image, too.

Here is an example, written about a re-issue of a classic astrology book by the late Howard Sasportas:

The Twelve Houses

An In-depth Guide to Interpreting Your Horoscope

Author: **Howard Sasportas**

Keynote/Publisher's Comments

The acclaimed textbook on the astrological houses – now with additional essays from well-known contemporary astrologers.

Description

In 1985 *The Twelve Houses* became an instant astrological classic—the first time this area of astrology had been explored with modern psychological insight. Over twenty years later, this best-selling handbook remains fresh, contemporary and relevant—an essential volume that is still considered *the* definitive work on the subject, and a favourite among students and professionals alike.

The houses of a horoscope give the reader the means of assessing how an individual's character (as shown by the planets and signs) will express itself through specific areas of everyday life. The houses describe *where* the action takes place. Howard Sasportas' comprehensive volume, both spiritual and psychological in its approach, explores in detail the field of experience associated with each of the houses, elucidating not only the tangible but also the more subtle, inner meaning of the various spheres of life.

This 2007 edition contains a new Foreword by Liz Greene, the pre-eminent astrologer of our times, as well as tributes to Howard Sasportas from well-respected psychological astrologers Melanie Reinhart (an authority on Chiron), Laura Boomer, Darby Costello, and Erin Sullivan (editor of the Arkana Contemporary Astrology series).

Sales Points

- A pioneering work in both psychological and spiritual astrology.
- Presents the most complete guide to the houses ever written.
- The author was a highly-influential, award-winning astrologer and writer.

Author Biography

Howard Sasportas (1948–1992) was an American astrologer with a Master's degree in Humanistic Psychology. He was co-founder, with Liz Greene, of the Centre for Psychological Astrology in 1983. With Greene he gave a series of seminars on psychological astrology, later published by Samuel Weiser, and wrote *The Gods of Change* (Arkana). *The Twelve Houses* remains his most important and popular work.

Publisher: Flare Publications

ISBN: 978-1-903353-04-2

Binding: Paperback

Publication date: 25/7/2007

BIC subject: Astrology

Extent: 324 pages

Price: £18.99

New/Reissue: New edition

Illustrations: 20 diagrams

Finally ... Just do it!

... said the Aries. Some of us write for pleasure, some for possible accolades and respect, while some of us feel a profound need to communicate our ideas to the public. Most of us write for all three reasons.

Having an article or book published is a great achievement. Seeing your book in the hands of buyers or on a bookshelf is a tremendous feeling. The process is hard work and won't pay much, but it's rewarding on so many other levels. In this chapter, I hope I've motivated you to consider your options and move forward with your writing. But if you need more, then each of the twelve signs has some advice for you:

Aries: Get started!

Taurus: Plan the project; be realistic about your time, the finances and size of the book, and the deadline.

Gemini: Read around the subject; find your voice.

Cancer: Research what others have written in the past; know where you're coming from.

Leo: Express yourself; have fun and make writing a joy.

Virgo: Think "quality control": edit; spell-check; tidy up; reorganize chapters and headings; rewrite; edit again; back up files and print off a hard copy.

Libra: Get feedback from others you respect; ask for endorsements.

Scorpio: Go back to the text and purge; be ruthless and eliminate dead wood.

Sagittarius: Sell it to a publisher, show them how marketable you are – or self-publish and set the astrology publishing business alight.

Capricorn: Talk business; negotiate the contract; present yourself as an authority.

Aquarius: Connect with your community and audience; get reviewers lined up.

Pisces: Then, put it in the hands of the fates and let it go ...

Frank Clifford has built an eclectic career as a consultant, publisher, lecturer, and a writer of a dozen books (including Getting to the Heart of Your Chart: Playing Astrological Detective). Frank lectures internationally and continues to write for (and guest edit) The Mountain Astrologer. In 2012, Frank won The Charles Harvey Award, a lifetime achievement award for "exceptional service to astrology." In 2016, he will begin courses online via The London School of Astrology.
Websites: www.flareuk.com, www.frankclifford.co.uk

Chapter 12

The Power of Peer Group in Astrology
Alexandra Karacostas

What is a Peer Group?

Have you ever had a session with a client that left you feeling awkward, perplexed or, even worse, like you fell short in your role as a helpful and skillful astrologer? If so, how do you regain perspective? For years this type of reading had been part of our experience yet we had no forum to share our thoughts. During the 1980's, Bob Mulligan, the founder of The Organization for Professional Astrology (OPA), recognized the isolation of the professional astrologer, and proposed a system to respond to our unique issues and needs.

The Peer model was originally developed as the centerpiece of OPA to create a format where astrologers can come together to discuss fees, effective advertising, business ethics, methods of earning a living, geographical and cultural differences, distinctions between psychology and Astrology, challenging client or professional situations, and how astrologers can support each other.

These are the kinds of issues which can be brought to a peer group and examined together. We study sample horoscopes, investigate difficulties that have emerged with clients and colleagues, and discuss ways to prevent problematic dynamics from playing out in the future. Together we discover new solutions.

When sharing these experiences we are presented with new perspectives and solutions to challenging situations. Sometimes, through simple discussion, the events that triggered us become diffused. As like-minded astrologers, we usually "get" one another and can serve as mirrors for each other, as the following examples will show.

OPA peer group origins

A peer group is a group of individuals with similar interests who come together for the purpose of benefitting from other's beliefs, insights and behaviors.

In our professional world of Astrology, we can look back to July 14, 1989, at 10:32 pm in New Orleans, LA at the United Astrology Conference (UAC) for the formation of the first professional peer group. That evening in New Orleans a group of like-minded individuals formed the special interest group, ProSig, the Professional Special Interest Group, under the wings of the National Council for Geocosmic Research (NCGR). ProSig was created to help astrologers discuss all aspects of making Astrology a professional and viable career.

Eleven years later, on October 4, 2000 at 01:45 pm in Tallahassee, FL., ProSig reorganized and was incorporated as an independent organization, becoming what is known today as the Organization for Professional Astrology, OPA (see chart 1). Since its founding, OPA has been a role model for networking, astrological peer group work and the associated peer review process.

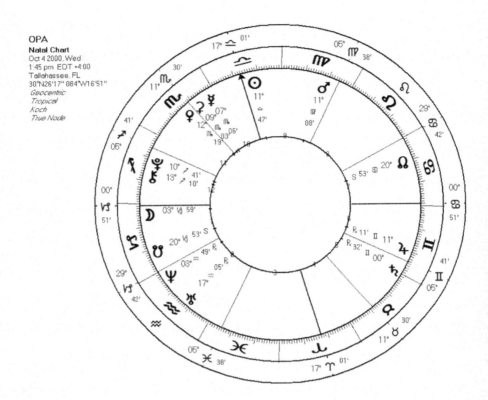

Chart 1 - OPA

A few well known peer groups

Over the last 80 years several powerful organizations that began as peer groups have flourished nationwide. Examples include the National Organization for Women (NOW) and the Neighborhood Watch movement. The Re-Evaluation Co-Counseling (RC) system founded by the late Harvey Jackins has been practiced throughout the US and Europe for over five decades. In the 1930's Alcoholics Anonymous started with a few individuals gathering to discuss problems, share insights, and explore solutions to their common malady. Since then it has become one of the largest and most successful international peer-based groups, along with its numerous 12-Step offshoots. Weight-Watchers is another peer group which had its origins in one woman's living room in 1961 and has since spread worldwide.

The purpose and advantage of utilizing peer groups in Astrology is to better understand ourselves and our clients. Through the process of working together we deepen our practices as we access the variety of personal and professional perspectives of the group. We expose ourselves to other viewpoints while receiving immediate feedback regarding our own. We gain a more profound understanding of our own strengths, virtues and limitations. This helps us deepen self-awareness and confidence so we can meet with greater success and become more skillful in our personal and professional lives.

Peer groups help us expand our sphere of relationships and provide greater networking opportunities. They facilitate personal insight and a healthier sense of self. Peers can provide a staging ground for practicing new ways of being. Through peer groups we can develop a sense of self which Erik Erikson, a developmental psychoanalyst and researcher, emphasized as necessary for a healthy ego. Personal growth becomes an ongoing and life-long journey. Harry Stack Sullivan, another well regarded psychiatrist and clinical researcher, further describes the benefits of these interactive environments as offering consensual validation and bolstering feelings of self-worth.

How peer groups work best

Participants must feel safe in order for peer groups to function effectively. Confidentiality is an essential element. It allows participants to be completely honest without fear of feeling humiliated, unheard and unacknowledged. An effective peer group is one in which each participant feels valued and accepted. Everyone has something to offer!

This format continues to guide the OPA retreats and provides a rich backdrop for networking. OPA helps both professional astrologers and laymen expand their horizons personally and professionally. Since its inception the impact of the organization has been far-reaching. This type of peer work and supportive network has been adopted by other astrological organizations like the National Council for Geocosmic Research (NCGR) and the International Society for Astrological Research (ISAR). NCGR uses the peer group format for segments of their certification programs. ISAR has also borrowed from this peer group format and applies it in their well-regarded Consulting Skills Certification Program.

Many people may feel uncomfortable, perhaps even a bit terrified, when they first enter a peer group, thinking "what will others think of my astrological insights? Am I good enough, smart enough, a worthy astrologer?" The monkey mind gets busy destroying internal equanimity. Giving voice to these fears and feelings of inadequacy somehow takes the edge off and magically transforms those emotions of discomfort into a greater sense of personal empowerment and freedom. Our connection to one another and our sense of acceptance, both for ourselves and others, deepens. Common resonance springs from understanding the tenderness in our psyche, which we experience simply by being human.

Through exposing our vulnerabilities within the safety of a peer group we can discover a greater sense of strength and unity, both individually and collectively. Through these interactions our body of knowledge and wisdom increases and multiplies. Unexpected and precious gifts emerge. This practice not only helps foster intimacy but also generates space for amplified awareness and personal insights. In order for any of this to happen, three essential qualities are required: mutual trust, respect and confidentiality. These qualities are critical to successful peer work and the review process, whether in Astrology or in other circles.

OPA's Peer Group Process

OPA's peer groups are not about learning Astrology, but rather using Astrology to learn with and from our peers. We enhance our astrological and interpersonal skills through interpreting the charts presented and the feedback received from our peers.

The theory behind this type of structure is that as astrologers we are exceptionally qualified to help other astrologers. We understand the challenges we face in our work, whether it be with clients, ourselves, or the working environment. We speak the same language, a lingo that can be difficult for others to understand. Acknowledgment and appreciation of our experience is fundamental to our success, both personally and professionally.

Part of the consulting astrologer's dilemma is that we often work in relative isolation. We typically spend time alone preparing for our clients and any research we conduct is a solitary activity. This is very different from careers where people engage with colleagues or associates throughout the day. It can be a very private vocation with no "partner" dialogue.

Here is one illustration of what can happen in a peer group. A group participant presented the chart of a client who had repeatedly invalidated and disagreed with much of what was said during consultations. After several sessions the astrologer finally suggested the consultations weren't helpful or constructive and offered referrals to other astrologers. Again, and not surprisingly, this client replied NO and said they would prefer to continue the professional relationship. Despite this positive feedback, the astrologer felt a bit abused and bruised after each session. What was going on?

With the help of additional competent eyes on the displayed charts we were able to identify patterns in the client's chart that were in the astrologer's blind spot. This was partly due to the astrologer's own family of origin issues. The relationship had bound them to mutually unhealthy patterns. Through seeing this dynamic more clearly, the astrologer was able to politely disengage from the client and in the process felt more empowered and confident in their astrological skills.

In another situation, a client experiencing domestic and emotional difficulties brought them to an astrologer in hopes of finding insight and a path toward resolution. The astrologer was unable to detect why certain events were manifesting at that particular time and could not offer much useful information.

With the help of peers, a simple error in the astrologer's calculations was discovered due to an extreme southern latitude birth locale. The benefits of this peer session greatly outweighed any embarrassment the astrologer may have felt over the miscalculation. We all make the occasional error, and it is freeing to work in an environment where we are comfortable enough to expose our fallibilities. Sometimes when we look at horoscopes long enough by ourselves, we miss the obvious.

On the psychological level, it is easy to become isolated while working alone. The dynamic cuts us off from others, which goes against the human need for connection and community. Most people need to feel they are part of community. Participation is where and how we thrive.

In gathering with friends and colleagues, a precious community is naturally created and maintained. The group becomes a safe harbor to share knowledge and techniques. Disclosing our insecurities and fears often feels scary, but doing so results in acknowledgement and realization of our unique gifts, which boosts our self-confidence. Most importantly, we discover that we are not alone.

Nuts and bolts of peer groups

Let's say you and some of your associates are interested in organizing such a group. How do you begin?

There are various ways to start a peer group. It is important at the onset to specify and identify the group's purpose and intention. Is it a lay or professional group? How many participants will best serve the purpose? Research shows that five to eight participants is ideal. More than ten is excessive. Sufficient time is required for all to share and digest the intimate work involved. Is there a subject matter or topic? Will there be a facilitator or leader, and what will that role entail?

Group leaders must be skilled at keeping the goals of the group in mind and monitoring time. Everyone should have the opportunity to speak and be given equal time to do so. These are simple but essential prerequisites for success in the group experience. Determine group size, when and where you will meet and for how long. Ninety minutes or two hours is a recommended starting point for meetings. The size will help you reach a decision. Next, choose a topic and a person who will serve as facilitator at the meeting. This is a position which can rotate.

It is useful to get the chatter done outside the peer group setting. Some groups share a potluck meal before the meeting starts to make space for more casual social conversations. To begin the session, focus on where you are feeling stuck and experiencing challenges. It may be helpful to begin by sharing a bit about what is going on in your own chart/life. This is always an easy ice-breaker, interesting, and a fun way to become more familiar with one another. Be sure to ask all participants to bring their natal chart and enough copies for everyone in the group.

The participants are asked not to interrupt while someone else is speaking. Active listening is a powerful component of this group process, and is a skill always worth improving. After an individual has shared, others can voice their observations, share their insights and add constructive feedback. There may be questions or additional information requested. The facilitator keeps track of time and ensures that everyone gets a chance to share his or her thoughts.

You may want to discuss celestial weather patterns (transits) as they pertain to yourselves or current social conditions. You may choose a certain planet, asteroid or aspect to go into in great detail. Whatever topic is chosen, you must always bring charts to accompany discussions. This provides the mechanism by which we engage and learn from each other.

The Rules

Below are several rules for providing safety and trust.

1) Maintain confidentiality. It is imperative that the charts we present are anonymous. In this way the identity of those individuals discussed is not shared. The rule of anonymity establishes safety for all involved.

2) Respect Privacy. Do not talk outside the session about what and who was discussed. What is shared in the group stays in the group. Again, confidentiality is paramount for a sense of safety.

3) Group sessions remain closed. If a group already is engaged (this primarily applies to multiple day events) new participants are not allowed to enter mid- session. In an ongoing group, keeping it closed strengthens the bonds among participants. Set a time, perhaps once or twice a year, when you will accept new members.

4) Be constructive. Suggestions must be positive and supportive to the person sharing. Avoid negative criticism. If hostile behavior arises between participants, it can be recognized and then addressed at another time with a therapist or other astrologers outside of the peer group. The facilitator has an obligation and responsibility to intervene on behalf of the group.

5) Focus more attention on personal interaction and less on content. This process emphasizes the interactions we have between ourselves as astrologers as well as our clients. Peer group work is not meant to be instructional regarding astrological technique. We use the style of charts and methods with which we are most adept.

6) Actively participate and be honest with one another. Again, this builds trust and meaning. If someone withholds, others feel less comfortable sharing.

7) Recognize our limits. Sometimes it is beneficial to the client (and the astrologer) if we use our referral network. We are not expected to be the right fit for everyone. We can support one another in establishing healthy boundaries and recognizing our limitations through the feedback offered.

8) Accept different styles and approaches. As mentioned above, we need to allow astrologers to use their preferred application of Astrology. The group must be inclusive, not exclusive. The use of Vedic, Chinese, Western, etc. horoscopes are acceptable if applied accurately and yield helpful results.

9) Discussion must be limited to actual experiences. Talking about future clients, consultations or theoretical situations must be secondary to the real experiences we encounter in our practices.

If you are drawn to creating this kind of group in your community it is easy to accomplish, even though it requires organization and effort. You can spread the word through mailing lists and social media that you are interested in meeting individuals with similar interests and concerns. You may also ask a certified OPA group leader to help you with the process. The possibilities are plentiful, depending on the size and location of your community.

The experience can be rich, powerful and empowering! But let's not take ourselves too seriously, as that spoils the fun and effectiveness of the work.

OPA's certification program

In 2009, the vision for OPA's Certification Program came to life. Unlike other certification programs offered in our astrological community, OPA's process does not entail testing on mathematical calculations, astronomy, history, consulting skills, etc. OPA anticipates that participants already have a solid foundation of astrological knowledge if they are to be accepted into the program. In this context, everyone who applies is admitted.

OPA wanted to offer qualified professional astrologers an opportunity to become authenticated through certification as proficient, capable, ethical and compassionate. Certified Astrologers are then recommended by OPA to the larger public. The certification process was designed for astrologers to provide hands-on demonstrations of their skills and character, regardless of their astrological orientation. The curriculum takes place over three days and is comprised of 3-5 people in a group, including the leader.

Day One, participants become acquainted with one another through sharing something about themselves. Then, starting with the group leader, each participant describes a problematic consultation with a client that has remained unresolved. Every member presents a case history which their peers have the opportunity to contribute to in a helpful and meaningful manner.

Day Two, consists of chart interpretation between participants. The previous night everyone is assigned the chart of another group member, which they will interpret the following day in front of their peers. This is a unique opportunity for astrologers to take the client's position and experience what it feels like to receive guidance from another astrologer. Moreover, each participant has the opportunity to learn from another's perspective and see what they choose to emphasize in a chart. After each session, members can offer suggestions or ask further questions.

Day Three, participants present a plan listing their professional aspirations for the coming year and how they can realistically achieve these goals. This is an important step for cultivating vision and supporting growth in their practice. All participants are invited to offer suggestions and insights, possibly using the chart of the presenter for reference. This entire process is rich, challenging and deeply rewarding.

In order to become an OPA Certified Astrologer, the astrologer must **participate in the program three times, each with a different group leader.** They need to be fluent in the language of Astrology and effectively analyze charts in their system of choice

Character is also evaluated and astrologers must demonstrate professionalism, dedication to the vocation, integrity, compassion, and a deep understanding of personal and professional ethics.

How to become an OPA group leader

Once certified by OPA, the astrologer can also choose to become **a group leader for the Peer Group Process**. Successful completion of the certification process is a necessary prerequisite.

In addition to completing the program, a potential group leader must be in professional astrological practice for a minimum of seven years and be engaged in a leadership role within the astrological community, i.e. being a board member, event organizer, author, or teacher. Moreover, participants must have an active practice and earn a certain percentage of their income through astrology work. These criteria serve as benchmarks for appointing Group Leaders to lead OPA's Peer Group work.

Peer groups are so invaluable that OPA has created several programs revolving around working together in small groups at the annual OPA retreat. It's a most effective and inspiring method for personal and mutual growth.

We all are on a journey of self-exploration. Each of us contributes our unique and extraordinary gifts as specks of stardust to the universe. Each of us has something special and divine to offer. Through peer group work, we get to benefit from one another's light and wisdom and deepen our understanding.

We serve as mirrors for each other. Let's be seen, heard and supported by our community. We all count more than we imagine. Get involved in a peer group today!

Alexandra Karacostas is a professional astrologer based in Chico, California. She has been a student of astrology since 1975. She teaches, lectures locally and internationally, and works with an international clientele. Alexandra currently serves on the board of OPA, the Organization for Professional Astrology and is a columnist for The Mountain Astrologer magazine. Website: www.wisdomastrology.com

Chapter 13

Professional Development
and the Community of Astrologers
Kay Taylor

Like many astrologers, my interest in astrology began as a child. It was interesting to know the signs of various family members and my Libra mother (who didn't 'believe' in astrology) would sometimes say in exasperation "I must have done something terrible in my past lives to get two Aries daughters" (even though she didn't believe in reincarnation either!). Back in the 50's astrology had permeated our vocabulary and culture through Sun sign columns.

As a teen, like many of you, I was the one with a tattered copy of an astrology text, trying to calculate whole charts from the simplified planetary tables in the back. In my twenties I had my first professional reading. I had no idea who this astrologer was; he was referred by a friend. I later found out he was accomplished in the field and had written a book on the esoteric subject of declination. But as a novice client, like many, I didn't know how to discern whether an astrologer was reputable or not.

My interest grew and I began to read more and more astrology books, integrating what I was learning into my other healing work. Soon I was offering astrological readings. Clients came to see me and often were pleased, but I sensed something was missing.

One day I woke up with the idea I should go to an astrology conference. I didn't know if astrology conferences existed, but a quick trip to buy a copy of Mountain Astrologer magazine revealed a NORWAC conference in Seattle coming up in a month. I attended, enjoyed meeting many astrologers, connected with my first serious teacher and soon belonged to several professional organizations. As I attended numerous conferences over the years I began learning from teachers in a structured way, eventually getting certified and feeling much more confident in my professional skills. Within several years I became a teacher and lecturer at these same conferences.

This is a common story, which is why I share it. We often find ourselves gently drawn into astrology without knowing we are going to become professionals. It begins as a hobby or a curious interest, and no matter how much we study ourselves, there are likely to be gaps in our knowledge because we read the books we are interested in and might ignore other useful perspectives or techniques. If you are an older professional, I almost guarantee this was how you became an astrologer: self-study through books, perhaps finding a teacher, and then learning about the professional organizations to join.

If you are younger, you have had the advantage of many decades of the evolution of astrological professionalism. There are wonderful schools, an abundance of books, and many excellent teachers in virtually every country in the world. Perhaps you were able to think of astrology as a career option and go to school to become proficient and certified. Maybe you're thinking of astrology's educational possibilities right now.

This chapter will explore how astrology went from being a nearly lost and taboo art to a valid profession during the last 100 years.

The History of Astrology and the Development of Organizations

Astrology is an ancient art that flourished during certain eras in history. Although no one knows for certain when astrology began, there is evidence it began as soon as humans began to measure, record and predict seasonal changes by following the stars and planetary movements visible to the naked eye, as early as 25,000 years ago.

By the 3rd millennium BC, various cultures around the world were developing sophisticated knowledge of celestial cycles, with definitive evidence from Babylonian culture emerging at approximately 1700 BC. Hellenistic astrology evolved into a powerful force in Greece after Alexander the Great conquered Egypt in 331 BC.

From these early years of recorded astrological history, Claudius Ptolemy (90 CE - c. 168) might well be considered the father of Western Astrology. A Roman living in Alexandria, Egypt which was under Roman rule at the time, he was skilled in astronomy, mathematics, geography and music. As was the belief of the day, he imagined the earth was the center of the astrological system and that the sun, stars and planets revolved around it. This belief was generally accepted until Copernicus. Ptolemy attempted to organize and structure all of the astrological information known up to that time in a book called *Tetrabiblos*, from which astrological knowledge grew and was learned throughout the world.

Astrology was kept alive in Middle Eastern culture when the European Christian churches attempted to destroy all alternative belief systems. By the 1700's the Age of Enlightenment demanded scientific proof in all matters and the few remaining astrologers tended to be associated with occult practitioners.

In 1781, the planet Uranus was discovered by William Herschel, the first planet to be discovered in 2000 years. It is interesting that Uranus came to be considered the planet 'ruling' astrology because at this time astrology began to gain some momentum, although astrologers could still be classified as vagrants and face imprisonment for being a public nuisance.

By the 1800's the revival of astrology had begun in England and America. Spiritualism, the process of communing with the dead in seances, became fashionable. France too became interested in astrology blended with magic and tarot.

In 1844 the British Association for Astral Science was established, perhaps the first astrological organization in recent centuries. In the late 1800's, Helena Blavatsky brought a type of spiritual esoteric astrology into America and Europe with her Theosophical Society in New York, founded in 1875. Slowly, more and more astrologers published books and journals and schools and platforms for learning were established.

Alan Leo (1860 - 1917) was a prominent British astrologer, author, publisher and theosophist. He too is referred to as the Father of Modern Astrology, primarily for his role in publishing. He used the Theosophical Society's international connections to publish, translate and disseminate his work throughout Europe and North America. Theosophy also influenced him to include the concepts of karma and reincarnation into his understanding of astrology. Leo was prosecuted for fortune-telling twice and no organizations existed at the time to help him in a legal battle. Some of his friends believe the stress of the persecution contributed to his untimely death from a cerebral hemorrhage.

The theories of Carl Jung (1875-1961) and his keen interest in astrology also helped promote professionalism in the art of astrology. The psychology of archetypes and the collective unconscious was a natural match for astrological wisdom. At the same time, Dane Rudhyar (1895-1985), the Grandfather of Humanistic Astrology, was deeply influenced by the expanding openness in the culture to psychological concepts. Rudhyar led astrology away from event prediction to a deeper emphasis on personality, psychology, and transitions related to the developing soul. Rudhyar immersed himself throughout his life in music, theosophy, poetry and art, continually synthesizing a deeper understanding of psychology into astrology. He wrote numerous articles and books that are still widely read today.

Although the quality of astrology was improving at this time, it was also becoming more popular with the general public through Sun sign columns.

Professional astrologers, seeking a deeper level of credibility and a separation of magic and occult interests from astrology, founded the American Federation of Astrologers (AFA) in 1938. This is the first U.S. based organization designed to bring greater credibility and professionalism to the craft of astrology.

Strength through Professional Organizations

One of the primary functions of astrological organizations is education and the expansion of astrological information throughout the world. Whether it is through conferences, webinars, journals or newsletters, organizations have the power to bring ancient and cutting edge information to students and seasoned professionals.

Many organizations have testing and certification processes to uphold core standards.

Conferences

One of the main advantages of astrological organizations is the many conferences they present around the world. These events give astrologers a venue for learning and the exchange of current ideas. There is an exciting alchemy that occurs at a conference where seasoned professionals listen to each other share their current theories and research while newer students and professionals can be exposed to different viewpoints. Often we learn even more at meals or during evening social activities as we discuss the lectures of the day. Personal astrological data is peppered into conversations, an amazingly deep shorthand that allows us to get to know each other very quickly. Advice, laughter and sometimes intense feelings are exchanged in social situations that would normally be much more superficial without the lens of astrology drawing the focus of conversation.

At conferences you can listen to the best astrologers in the world share their particular expertise and choose which astrological subjects and theories you are most drawn to. This is a great environment in which to decide what school or teacher you would like to study with. You have the opportunity to listen to short lectures or study in-depth with pre-and-post conference workshops, many of which feature panels of astrologers discussing and debating current issues.

In the marketplace room you can buy books, DVDs, CDs and the latest astrology software. Often the software developers are available at their booth to answer any questions and you can have a hands-on experience with each available product before you buy. There are all manner of astrology-themed products, clothes and accessories available to peruse or purchase.

Some astrologers feel isolated because they work from home and don't know other astrologers personally. At a conference you can meet new friends and colleagues and catch up with those you've met on previous occasions. If you are a consulting astrologer, you might meet astrologers with particular skills and specializations to refer clients to who are beyond your scope of expertise, an important ethical issue.

At this point in history, we take the existence of astrological organizations as a given; there are so many choices of conferences, webinars and activities that we can't possibly attend them all. This has not always been the case. As we will see, AFA began in 1938 and the other organizations later began as a response or even in rebellion to perceived limitations of AFA.

Chris McRae, an astrologer for more than 50 years says:
"I had been studying astrology in isolation all by myself up in Western Canada, learning from books ordered from the AFA. I went to my first AFA conference in 1972 to meet other astrologers and assess my knowledge. I recall how thrilling it was meeting Dr. Marc Edmund Jones, listening to Dane Rudhyar from the podium, being in the swimming pool with Doris Chase Doan and Isabelle Hickey, and listening to T. Patrick Davis. I was a charter member of NCGR and relished it coming into being. I was at the very first OPA meeting listening to the dreams of Bob Mulligan and a room full of excited participants. When I arrived with Joyce Wehrman the room was so packed that we had to stand at the door. It seemed everyone was there. ISAR's birthing came shortly thereafter with further promises of international expansion. It was exciting in those expansive days and equally as exciting today as new frontiers of excellence keep developing."

Although the astrological organizations offer large conferences annually or semi-annually, there are many smaller regional conferences offering quality local and internationally known speakers, a marketplace for goods and services, and the opportunity to meet people and network in a much smaller environment. Northwest Astrology Conference (NORWAC) in Seattle is particularly known for its personal environment because meals are eaten together and the speakers each sit with a table of participants. State of the Art Conference (SOTA) held in Niagara Falls now each year (formerly in Toronto) and the Great Lakes Astrological Conference (GLAC) in Ann Arbor Michigan are also known for excellent speakers in a smaller venue.

Astrological organizations are beginning to create a better public relations image for the profession than ever. In the past, many people had no idea that astrology could be a legitimate professional occupation. Some of the organizations, most especially AFAN in the U.S., focus on advertising and public relations, responding to negative press in a positive way, and educating the public about the value of astrology. Over time, many of the anti-fortune telling laws have been withdrawn or are no longer applied to astrology.

These changes occurred through long and expensive legal processes. Four major court cases have been won and dozens of cities have changed their laws or have been unable to enforce punitive ordinances designed to circumvent the laws. These measures have included bonding requirements that would be impossible for most astrologers to obtain, business license fees ranging from $300 per year to $100 per day, and other punitive measures setting astrology apart from other consulting professions.

This battle is critical for astrology to be taken seriously, similar to the battle chiropractors fought for years before claiming full rights as a healing profession. Just like the chiropractors, who filed an antitrust suit against the AMA for decades of prejudice under the guise of 'anti-quackery', it was a major California Supreme Court victory in the Azusa case that spread a string of victories for astrology throughout the nation.

In that case the Court declared an Azusa, California ordinance that banned fortune-telling an unconstitutional infringement on free speech (Spiritual Psychic Science Church of Truth, Inc., et al. v City of Azusa L.A. 31926). The Court held that astrologers and fortune-tellers have the same constitutionally protected right to express and charge for their opinions as other mainstream forecasters.

While fortunetelling ordinances are normally local and include a list of many banned activities, including witchcraft and clairvoyance, they may also include psychology, hypnosis and even a catch-all phrase of 'any similar art.' Unfortunately, this broad classification is supported by police and citizens who feel it will protect an unsuspecting public from gypsy fortunetellers and con artists, but at its core are ancient fears of any belief system that is unfamiliar, unknown, and not in accord with conservative religious thought.

Other membership benefits

Joining an astrological organization offers many other benefits to astrologers at all levels.

Webinars & Lectures

Many organizations offer distance learning through webinars or conference calls, an easy and affordable way to keep up with the latest thinking in astrology and offer your expertise to colleagues. Some organizations (NCGR perhaps the most notable national group in this regard) have local group meetings where speakers give two hour lectures or offer longer workshops. These meetings provide an opportunity for newer astrologers to speak in front of an audience.

The meetings will normally offer a blend of local professional astrologers, regional speakers and any international speakers able to travel to that area.

Networking and Professional Lists

Many of the organizations maintain an online list of certified professional astrologers that allows potential clients to learn about their services. These member lists combined with the opportunity to get to know other astrologers at meetings facilitate a professional referral network. As one contemplates ethics in astrological consulting, it becomes essential to know where one's professional limit of expertise is. You may be a great astrologer in general, but there are experts in financial astrology, horary, rectification, pregnancy, fertility and other medical or specialized issues who might be a better match for your client's questions.

There already exists among educated consumers of transformational therapies an understanding that professional astrologers exist and can be called upon for important matters. Enid Newberg of Kepler reported that many people contact the college to find out how they might locate a qualified astrologer.

Newsletters & Book Reviews

Organizations often provide book reviews in their newsletters that would not normally be covered in mainstream press. Here you get a chance to preview the latest releases that can enhance your knowledge of astrology.

Legal & Medical Support

Some organizations such as AFAN provide professional legal support for astrologers who find themselves under attack in their communities, most often through outdated laws and statutes. They have helped raise money for astrologers facing unexpected medical crises and expenses, as astrologers have seldom had easy access to medical insurance.

In the U.K. the APAI offers Professional Indemnity and Public Liability insurance, offering a competitive group rate. Hopefully this type of insurance will be available to all astrologers in all countries as the profession becomes more organized.

Certification

Several organizations offer certification. Through certification testing, organizations determine and validate the professionalism, education, and ethical awareness of their members, offering the public greater security in choosing an astrologer. Most agree the AFA test and certification process is the most challenging, although each certification process is challenging and validating in its own way. NCGR has a four level testing process involving all facets of astrological knowledge, including the hand casting of various charts and various specialization possibilities at the Level IV. ISAR created their certification process less than 15 years ago with an emphasis on Consulting Skills and Ethics and a six hour astrological examination. OPA's certification focuses on different criteria, such as the management of one's practice, capacity and skills in reading and counseling, and demonstrating compassion, ethical behavior, and integrity, honed through peer counseling experience.

Ena Stanley, founder of OCA (Online College of Astrology—now International Academy of Astrology), remembers when certification was a hotly debated issue:

"In 1990, I sat on a panel to discuss the pros and cons of certification at the Cycles and Symbols Conference in San Francisco. Aside from myself, I don't recall any person on that panel—nor in the audience, for that matter—who supported certification…That was 1990!"

We can see how far we've come toward the idea of professionalism through certification, although there are some who still believe certification falls short of proving an astrologer is capable of giving an excellent consultation. Perhaps the continued development of educational programs will bring astrology to the point where we are confident that every graduating astrologer is fully equipped to pursue their specialized career path.

Astrological Organizations – US Based

AFA - American Federation of Astrologers

AFA is the first astrological organization, founded *May 4, 1938 at 11:38 am in Washington, DC* when the organization's convention was called to order and incorporation papers were filed simultaneously, a prime example of how astrologers run their lives! Although it was first called The American Federation of Scientific Astrologers, the constitution was amended in 1945 and the name was changed to the American Federation of Astrologers.

The stated mission of AFA is "to encourage the study of all scientific methods of astrology, both current and future, leading to the spread of astrological knowledge and its understanding throughout the world. AFA's mission is education, research cooperation, and progress."

To become a member, one must commit to the AFA Code of Ethics and <u>pay a membership fee of $45</u>.

One of the ways AFA fulfills its mission of education is through its correspondence course. AFA also offers an examination and certification process considered to be quite rigorous. There are three levels of certification (student, professional and teacher) each requiring an 8 hour exam.

AFA holds annual conferences over three day weekends and members teach local astrology classes, the listings for which are on the AFA website.

L↑

A journal for members, *Today's Astrologer*, is published monthly.

ᔆ NCGR - National Council for Geocosmic Research

The purpose of NCGR is to "provide an environment to foster and publish research of a geocosmic nature and to pursue educational programs in various interdisciplinary fields related to geocosmic *(X)* studies." The term geocosmic is defined as "of or pertaining to the study of correspondences and cycles involving earthly phenomena and cosmic (celestial) events." *CONSIDER*

The group publishes various journals, newsletters and books. They also provide financial and technical assistance or guidance to individuals or groups seeking to conduct astrological research. NCGR charters regional groups, encouraging high professional standards and ethical behavior among these chapters.

NCGR was formed by a group of individuals who broke off from AFA in 1971 for the purpose of raising the standards of astrological education and research. Seven men and women met in *Wareham, MA, on March 6, 1971*, at the home of Harry F. Darling, M.D., who became the first Chairman. The founders included astrologers, medical professionals, scientists and scholars, all interested in exploring astrology as it related to other disciplines. The name they chose, Geocosmic, sought to avoid the popular misunderstanding of astrology and set the tone for their purpose with a serious and scholarly approach to the study of correspondences between life on earth (geo) and the cycles of the cosmos, in particular the solar system.

NCGR holds conferences approximately every three years in cooperation with the schedule of UAC (United Astrology Conference), of which NCGR is a main sponsor. Local chapters have their conferences and other events on their own schedules. There are many local chapters across the U.S. as well as in Mexico, Turkey, Japan and Thailand, with new chapters forming across the world yearly. These chapters often hold monthly speaker meetings with a mix of prominent local and visiting speakers.

In 1979, NCGR developed and launched a **four-level education and testing program** leading toward certification for astrologers. In 2008 this program was transferred to a new organization for the sole purpose of overseeing the certification process. It is called NCGR-PAA (Professional Astrologers' Alliance). Levels I through III require a five hour exam. Level III requires an extra analytical written submission after passing the exam. Level IV requires specialized submissions such as a recorded consultation or lesson, published research, or a class syllabus on the area of your teaching specialty.

Geocosmic Journal and the *NCGR Research Journal* are published annually. An online member letter comes out bi-monthly and the E-News is distributed by email every other week.

Membership requirements include annual dues of $55 and an agreement to uphold the Ethics Code of NCGR. There are memberships for couples, three year terms and lifetime membership.

༄ ISAR- International Society for Astrological Research

ISAR's mission is to "uphold the highest standards of competence and ethics in astrology, and support the highest standards of education in the field."

The organization began as an Ohio-based, research-oriented astrological group formed by Peggy Lance in 1968. In 1978 she met with Juliene Mullette at an AFA Conference to discuss breathing new life into her organization. Juliene became the first President of the new ISAR and on *December 5, 1979 at 10:30am* the organization was incorporated as a nonprofit in *Sacramento, California.*

The Los Angeles Chapter was very active, meeting monthly at Zip Dobyns' chapel to hear local, national and international speakers such as John Addey, Michel and Francoise Gauquelin, Alex Ruperti, Charles Harvey, along with American researchers Rob Hand and Lee Lehman. Most of the prominent astrologers of the 70's and 80's came through Dobyns' chapel where a group of 30 to 40 regular attendees participated in lively discussions. A social hour always followed so a great collegial bond was formed. Many of the conversations centered around the new, cutting edge computer data that was changing the nature of the profession.

This was the infancy of the computer age, when early computers like the Osborne I, TRS-80 and the Kaypro required lots of scrolling and disk swapping. Mark Pottenger was responsible for training many ISAR members to use astrology software and integrate computer technology into the profession. Over the years a Membership Directory was created to allow members to meet in local areas and form research pods.

ISAR's membership dues are $49 annually and the organization usually holds a conference every two years to promote education and the exchange of ideas. Members from around the world gather to listen to prominent speakers and participate in a variety of educational programs. The ISAR CAP (Certificate of Astrological Proficiency) is awarded to candidates who have completed (in addition to educational preparation), the following:

- **Consulting Skills Training Course:** a two and a half day training program to teach the professional astrologer active listening and empathic consulting skills to integrate into their chosen style of astrological consultation.

- Ethics Awareness Training Course and Test

- The ISAR Competency Exam (a six hour comprehensive examination offered at conferences).

In addition, the applicant must have completed three approved Elective Courses.

ISAR's Certification Program has been translated and incorporated into astrological schools and organizations in several different countries including Argentina, Russia, Turkey, Ukraine, Serbia, Israel, and China.

ISAR offers grants for original astrological research and publicizes comprehensive research studies in astrology. It distinguishes between scientific, empirical and qualitative research and establishes guidelines and support for each. ISAR also gives scholarships to promising students to help them expand their astrological education.

ISAR publishes the *International Astrologer* three times annually. This journal contains articles written by both established and upcoming astrologers in every specialty of astrology. In addition, the weekly E-zine, the ISAR online newsletter, provides a forum through which astrologers can communicate with each other, share new concepts, and exchange the results of astrological research.

✖ AFAN - The Association for Astrological Networking

AFAN "exists to enhance, protect, and validate the important role astrologers and astrology have in today's society." They do this by taking a leading role in protecting astrologers' legal right to practice, assisting astrologers who are experiencing medical or legal challenges, and creating a powerful Media Watch group. This group has been formed to effect positive change in the way the media portrays astrology, through a program of proactive outreach to promote accurate information and the training of spokespeople to present astrology in a favorable light.

AFAN originally began in 1980 as the Association for Professional Astrologers. It was formed "to create and support the profession of astrology amongst astrologers and the public." Although this organization only survived a few months, it created an urge among younger astrologers to form a new organization, brought about in part by discontent with the leadership and policies of the main astrological organization of the time, AFA. These astrologers wanted to participate from a grass-roots level and wished to encourage an interface between the astrological profession and the larger society.

Clearly this was a divisive time for astrological organizations. Ray Merriman was actively involved in the formation of AFAN and remembers the breaking away from AFA fondly as a necessary step in the professionalism of astrology:

"...we formed a group at one of the ARC conferences in 1982 called PACT: 'Professional Astrologers Coming Together'. We raised money and rented a room at the Marriott Hotel in Chicago where AFA was conducting their conference that year; there were about 200 of us. For one thing, we wanted AFA to not charge us to speak. Back then, you had to pay to speak. You had to pay all your expenses and we thought, you know, we're professionals too and this is our living. If we're going to make presentations, we want professional respect. So, we decided to talk with them about this injustice.

"At first, they said they were interested, but it turned out they really weren't interested in working with us as professionals at all. So, AFAN grew from that meeting and the disappointment of its aftermath with AFA. I was one of the founding fathers of AFAN. Basically if AFA wasn't going to treat us as professionals, then we needed to band together and have an organization that dealt with our needs—our careers—as professional astrologers. Well, it didn't take long after that, at the 1984 conference, for us to realize that we also needed to develop our own conferences for professional astrologers. So, AFAN, NCGR and ISAR all got together and we formed UAC, creating our first conference in 1986. UAC of course has had a wonderful history of success ever since then.'

Ena Stanley: "I was in that hotel across the street from the hotel where the AFA conference was being held...I wouldn't sign the document proclaiming that I would not meet, nor converse about the political structure of AFA during the conference...And I was there when Neil Michelsen came back from his meeting with Cooper...Neil choking back tears as he told us he had not succeeded, but as well, he had been excommunicated from AFA. I became a member of AFAN that very night..."

Not everyone fully supported the breakaway from AFA...

Monica Dimino: "I did not really understand why the astrologers had such problems with the AFA. My husband was a doctor and he didn't get paid or anything to speak. It was considered to be a privilege. Everyone was so angry. I didn't feel in tune with them. By the end of the conference Neil was thrown out of AFA. There was lots of animosity. That's when the real shift got into high gear. People who were against AFA had set up a separate conference in a separate hotel next door. By the time it ended, we were asked to show if we supported the new or the old one. I actually don't know how any of us voted to be on one side or another. But we had to put our name down to go check out the new conference. Later I learned I was the networking coordinator for AFAN in Latin America! Certainly Dr

Cooper was a very intransigent man. He wouldn't listen to anyone. So it was difficult for a truce to be reached."

Thus, at the AFA convention in 1982, a group of some 300 AFA members agreed on the name AFA Network (AFAN) *at 11:52 pm on August 31, 1982* to create a network among members of the AFA and to improve communications between membership and the board of directors of the AFA. With the illness and subsequent death of an astrologer named Johnny Lister, AFAN soon became concerned about the support and wellbeing of astrologers with medical and other troubles. Various legal challenges faced by astrologers focused AFAN on helping professional astrologers navigate the legal system. Over the years AFAN's Legal Committee has directly supported and advised many astrologers on how to legally negotiate attacks on astrology or themselves personally in their community.

In 1987 the name was changed to "The Association for Astrological Networking" and on *January 29, 1988* AFAN applied in San Francisco for nonprofit status after incorporating under California law.

The membership requirements are simply the payment of a $30 fee.

AFAN does not hold individual conferences but still plays a significant role in the creation of the largest international conference, UAC (United Astrology Conference), which is usually held every four years. Three astrological associations have been the main producers for this event: ISAR, NCGR and AFAN. CVA has been involved in the past two conferences due to the increasing interest in Vedic astrology.

AFAN's role of supporting professional astrologers in practical ways is also shown through their Mentoring Program. AFAN Advisors and Networkers are willing to mentor other AFAN members for a minimum of three months. They may also provide scholarships to attend conferences or Study Stipends for further education.

ॐ   CVA - Council of Vedic Astrology

The prime mission of CVA is to establish and maintain a professional association for Vedic astrologers. Additionally, they establish educational and professional standards and certification for practicing Vedic astrologers and teachers, promote the national and international practice of Vedic astrology and encourage the free exchange of ideas and research among the various schools of Vedic astrology. There is an international community of CVA recognized teachers and practitioners who can promote their educational and professional services via the CVA website and CVA co-sponsorship of conferences

CVA began in *November of 1993* as the American Council of Vedic Astrology (ACVA). ACVA was modeled on the Indian Council of Astrological Sciences (ICAS) with the blessing of Dr. Raman, the founder and first President of the Indian Council. The Council appointed Chakrapani Ullal honorary chairman of the organization, as he was close to Dr. Raman and in regular contact with him. David Frawley was appointed the first President of the Council and Dennis Harness was appointed Executive Vice President. ACVA was renamed the Council of Vedic Astrology (CVA) in 2004 to reflect the growing international role of the organization and to avoid confusion with other existing organizations.

The Council passed an important milestone on *April 5, 1995* when it earned its 501(c)(6) non-profit status with the IRS. This legally recognized the Council's function as being "operated to promote a common business interest and to improve business conditions in the industry."

This was legally distinct from the status achieved later by the American College of Vedic Astrology, that was recognized later on *November 22, 1999*, by the IRS as a 501(c)(3) organization being operated exclusively for educational purposes.

General Membership is $65 annually and Professional Membership is $95.

The CVA, dedicated to the education, training and certification of Vedic astrologers through an international community of over 100 teachers, provides the opportunity to study within a network of recognized teachers in over twelve different countries.

To become certified by CVA one must first be sponsored by a CVA-recognized practitioner with Professional Membership status who will verify the applicant's completion of requirements. For the Jyotish Visharada, or Proficiency in Vedic astrology, the examiners assess the applicant's knowledge of the foundation principles of Vedic Astrology. Jyotish Visharada applicants need to complete 600 hours through CVA-recognized teachers and practitioners in the following categories: Approved classes, courses, audio recordings and private mentoring sessions with CVA recognized practitioners. A maximum of 200 hours can be accrued through CVA approved teachers correspondence courses and a maximum of 200 hours can be accumulated through audio recordings with CVA recognized teachers and practitioners.

The CVA Jyotish Visharada examination fee is $200. Each student must also complete 10 written chart interpretations.

CVA publishes the *CVA Journal* twice a year.

CVA was one of the sponsors of the United Astrology Conference (UAC) in 2008 and 2012. CVA holds conferences individually; the last CVA conference was its 20th Anniversary Conference "The Return of the Light" in 2014.

∾ OPA - Organization for Professional Astrology

OPA is a non-profit organization 501(c)(6) whose stated mission is to "advance the cause of professional astrology by providing a support system for professional astrologers, and by helping students and practicing astrologers get the information, insights, and experiences they need to foster their understanding of astrology, and launch and enhance their astrology practices."

OPA was founded by Bob Mulligan and Monica Dimino as a special interest group of NCGR known as Prosig. Its mission was to give working astrologers a place to share information on the intricacies of the profession and receive support from other astrologers. In 1994 Prosig held a conference called "Astrology at Work" in Annapolis, Maryland. It was the first of its kind—a conference dedicated to the many facets of *being* an astrologer as opposed to learning astrology. Marion March said it was the best astrology conference she had ever attended and encouraged Prosig to do more of these kinds of conferences. Prosig continued to hold conferences oriented towards professional work and introduced retreats in 2001. The idea was to foster deep communication among astrologers in a safe environment.

In 2000, when Prosig's progressed Sun came to conjunct natal Pluto, Prosig left NCGR to incorporate autonomously as OPA, the Organization for Professional Astrology. The incorporation date was *October 4th, 2000 at 1:45 pm in Tallahassee, Fl.*

OPA is a place where astrology enthusiasts meet to exchange information, compare skills of the craft, and explore new frontiers of the field. There is a strong emphasis on peer support and development, with an emphasis on the professional astrologer as a colleague and perennial student. OPA encourages members to work together to develop solid professional practices while improving conditions for the profession as a whole.

OPA supports astrology in its different manifestations and advocates tolerance, ethical practice, high standards, and continual growth of the profession.

> *"We are a family, we are friends, we live in different nations,*
> *and we bring together different schools of thought."*

As OPA originally developed, it started many discussion about professional standards, ethics, setting fees, methods of forecasting, accounting practices, and many other professional issues. The practice of observing fellow members reading charts in small groups was instructive for the participants who had the opportunity to learn about different reading styles and take the role of the client, something many practicing astrologers have not had the opportunity to experience recently or regularly.

From these meetings, OPA developed a model call *Peer Group Work* where this process of mutual exchange and discussion was organized into a three day workshop where astrologers would meet in small groups to talk about their professional challenges, demonstrate their reading style, and prepare a business plan to enhance their practice.

Today, OPA retreats last four days and include additional study activities besides the Peer Group Work. The retreat includes participants with varying levels of expertise in astrology, some of whom are not practicing professionals. There is the 'large group experience' of everyone together listening to a variety of presenters, and the 'small group experience' for detailed training. While OPA supports the profession of astrology and astrologers in their practice, its programs are open to every level of expertise.

OPA has a unique certification process. The purpose of this certification process is to assess the quality and ethics of the applicant's professional practice. Once the astrologer is certified, he or she is sanctioned by OPA as reliable and effective. To be certified, you demonstrate proficiency, ethical and responsible behavior, and compassion in your astrology practice.

OPA has designed a unique program called *I-Astrologer* to provide aspiring astrologers guidance, references, and tools to launch their practice or enhance their existing one. Participants meet with editors, web designers, and professional mentors to increase their clientele and enhance their practices.

OPA members benefit from free monthly teleclasses by fellow members speaking on a specialized topic within their area of expertise.

Annual membership at OPA is $60, or $150 for 3 years. OPA offers membership discounts to some countries.

OPA publishes their magazine *The Career Astrologer* quarterly.

✎ AYA - The Association for Young Astrologers

AYA is a non-profit dedicated to providing educational and networking opportunities for members with a focus on younger people, novices, and aspiring professionals.

Their mission is to ensure the continuity of the astrological tradition across generations. They support aspiring astrologers and offer a social networking community where members can learn, be inspired and connect with peers and mentors.

AYA started in 2003 when a couple of young astrologers noticed a paucity of young people attending workshops and conferences, with even fewer speaking at them. These astrologers talked to others and a conversation began about why this was the case and what could be done about it. Six months later, the Association for Young Astrologers was born.

AYA has made it possible for young astrologers to attend and speak at a number of conferences and workshops. AYA has facilitated online and in-person networking, fostering community between peers and relationships across generations. AYA has also accumulated an archive of educational materials for its members. The group makes attending astrology conferences more accessible by providing scholarships, arranging volunteer opportunities and coordinating room shares. Their networking mission is fulfilled by a website that includes social networking features which allow members to connect with those with similar interests. Special interest groups include schools of astrology, geographical regions, and sharing ideas on working with clients or building a business. AYA offers publishing opportunities for those who are interested. AYA also boasts that it has hosted some particularly fine parties. *(AFAN and others might claim they too can provide excellent social events for conversation and networking).*

<u>Members can join for $20 a year</u>. Seasoned astrologers are encouraged to join as <u>Benefactors for $25 a year</u> and are encouraged to offer additional financial support or provide mentorship for younger members. AYA hopes that benefactors will support and empower the coming generation of astrologers through participation in the dynamic organization.

AYA has held several conferences in the past and is in the planning stages for another conference.

AYA publishes a yearly journal *The Ascendant*, offers members access to free educational resources, scholarships to astrology conferences, and other benefits.

∾ UAC - United Astrological Conference

UAC is not an astrological organization in the traditional sense, but rather is a large international conference produced by several organizations every four years. It is a powerful event, hosting more than a thousand of participants, where you will see every imaginable type of person, discover current trends in every astrological discipline, and hear the world's languages spoken in hallways and elevators as you move through the throngs of international participants.

It's possible to spend days at UAC and not run into everyone you know, and yet by the end you're likely to have an entirely new group of colleagues and friends to connect with.

UAC began in 1984 as the idea of a blockbuster joint conference to be held by NCGR, ISAR and AFAN. UAC was incorporated in 1985 and by that time conference planning for UAC '86 in San Diego, California was well underway. In recognition of the growing interest in Vedic astrology, CVA was one of the sponsors of UAC in 2008 and 2012.

Groundbreaking Astrology Schools

There are a number of schools offering a strong astrological framework via cosmology studies. This includes

- California Institute of Integral Studies in San Francisco,
- The University of Philosophical Research in Los Angeles,
- The Cultural Astronomy and Astrology program at the University of Wales, and
- The Warburg Institute in London.

Three colleges in the United States that deserve special mention for their groundbreaking contribution to astrological education are
- Kepler College,
- Online College of Astrology
- Avalon School of Astrology.

These schools provide in-depth training that supports an astrologer at the early stages of their professional journey.

Kepler College

In 2000, Kepler College began a liberal arts degree program examining astrology and its role in the development of science, the arts, politics, medicine, mythology and religion. The accreditation process proved long and expensive and Kepler's authorization to grant degrees ended in 2012. Since then the focus has shifted to the development of a new certificate program.

Online College of Astrology

In 1997 Ena Stanley founded what would become the Online College of Astrology. This was the first online astrology school and was a groundbreaking idea when the internet was still gaining widespread acceptance. OCA is now called *the International Academy of Astrology (IAA)* and is headed by Julene Packer, who has helped create a multi-faceted curriculum.

Avalon School of Astrology

In 2002, David and Fei Cochrane formed the Avalon school in Gainesville, Florida as an accredited vocational school. Avalon offers a Professional Astrology Certificate (10 courses, 450 classroom hours) that allows one to apply for ISAR certification as well as an advanced path to a Diploma of Theoretical and Applied Cosmic

Cybernetics (also 10 courses, 450 hours) that permits one to apply for NCGR Level IV certification.

The Path of Research

How often do we believe and speak an astrological truth without knowing for certain that it withstands the test of research? How many astrological techniques were lost over the centuries as astrologers were persecuted and documents were destroyed? The professionalization of astrology will require that the organizations continue supporting this critical research.

Association for the Retrieval of Historical Astrological Texts (ARHAT)

This organization began informally in 1992 as Project Hindsight with Robert Hand and a group of dedicated researchers, historians and translators. Their goal was to protect, translate and publish historical astrological texts, retrieving lost traditional and medieval astrological wisdom.

Project Hindsight lasted about three years. ARHAT was formed subsequently by Robert Hand to continue this valuable work.

Astro-Data Bank

Astro-Databank is a collection of astrological data collected by Lois Rodden and many others over the years that is now available online as the Astro-Databank Wiki Project.

This project began in 1981 in Los Angeles with members of ISAR (International Society for Astrological Research) and other organizations who began to design a database for astrologers to have accurate information for research.

Mark Pottenger, ISAR Research Director at the time, provided volunteer programming and others volunteered to enter data. However, in 1985 the group decided that instead of continuing forward with their more complicated plan, it would be expedient to use data already collected by Lois Rodden. Rodden was known for her rating system of birth data. She believed it was extremely important for astrologers to be using the best possible data and to know its source, or to be aware that the data was possibly inaccurate.

Rodden Data Rating System:

AA for *Accurate Accurate*: data as recorded BC (birth certificate) or a BR (birth record such as a baby book or baptismal certificate)

A is considered *Accurate* and is data quoted by the person, relative, friend or associate.

B is from a *biography* or autobiography

C is for *Caution*, there is no real source

DD is *dirty data*, meaning two or more conflicting quotes that are unqualified are available

X is for data with no time of birth

XX is data without a known or confirmed date, especially likely for historical figures.

The project was originally called the Rodden-ISAR Databank. The first version was completed on February 13, 1988 at 8:07 pm in Los Angeles with almost 7500 birth data records, but the project was losing steam by 1991. Then in 1996, Rodden met Mark McDonough who offered to help with the databank, and AstroDatabank was born, with now approximately 30,000 records.

The AstroDatabank software developed by Mark McDonough and Param Software was sold to astrologers seeking quantitative analysis through many filtering and advanced research tools using

35,000 variables. For some years AstroDatabank was a commercial venture owned by Mark McDonough and ultimately by Richard Smoot in 2005, developing its capabilities through the site AstrologySoftwareShop. At its peak in 2008 the site had over 90,000 unique visits at an average of 90 minutes per user.

Richard Smoot sold the database to Alois Trendel, owner of Astrodienst (astro.com) in Switzerland, where the data was made available to the public for free. Aside from being on the astro.com website, directly as http://astrodatabank.com, the entire database and quantitative analysis routines are now in the Sirius 2.0 software sold by David and Fei Cochrane and *Cosmic Patterns*.

Astrodienst states they are committed to the spirit of Lois Rodden's work of providing the highest quality astrological data to the community for research. To further this goal they have now created the project known as Astro-Databank Wiki Project, which is the most current incarnation of this important research project.

Astrological Organizations - International

United Kingdom

The Astrological Association of Great Britain (AA)

Founded in 1958 in London. The founders, notably John Addey and Roy Firebrace, were members of the Astrological Lodge of the Theosophical Society. The Astrological Lodge of London was founded by Alan Leo in 1915 and is still in existence. As is often the case with the founding of new organizations, a splinter group felt their ambitions for astrology were restricted by the Lodge and the Theosophical Society in general. AA's initial aims were to demonstrate astrology's objective validity and to enhance its public reputation, especially within the scientific and healing professions.

Throughout the 1960s and 1970s AA encouraged philosophical depth, psychological understanding and scientific research.

The AA offers annual conferences bringing astrologers together from all over the world. The website seeks to educate all levels of practitioners, from beginners to professionals. AA publishes *The Astrological Journal and Correlation*, as well as *Culture and Cosmos* and the *Astrology and Medicine Newsletter*.

AA provides a birth database of thousands of notable people and events. They maintain friendly links with various other organizations and are currently teaming up with ISAR to offer ISAR's Consulting Skills Training at their next conference. Like many organizations based in the U.S. they respond proactively to issues raised within the media. The AA supports local and regional astrology groups, posting free listings on the website. Additionally, a directory of astrologers is available to facilitate networking.

The basic membership is £29.

The Association of Professional Astrologers International (APAI)

APAI is an organization serving professional astrology in the UK and abroad. Established in 1990, astrologers are required to study for and obtain a diploma from a recognized college and to abide by the APAI's Code of Ethics.

APAI represents the interests of professional astrologers to the public and the media. They support members experiencing hostility or legal pressure in their practices. They also offer professional liability insurance. APAI offers a Consultants List to promote the services of its members and publishes the magazine *Conjunction*.

British Association for Vedic Astrology (BAVA)

Founded in 1996 by British Vedic astrologers, Andrew Foss and Komilla Sutton. BAVA promotes knowledge of Vedic Astrology in Britain, especially the deeper spiritual aspects which Vedic Astrology can offer. BAVA works to increase awareness of this ancient science through lectures, courses, workshops and conferences. The founding patrons included the Late Dr. B.V. Raman and David Frawley. BAVA holds an annual conference, publishes a newsletter and offers a beginners' course in Vedic Astrology.

Turkey

School of Wisdom of Sky (Goklerin Bilgeliği Okulu)

The School of Wisdom of Sky in Istanbul, Turkey, has been offering astrological education, seminars and examinations since 2000. The curriculum provides an eclectic and hands-on approach combining modern astrology with its ancient roots through classes (Diploma) and online (Certification) education. The program spans three years and includes methods such as midpoints, Harmonics Theory, Relationship astrology, Chiron, Rectification, prenatal eclipses and lunations, History, Calculation and Astronomy. The school provides a master class in the fourth year for students who wishes to enhance their knowledge with traditional techniques in Hellenistic and Renaissance astrology.

Serbia

Kepler Association of Professional Astrology (KAPA)

The prominent organization in Serbia, KAPA offers ISAR's certification process.

Portugal

Associação Portuguesa de Astrologia (ASPAS)

Established in March 2012 in Portugal where there is a very large and active astrological school. Many Brazilian astrologers belong to it due to the language compatibility. ASPAS holds major conferences and supports the general purposes of most astrological organizations, such as upholding ethics, educating astrologers, facilitating research, and publishing the work of members. Following a reorganization in 2014, ASPAS structured more formal guidelines about how they might partner with schools and others for the benefit of astrologers. They publish a quarterly journal: *Four Seasons Astrological Journal.*

China

There are currently no astrological organizations in the People's Republic of China due to prohibitions and legal obstacles against the formation of national groups. However, there is now a major astrology school with a professional international faculty; this has been a remarkable development in this country.

As of 2000 there was virtually no western astrology present in China. All astrology had been banned since Oct 1949 and labeled as feudal superstition, including Chinese astrology. Public policies and attitudes relaxed during the 1990s as business interaction and involvement with the West increased. In the fall of 2000 the giant web server **sina.com** opened a horoscope platform, copying this format from the West. This would slowly evolve into a Sun Sign astrology internet website platform.

With access to the internet young people in China began to discover Western astrology online and became increasingly fascinated. They could quickly relate to the updated modern astrology of the West versus their own Chinese astrology, as Chinese astrology was still written in an archaic form of Chinese. Western astrology appealed to young people because they could relate to the twelve signs and found the language relevant to their modern life.

When American astrologer David Railey arrived in China in 2010 on a book tour, this was the state of astrology: a strand of Classical Western influence, a few scattered new practitioners but no educational structure or learning system in place. Sun Sign astrology had exploded in popularity. Railey's book *The Soul Purpose*, was only the second Western astrology book to be translated into simplified Chinese (Mandarin), the first being *Astrology Karma and Transformation* by Steven Arroyo in 2009.

Railey and Felicia Jiang (Jiang Ying) began a website called **www.nodoor.com** in June 2011, the first purely western astrology website in China. They also began a school located in Beijing using online education to teach basic to advanced astrology. The Nodoor School of Astrology became the first Western astrology school in the PRC. Railey increased his travels to cities that had never met or seen a western astrologer. In 2012 they invited Noel Tyl, Jeff Jawer and Steven Forrest. The online faculty began to grow and they developed two and three year curriculums for those wanting to become professional astrologers. Nodoor gained ISAR certification as an affiliated school in 2013. As of May 2015, Nodoor has 1,400 students.

India

In contrast to China, India has a long and well accepted history of astrology. There are many astrological organizations throughout India as well as a widespread acceptance of Vedic Astrology, known as Jyotish, within the culture. The most important and respected organization is **Indian Council of Astrological Sciences (ICAS)** formed in 1984 by Dr. B.V. Raman. Their stated goal is:

"...To strengthen moral and ethical values of our society in order to establish just social order. There is no better way of doing this than propagation of Vedic Wisdom, including knowledge of astrology."

They offer a one year basic astrology course, a one year advanced course and a two year research program for graduates of the first two courses. ICAS operates centers in many cities throughout India.

The Council of Vedic Astrology (CVA) was formed in 1993 to support the professional practice of Jyotish and is allied with ICAS. This organization seeks to maintain and raise educational and professional standards and offers levels of certification for both students and teachers of Vedic Astrology.

Australia

The Federation of Australian Astrologers (FAA)

Formed in 1971 and incorporated in 1995 as a non-profit, non-sectarian and non-political body. They offer the standard organizational benefits such as a biennial conference, examinations and certification, publication of a national magazine (FAA Journal) and the codification of a Code of Ethics for Australian astrologers. They also seek to encourage cooperation between astrologers in Australia and other countries.

Australian Society of Astrologers (ASA)

Formed in reaction to the perceived monopoly of FAA, they offer a full certification program and strive to educate all interested Australians in the basics of astrology. Another goal is 'to promote and create a conducive and fear-free astrological environment that is beneficial for all astrologers, students of astrology and novices."

Argentina

There are no national organizations in Argentina, but one can find various schools that offer coursework in astrology. These schools are professionally structured and offer many of the benefits of astrological organizations. One such school and research group, Centro Astrologico de Buenos Aires, was founded in 1961. Now it is the Buenos Aires Astrological Center Foundation, and is also an ISAR affiliated school. Instituto Superior de Astrologia is dedicated to supporting the profession of astrology by providing an academic setting to teach the necessary skills (theory, practice and ethics) to enhance client work. This school also seeks to motivate students to constantly update their global astrological knowledge and provide them with a legal framework for their professional practice.

There was a professional organization, ASTROAR, that organized annual conferences in the province of Cordoba, Argentina, up until 2013.

Brazil

CNA - Central Nacional de Astrologia

A national organization that does not offer training nor certification

SINARJ - Sindicato dos Astrólogos do Estado do Rio de Janeiro

This is not a national organization but is based in Rio de Janeiro. They are considered very active, have their own certification process, and organize large annual conferences.

Prospects for the Future

There are now many professional astrology organizations in the U.S. and around the globe. These organizations have been rapidly expanding in the past fifty years, which is a very brief time in the history of astrology. As organizations hold international conferences, technology permits instant communication, and websites make published material accessible, astrologers from many countries are getting to know each other. Research is shared easily, ideas cross international borders, and the professional prospects of astrology are growing.

Dedicated schools of astrology with qualified teachers are an important component for providing a full, complete astrological education. Although there have been challenges to the establishment of the discipline of astrology via accredited college degrees in the United States, other countries and some schools in the U.S. have created valuable, structured educational paths for the aspiring professional astrologer. We might hope and expect this trend to continue in the U.S.

It may be necessary for the organizations to come together to have the political power necessary to effect major cultural changes regarding astrology. When I suggested the possibility of creating one umbrella organization to astrologers who have been in the field for decades, many were skeptical this could ever happen. The politics of organizations is always tricky and few see a clear path to amalgamation. Perhaps as the years unfold and a younger, more collaborative generation evolves, we will see a coming together of the organizations to build a professional pathway similar to those created by chiropractors, naturopaths, financial advisors, yoga teachers and others. We could study their efforts to see how professional standards and cultural acceptance were realized.

Most of us believe the professional image of astrology is likely to be enhanced as high quality education, certification and testing is implemented. With Pluto transiting through the sign of Capricorn until 2023, we might expect higher levels of professionalism to permeate many career paths that have previously been seen as fringe or alternative. As with all Plutonian transits, we must work with the energies and choose consciously to transform, or the transformation will be thrust upon us. This is the challenge of the organizations going forward into the future over the next five to ten years.

An example of astrology becoming more accepted in mainstream society might be the budding acceptance among psychotherapists as psychological astrologers have brought their theories to the psychological world. It seems this trend will continue. Astrology provides an accurate personality typing system to provide assistance to psychologists, career counselors and other inner growth professions. Will astrological charts be used to determine if a person is right for the job? To consider what days off a person should have? To determine if a couple is compatible? Will your stockbroker be a trained astrologer? Will your doctor understand the astrological factors of disease as they did long ago?

The proliferation of astrological books and websites has affected the acceptance of astrology in the culture. Certainly organizational efforts to enhance the public's view of astrology have begun to pay off. According to a study by the *National Science Foundation* in 2014, Americans are believing in astrology at a higher rate than ever before. The percentage of Americans who think astrology is 'not at all scientific' dropped from 62% in 2010 to 55% in 2012. From the scientific community's perspective, this is a disaster, especially since among young people the statistics are even stronger. Close to 60% of 18-24 years olds believe that astrology is 'very' or 'sort of' scientific. Even more telling was in a poll of students in England in 2000. They found 100% of the students knew their Sun sign, 70% read their horoscopes regularly, and 85% agreed that the description of their birth sign described their personality. Clearly there is a growing acceptance of astrology among the young and this trend is likely to increase.

Astrology is ready to be a fully validated profession. Through the pursuit of quality astrological education and the efforts of astrological organizations to support research, certification, and the establishment of ethical and professional standards within the field, we have grown and developed significantly over the past hundred years. As astrologers we can participate in this revolution by supporting our organizations, developing professionally and contributing our skills and highest levels of service. As we work together, our profession has even greater opportunities for expansion in the next fifty years.

Kay Taylor *integrates an evolutionary and spiritual approach to astrology with her refined intuitive skills, psychosynthesis counseling, yoga and hypnotherapy. Her work focuses on illuminating soul path and transformational healing. She leads international retreats, is an ISAR Consulting Skills Trainer, has lectured at regional groups and conferences (ISAR, UAC, OPA, SOTA), and wrote for Astrology.com for many years. Kay is ISAR CAP and NCGR II certified. Known for her grounded, heart-centered approach, Kay has a thriving practice based in the San Francisco Bay Area for over thirty years. Website: www.kaytaylor.com*

Part 3

Interviews of Professional Astrologers

Learning from Life Experience

Seven Forrest

Professional Astrologer Interview

Borrego Springs, California
www.forrestastrology.com

Are you practicing astrology part-time or full-time?

FULL

What are the components of your astrology practice? Please share information about the different services you offer:

Private readings, international teaching, and writing.

If you offer more than one service, what were the different reasons for you to expand the range of astrology services?

They grew together organically.

What percentage of your overall income comes from your astrology practice?

Counting all of the above, 100%. I have no family money or other source of income.

Do you financially rely on one of your services more than the others, or do they all provide more or less an equal portion of your income?

> Probably about 75% of my income derives from personal private readings.

Is your practice mostly for local clients or do you practice internationally?

> Internationally.

Can you describe how you studied astrology?

> Self studies via books, 100%. I had published The Inner Sky with Bantam before I even MET another astrologer.

Were you certified for your astrology studies?

> Never. It's an elected position.

How long have you studied before you began your practice?

> About ten years.

How old were you when you first started to practice?

> I really started with palmistry when I was 13 and got into astrology at age 17. I did my first paid reading in summer 1973 when I was 24 years old. I worked full-time as an interviewer, computer programmer, and grant-writer on a big National Institute of Mental Health project from 1974 through mid-1977, all the while doing readings in the evenings and on weekends. I officially went full-time, quit work, in November 1977 at age 28. Within a year I was booked many months ahead. Four years later, the contract

with Bantam Books to write "The Inner Sky" fell into my lap. I blame God for all of it. :)

If you are a full time astrologer, how long did it take you to transition from a part time to a full time practice?

About five years

How do clients usually find out about you?

My books and word-of-mouth client-to-client

What makes it possible for you to be a professional astrologer— both in character and in practical terms?

I am articulate. I am serious, but fun too, I think. I practice a very choice-centered, empowering form of astrology rather than depressing people with fatalism and determinism.

How long does it take you to prepare for a typical private consultation reading?

15-30 minutes.

How do you cope with the general credibility questions that astrology is subjected to by the mainstream?

It is annoying sometimes, of course. Mostly I don't think about it. My actual daily experience is one of people respecting and appreciating what I do. I occasionally see a wisecrack about astrology on-line or in the press. So that ratio creates perspective.

Did you initially, (or do you now) feel self-conscious to a degree about being an astrologer?

Not anymore. I did when I was younger.

What are for you the great rewards of having chosen to become an astrologer?

They are infinite. Having meaningful work in this world is something that increases in value to me with every decade I live. I have gotten to see much of the world. I have developed relationships with many very interesting people, and several famous ones who shape the world we live in. I make a good living and I have a lovely, magical home in a beautiful place.

What are your most important guidelines and insights for a person who now contemplates the opportunity to become a professional astrologer?

You have to love people, have the gift of language, and have to have tolerance for living in an independent way without guarantees. Mostly, I like to say that you have to be careful about what kind of astrology you practice. In general, I believe the potential clientele has gotten beyond the level of current astrological practice. People want genuine help and support, not deadening "delineation" and prediction. That's where you strike the vein of gold in the modern world.

__Steven Forrest__ is the author of several astrological bestsellers including, The Inner Sky, The Changing Sky, The Book of Pluto, Yesterday's Sky, and most recently The Book of the Moon. His work has been translated into a dozen languages. He travels world-wide teaching his brand of choice-centered evolutionary astrology. A thousand people have passed through his Astrological Apprenticeship program since its inception in 1998. Currently there are two such programs in California, plus annual programs in North Carolina, Australia, and the People's Republic of China.

Melanie Reinhart

Professional Astrologer Interview

Old Warden, Bedfordshire, UK.
www.melaniereinhart.com

Are you practicing astrology part-time or full-time?

Full-time

What are the components of your astrology practice? Please share information about the different services you offer:

Private readings, teaching for established schools such as the Faculty of Astrological Studies, running my own workshop programme, speaking at conferences in the UK and abroad, writing books and articles, blog for subscribers to my website, publishing.

If you offer more than one service, what were the different reasons for you to expand the range of astrology services?

I like variety, do have many skills, and enjoy engaging with astrology in different ways.

What percentage of your overall income comes from your astrology practice?

> 100%

Do you financially rely on one of your services more than the others, or do they all provide more or less an equal portion of your income?

> This fluctuates from year to year, but income from private readings is usually the higher proportion.

Is your practice mostly for local clients or do you practice internationally?

> International (including local and nationwide).

Can you describe how you studied astrology?

> Initially self-taught up to professional level, then gained the Diploma of the Faculty of Astrological Studies. On-going education by attending seminars, doing courses (some certified).

Were you certified for your astrology studies?

> Yes.

How long have you studied before you began your practice?

> Sixteen years, if you mean 'professional practice'. (I had read a large number of horoscopes without payment before I began to charge any fees.)

How old were you when you started your practice?

> Twenty-six, but see response to previous question.

If you are a full time astrologer, how long did it take you to transition from a part time to a full time practice?

Ten years, although for part of this time I was also working as a psychotherapist, using astrology either 'background' or 'foreground', in addition to doing readings.

How do clients usually find out about you?

Word of mouth, website, meeting me at conferences, etc.

What makes it possible for you to be a professional astrologer— both in character and in practical terms?

As astrology has been central to my life since the age of 10, I don't recall a 'decision' to become a 'professional astrologer'. It was a logical outcome of my curiosity and passion—for seeing how astrology reflects our place in the cosmos, and how it provides guidance. Living in the milieu of London was very supportive to developing my professional work. So I guess 'total immersion' has been my way! In terms of character … I have a naturally 'forensic' kind of mind, 'enough' psychic sensitivity, good communication skills and a capacity to organize information. This rests on and also offsets a somewhat 'mystical' temperament.

How long does it take you to prepare for a typical private consultation reading?

Before a reading, I try to take time (maybe 30 min) to prepare myself, my desk and my working environment. I allow about one hour minimum to prepare the astrology for a 'standard' reading, but may need longer if it is a more complex situation, perhaps involving more than one chart, or a client who has requested an in-depth exploration of a particular theme.

How was your choice to become an astrologer received by your family and greater environment?

My parents were somewhat mystified, but as they did not oppose my early involvement with astrology, it was not an issue. My father was touchingly proud of me when I passed the Diploma exams of the Faculty, even though he was obviously puzzled by it! Likewise, when I did the most concentrated part of my 'solo' studies, the 'greater environment' was my life in a spiritual community focalized by Fazal Inayat Khan, who was then the director of Servire Publications, who published Dane Rudhyar's books! So astrology was mostly totally accepted there.

How do you cope with the general credibility questions that Astrology is subjected to by the mainstream?

I basically ignore them. Perhaps having such supportive environments in the early days of solitary learning has helped me feel that I don't have to prove anything to anyone. When I became aware of the hostility sometimes expressed towards astrology, I felt perplexed and sorry that otherwise intelligent people held such prejudices. I'm always happy to discuss things, but avoid situations where I might be expected to 'defend' astrology.

Did you initially, (or do you now) feel self-conscious to a degree about being an astrologer?

No, I didn't, initially (see responses above about supportive learning environment). Any self-consciousness I feel now is about anticipating a 'non-neutral' response once people learn I am an astrologer. However, I do take seriously the responsibility of 'representing' our great tradition to others and do my best to engage with sincere questions. Over time, however, I have also developed a repertoire of 'conversation stoppers' for the purpose of changing the dynamics if it seems necessary!

What are for you the great rewards of having chosen to become an astrologer?

The flash of 'seeing' astrological symbolism spontaneously occurring in the inner or outer world is something which never fails to nourish my mind, soul and body. I feel immensely privileged to share the deep 'soul conversations' that I have with clients, and I love the process of preparing and offering classes, seminars and lectures. I value the many exceptionally brilliant and gifted fellow astrologers I have met, some of which I have also studied with. The feeling of participating in an ancient tradition is precious to me.

What are your most important guidelines and insights for a person who now contemplates the opportunity to become a professional astrologer?

Best … read and take to heart the advice from Master Astrologer William Lilly in his 'Letter to the Student of Astrology' (www.skyscript.co.uk/letter.html - From 'Christian Astrology', 1647).

My own thoughts …

Becoming a 'professional astrologer' does not mean you have to conform to 'the ways of the world' in order to participate and be available. It may be wiser to be a 'willing outsider'. Find your own level, and learn the art of being 'in the world but not of it' rather than being 'of the world but not in it'! Respect our noble tradition and feel its support behind you; be humble enough to reach out to colleagues and mentors for advice and help. Avoid partisanship and evangelism within the astrological community; stay clear of grandiosity and having to be 'right'; focus instead on how best to be of service, and just keep doing the work.

Remember that astrology is a vocation rather than a profession, the difference being that if you are called to a vocation, it's your job to support this vocation, not the other way around! Develop a spiritual healing practice of some kind which serves the need to be skilled in processing the feeling content of your readings for people in crisis or acute need.

Melanie Reinhart has been a professional astrologer since 1975, and is a prize-winning Diploma-holder of the Faculty of Astrological Studies, of whom she is now a Patron; she also received the Charles Harvey award in 2004, for 'exceptional service to astrology'. She has taught for leading astrology schools in the UK and abroad, runs a thriving consultation practice, and offers workshops on her own programme. Her books have been translated into six languages and include: 'Chiron and the Healing Journey' , 'Chiron, Saturn and the Centaurs', and 'Incarnation'. Visit her website for articles, free downloads, and event calendar.

Kim Marie

Professional Astrologer Interview

Rapid City, South Dakota
www.EvolutionaryAstrology.net

Are you practicing astrology part-time or full-time?

Full-time.

What are the components of your astrology practice? Please share information about the different services you offer:

Private readings, teaching an Evolutionary Astrology course and public webinars.

If you offer more than one service, what were the different reasons for you to expand the range of astrology services?

I love to teach and desire for all souls to utilize the field of astrology as a natural guidance system in any area of life. The emergence of the webinar format allows astrological teachings to reach souls all over the planet regardless of time or space, and to take the visual of astrology to new levels of quicker understanding. The desire to study astrology tends to follow a client requesting a reading, and then wanting to know astrology for their own guidance, so it has been a natural combo for me.

What percentage of your overall income comes from your astrology practice?

About 50%. I also work in the field of energy medicine by choice, as it allows me to completely immerse myself in spirituality—both the type of astrology I practice and the quantum physics field of self-healing.

Do you financially rely on one of your services more than the others, or do they all provide more or less an equal portion of your income?

It ebbs and flows. Sometimes readings bring in more income, and at other times EAN's (Evolutionary Astrology Network) course segments provide more income. Public webinars have allowed another source of income without all the expenses of travel. Astrological income follows the planetary trends just like life in general does.

Is your practice mostly for local clients or do you practice internationally?

All of the above. The best advertising is word-of-mouth from clients. EAN strives to be on the leading edge of technology, and today it allows us to offer our services worldwide from the comfort of one's home. My husband, LeRoy Weimer, also does both occupations with me and manages our website, DVD production, streaming videos, etc. for the last dozen years.

Can you describe how you studied astrology?

Self-studies, immersing myself in books and then chart practice, practice, practice, which was followed up with writing monthly forecasts from 2000-2009.

Were you certified for your astrology studies?

Yes, Jeffrey Wolf Green School of Evolutionary Astrology, the school I managed from 2002-2008.

How long have you studied before you began your practice?

I started self-studies in 1983, and was teaching locally by 1987. I practiced with chart readings from the beginning.

How old were you when you started your practice?

26 the first time, then had a career in environmental politics. 35, the second time with commitment to really practice astrology.

If you are a full time astrologer, how long did it take you to transition from a part time to a full time practice?

About 3-4 years, transitioning out of my full time job one day per week per year (had a very supportive 9-5 boss). Quantum physics work came after I became a full time astrologer.

How do clients usually find out about you?

Initially, word-of-mouth advertising. I started before household computers. Word-of-mouth is still an active source of referral for me. Today, our free weekly forecasting podcasts bring in many new clients, as well as periodic free forecasting webinars.

What makes it possible for you to be a professional astrologer—both in character and in practical terms?

First, being a good listener. It is all about taking a complicated subject and making it understandable to each individual client—meeting the client where they have need and interest. Nothing replaces the ability to take the language of astrology and intuit that language to what is meaningful for each client.

Like any talent, it takes effort over time to become proficient and successful. Specializing in spiritual/karmic astrology, I always address both the distortions and natural expressions of any astrological signature—here is the situation and here are your opportunities for evolution. I always want to have any reading session recorded so that the client has opportunity for continued awakening—astrology is a very condense language and operates on many levels of understanding.

I also only work with "live" clients (in person, phone, internet) in order to have the immediate give and take that then reaches the client where it has value for them, and to minimize any projections of astrological archetypes. I have had many lifetimes as a healer/shaman. In the consensus world, I only have a high school degree.

How long does it take you to prepare for a typical private consultation reading?

> After 30 years of practice, I can "read on the fly." Starting out, I would spend more time on prep than the actual reading. Over the years I have "trained" myself to read in one-hour sessions—if I cannot answer your questions in an hour (my opinion), I'm not doing my job.
>
> Typically, I spend 15-30 minutes in prep for a single chart, and 30-45 minutes prep for composite charts (three charts and synastry grid). Health and wellness astrology, and choosing surgery dates, is another story that takes more time.

How was your choice to become an astrologer received by your family and greater environment?

> In the mainstream world, I call myself a counselor to save time and eyebrow reactions. Over the years, my family has always known me as the alternative one, and now want to know if Mercury "is in retrograde" all the time. Dad doesn't understand any of it, however, his oldest daughter always pays her bills and doesn't ask for money. Mom came through the metaphysical door with me in my 20s, and has always been my biggest cheerleader (so blessed to have her support). I am also blessed to have a husband who enjoys doing this work with me.

How do you cope with the general credibility questions that astrology is subjected to by the mainstream?

> I allow others the freedom of choice in their beliefs as I wish the same to be allowed for me. I do not have time to

convince and convert. Souls exist at different stages of
awareness or consciousness, and until the student is ready,
the teacher will not arrive and time is wasted. I prefer to
attract those who are ready for spiritual truth as best as I can
understand it myself.

When mainstream religious souls knock on my door,
however, they usually walk away before I am done with the
conversation (sharpens my debate skills).

**Did you initially, (or do you now) feel self-conscious to a degree
about being an astrologer?**

Never really did feel self-conscious, I love my work and feel
blessed and valuable.

**What are for you the great rewards of having chosen to become an
astrologer?**

The feedback of appreciation and endorsements from clients
and students. The energy of those exchanges is priceless.
Also, the freedom to live my life as I choose, knowing I am
helping others live more harmoniously with all species on
planet Earth.

**What are your most important guidelines and insights for a
person who now contemplates the opportunity to become a
professional astrologer?**

Practice, practice, practice with live clients for feedback in
order to improve your skills. Nothing replaces good reading
qualities and abilities. Pay attention, learn the practical side
of running a business and how to market in today's fast-
changing internet world. Astrologers rarely achieve

overnight success, and most have other sources of income, so practicality is necessary through Pluto in Capricorn.

Remember, astrology is natural law, and while it can be suppressed and distorted, it can never be destroyed. Universal truth is on your side and supports you. I do believe, think and feel that an astrological renaissance is upon us. Be a part of it however small or large your role may be. Wishing you all the success in the world.

Kim Marie is the Director of the Evolutionary Astrology Network. She has studied and practiced Evolutionary Astrology for 30 years and counsels an international clientele. Her background includes experience in alternative healing and environmental politics. Kim Marie is a certified Master Gardener and a Deep Memory Processing past-life regression therapist. She resides on a beautiful piece of paradise in the Black Hills of South Dakota with her husband LeRoy – Media Manager for EAN.

Chris Brennan

Professional Astrologer Interview

Denver, Colorado
www.ChrisBrennanAstrologer.com

Are you practicing astrology part-time or full-time?

Full-time.

What are the components of your astrology practice? Please share information about the different services you offer:

I offer private consultations in natal astrology, electional astrology, birth chart rectification, relationship analysis, and horary questions. The majority of my consultations focus on natal or electional. I also teach online courses on Hellenistic astrology, electional, and horary.

If you offer more than one service, what were the different reasons for you to expand the range of astrology services?

Since I'm proficient in several different branches of astrology I didn't see any reason to limit myself by only offering one service. Offering different services also generates more income, and I find it more interesting because it adds more variety to my work schedule.

What percentage of your overall income comes from your astrology practice?

> 100%. I rely solely on my income from astrology in order to make a living and support myself financially.

Do you financially rely on one of your services more than the others, or do they all provide more or less an equal portion of your income?

> I would say that at this point my income is split pretty evenly between consultations and the online courses I teach. In terms of consultations, right now I make the majority of my income from doing natal astrology consultations. In terms of classes, I make the majority of my income from my online course on Hellenistic astrology, since that is the course that I have put the most work into, and Hellenistic astrology is the main thing that I'm known to specialize in.

Is your practice mostly for local clients or do you practice internationally?

> Since people usually tend to find me online through one of my websites, the vast majority of my business tends to come from people who are either in different parts of the country or different parts of the world. In terms of clients, it is probably 80% from the US. In terms of students, it is maybe 70% from the US, and 30% international, give or take. Because the majority of my clients are from out of state, I have never felt the need to set up an office locally, although this can be problematic sometimes when a local person does want to meet up with me in person.

Can you describe how you studied astrology?

I studied astrology on my own for the first four years, by reading books and online articles, and studying the charts of friends and family. Then I attended Kepler College for about 2 years and received an associate degree from them, when they were still authorized by the state of Washington to grant degrees. After that I spent two years studying at Project Hindsight, which is a translation project for ancient astrological texts. Around this time I began doing consultations and moving towards becoming a professional astrologer.

Were you certified for your astrology studies?

I have an associate degree from Kepler College, which also grants me NCGR Level 3 certification. I feel somewhat ambivalent about the value of being certified at this point in time though, since I think that the quality of the education you receive from any certifying body is much more important than the actual degree itself.

How long have you studied before you began your practice, and how old were you?

I studied astrology for about 6 to 7 years before I really started doing consultations professionally. I was about 21 or 22 by the time that I began to make that transition. I didn't become a full-time practicing astrologer until I had been studying astrology for about 10 years. I was 25 years old at that time.

If you are a full time astrologer, how long did it take you to transition from a part time to a full time practice?

It took me about 4 years before I was able to transition into practicing full time. I had day jobs off and on until I was 25. Then one day I realized how much time I was wasting by working a normal job, and that I could be using that time to advance my career in the field of astrology. I decided to quit my day job suddenly that day, and devoted myself to making it as an astrologer full time. I was pretty broke that first year or two, but I was happy to be doing what I loved, and I've never looked back.

How do clients usually find out about you?

Usually they come across one of my websites after doing an internet search for a specific topic related to astrology, and they find something I've written about. In order to promote my practice and draw in clients and students I have several different websites that I write articles on. At the moment one of my primary sites is a podcast that I started a few years ago called The Astrology Podcast. I also have a blog called the Horoscopic Astrology Blog that I write articles on from time to time, as well as other sites that I write on sporadically such as The Astrology Dictionary, Saturn Return Stories, The Hellenistic Astrology Website, and The Political Astrology Blog. Over the past few years I've also written a bi-monthly column in The Mountain Astrologer magazine on auspicious electional dates.

What makes it possible for you to be a professional astrologer—both in character and in practical terms?

> The main thing that makes it possible for me to be a professional astrologer is that I have a deep interest in and fascination with astrology. I really enjoy doing it, and I couldn't imagine doing anything else. Or at least, I can't really imagine myself being happy doing anything else, because I really love doing astrology.

> In practical terms, I would say that the internet has really allowed me to develop my professional practice much more quickly and effectively than I think I would have been able to otherwise. So, without the internet and some of the things connected with it such as blogging or podcasting, I don't think my practice would be possible, at least not in the form it is in today.

How long does it take you to prepare for a typical private consultation reading?

> I spend one hour preparing before each natal astrology consultation. Most of this time is spent preparing some notes on different timing periods, which are then sent to the client before we talk. A lot of this is due to an advanced timing technique that I use that I like to write out notes for ahead of time. If I didn't approach the technique in that way then I could probably cut my prep time down a bit more, if I wanted to.

How was your choice to become an astrologer received by your family and greater environment?

> I was lucky in that my family was very supportive of my decision to pursue astrology as a career, even though I was still in high school when I made that decision. A large part of the reason for that is because prior to that time I did not have any real educational or career aspirations, but after I discovered astrology I felt like I had discovered what I wanted to do with my life. My family was happy that I had found something that I was passionate about, and they helped to cover my tuition when I went to Kepler College to get a degree in astrological studies after high school.

How do you cope with the general credibility questions that astrology is subjected to by the mainstream?

> This is actually something that I usually feel moderately embarrassed about, not because I view astrology as false, but because I understand what the public perception of astrology is, and thus what many people must think of me when I say that I'm an astrologer. Usually in casual conversation with strangers I don't say that I'm an astrologer, because I don't want people's initial perception of me to be colored by whatever misconceptions they have about astrology. I do spend a decent amount of time thinking about the different arguments for and against astrology though, so that when the subject does come up I can have a reasonable conversation about it, and defend my views if necessary. For the most part these sorts of arguments only happen online though, and I've never really had a disagreement with someone about astrology in

person. That may be because I generally avoid putting myself in situations where it might come up.

Did you initially, (or do you now) feel self-conscious to a degree about being an astrologer?

Yes, I do feel somewhat self-conscious about being an astrologer, partially because of the negative public perceptions of the subject, but also partially because astrologers don't always present themselves in a very respectable manner.

One of the things that I sometimes have to remind myself is that astrology itself is incredibly weird. Oftentimes astrologers get so used to looking at the world through the lens of astrology that they forget to step back every once in a while and look at it from the perspective of a normal person. When you do this you realize how odd it must look to someone who doesn't have any familiarity with the subject, and you can start to understand why most educated people assume that astrology is false. I feel like this is kind of an important realization to have because it is kind of humbling, and it puts you in a better position to deal with and relate to people who may be somewhat skeptical about astrology.

What are for you the great rewards of having chosen to become an astrologer?

The most rewarding thing for me about becoming a professional astrologer is that I feel like I not only found something incredibly interesting that I'm happy to spend the rest of my life studying, but it also gives me a greater sense of meaning and purpose in my life. I also appreciate the fact that I get to share that with my clients by helping them to see the meaning and purpose in their own lives as well. There is something very rewarding about that, because it makes the practice of astrology a lot more than just some day job or career that I fell into, but instead it makes me feel like I'm having a positive impact on people's lives.

What are your most important guidelines and insights for a person who now contemplates the opportunity to become a professional astrologer?

My primary piece of advice for anyone who is contemplating becoming a professional astrologer is just to study as many different forms and traditions of astrology as you can early on in your career, before you get locked in to a particular approach. This is important because most of the time people just end up sticking with whatever approach to astrology they learned when they first started studying the subject. This can be kind of limiting though, and the longer you go without exposing yourself to other forms of astrology, the harder it will be later on in your career to incorporate new or foreign concepts into your existing practice.

My other piece of advice is to start a blog as soon as possible, and start writing. It doesn't matter whether you are still a student or you are already seeing clients, you need to start writing and generating a body of work. Even if your approach to astrology is still in development or is in transition, you should write out and document whatever your current thoughts on the subject are. This will benefit you in multiple ways. The most important way is that you will start to develop an audience of people who read and follow your writings and know who you are. Building an audience is the first step in eventually getting clients or students. Additionally, as you write more and more you will get better at writing. This is important because someday you may want to write a book on astrology or an article in a journal, but you won't be taken very seriously if you don't know how to write. So it is good to start practicing now. Finally, by starting a blog this will force you to start learning some of the things you will need to know in order to start, manage, and promote a website. So, even if you aren't a technical genius right now, by starting a blog it will force you to start learning some skills that will become very useful for you down the line. So, start a blog, and get to work writing some articles on it now.

Chris Brennan is a professional astrologer from Denver, Colorado. He was educated at Kepler College, where he focused on cross-cultural comparisons between the astrological traditions. He is the former President of the Association for Young Astrologers, and the former Research Director of the National Council for Geocosmic Research. He specializes in the Greco-Roman tradition of astrology known as Hellenistic astrology, and his forthcoming book on the subject is titled Hellenistic Astrology: The Study of Fate and Fortune.

Linea Van Horn

Professional Astrologer Interview

 San Mateo, California
www.astrologeratlarge.com

Are you practicing astrology part-time or full-time?

Part-time.

What are the components of your astrology practice? Please share information about the different services you offer:

I offer private sessions for individuals and couples covering a wide variety of services such as natal charts with transits and progressions; solar returns; children charts and family readings; vocational readings.

I teach classes and mentor students at all levels from Fundamentals of Astrology to Advanced and beyond including manual chart calculation and preparation for certification exams.

In addition I give presentations and workshops and I have had several articles published. I ghost write for another astrologer once a month.

Also, although it is not a direct component of my practice, I have created and guided a successful local astrology group, and have served on Boards of bigger astrology organizations. Finally, I worked in the astrology internet industry for many years; an "actual" job with an office, benefits, etc.

If you offer more than one service, what were the different reasons for you to expand the range of astrology services?

After leading a small monthly astrology group in my area for about four years, during which time I prepared a lesson for each meeting, I realized that I had enough knowledge and experience to teach. By that time I had passed my first certification exam, and there was a demand in my area from others who also wanted to pass the exam. So my first class, I co-taught but since then I have taught by myself. Additional classes were added in response to student demand.

For a long time, I had many more students than clients (I was also working full time) and found teaching to be far more lucrative since my classes filled up. Now that I am not working outside the home, there is more time for client work. I have about an equal number of clients and students now. I really enjoy both types of work.

The writing and speaking part developed as a result of my various areas of deeper interest and a desire to share the results with a larger group.

What percentage of your overall income comes from your astrology practice?

> Virtually all of my income is from astrology. Fortunately for me, I am supported by my husband so the financial demands on me are not great at the moment. Back in the days when I was a single mom, I needed a regular job to make ends meet (happily I was able to work at astrology websites). Frankly it would be very nerve wracking if I had to support myself doing only astrology.

Do you financially rely on one of your services more than the others, or do they all provide more or less an equal portion of your income?

> This balance has shifted over the years but now, teaching and clients are about equal. Much less from writing and speaking.

Is your practice mostly for local clients or do you practice internationally?

> Teaching is local. I will offer my first virtual class this fall. Most clients are local, but the ones who aren't are mostly American, with a few expats living in other countries in Europe and Asia.

Can you describe how you studied astrology?

> I took a series of 3 classes from an astrologer friend and then did intense self-directed study for several years. I started going to lectures and conferences and then formed a local group myself, which met monthly and gave me a wonderful foundation because we covered a wide variety of subjects and I prepared a lesson every single month. That really

solidified my education. I also passed all four levels of the NCGR certification exams (I am proud to say I took the tests; I didn't grandfather in) and this also contributed to a well-rounded body of knowledge.

Since then I have continued to attend lectures and conferences and to study with specific high level astrologers to expand my knowledge base and to keep abreast of current developments. I still consider myself a serious student of astrology.

Were you certified for your astrology studies?

Yes. I am fully certified through NCGR.

How long have you studied before you began your practice?

About 4 or 5 years. I didn't actually start a practice. It created itself when a small home business I was doing suddenly folded, and then next morning in the mailbox there was an envelope from my neighbor with $50 in it and a request for a reading. She was my first paid client. It was quite a few more years before I legitimized my astrology business with a business license, etc.

How old were you when you first started to practice?

I was at my Saturn Return when I discovered astrology. So I was in my early 30's when I started seeing clients. Wow! 30 years now!

If you are a full time astrologer, how long did it take you to transition from a part time to a full time practice?

My situation was unusual since I worked at a couple of

astrology websites for a long time as well as seeing clients and teaching.

How do clients usually find out about you?

Referrals from previous clients continue to be my best source of new clients. Other clients come from my student groups, the organizations I participate in, and internet searches.

What makes it possible for you to be a professional astrologer—both in character and in practical terms?

In a practical way, I've done my studies. I know what I'm talking about. Also, I don't have to worry about being anything else, because this is what I do. The experience of parenting has been instrumental in being a good astrologer, although there are many fine astrologers who do not have children. Being able to listen and hear deeper meaning and making connections between a client's chart and their experience. Having a healthy intuitive capacity also helps. The most common word used by clients about their sessions is "insightful."

How long does it take you to prepare for a typical private consultation reading?

At the beginning it took hours. Then I started limiting the preparation time so it was not greater than the scheduled consult. Now I can do it much faster; in probably half (or less) of the amount of time for the consult. I always prepare: I think it's really important to be familiar with the chart before the client arrives. When they are present, I want to focus on the client, not the chart wheel!

How was your choice to become an astrologer received by your family and greater environment?

> Pretty well. No big problems there. In the area where I live it's considered "cool."

How do you cope with the general credibility questions that astrology is subjected to by the mainstream?

> I would be mentioning its historical importance and modern day practical applications.

Did you initially, (or do you now) feel self-conscious to a degree about being an astrologer?

> To a small degree. But not anymore.

What are for you the great rewards of having chosen to become an astrologer?

> Oh, so many! What a gift to get paid well doing what I love!!! I love the greater perspective and acceptance that astrology provides, and I love being able to give practical and insightful counsel to my clients and students.

What are your most important guidelines and insights for a person who now contemplates the opportunity to become a professional astrologer?

> Have several teachers so you're not inculcated into one narrow system. Practice the art of symbol synthesis—this is a skill that can be and must be developed for a person to be an effective astrologer. Keep current in the astrology world—there are so many promising younger astrologers nowadays who are doing remarkable work. Have a spiritual

practice to complement the astrology. Do as many charts as you can and ask for feedback. Have faith in yourself!

Linea Van Horn, *C.A., NCGR, is the Astrologer at Large. A professional astrologer since 1998, her career centers on teaching, client work and community building. She is founder and past President of the San Francisco Astrological Society, has served on NCGR boards, and spearheaded the West Coast Astrology Groups coalition in 2012. Linea was employed in the astrology internet industry from 1998 – 2009. A published writer, respected teacher and a lively, popular presenter, she now devotes herself to client work, teaching, mentoring, writing, lecturing and networking in the San Francisco Bay Area. Member of AFAN, ISAR and OPA.*

Aleksandar Imsiragic

Professional Astrologer Interview

Belgrade, Serbia
www.keplerunited.org

Are you practicing astrology part-time or full-time?

> Full-time.

What are the components of your astrology practice? Please share information about the different services you offer:

> Teaching at the Astrological Institute in Serbia, giving lectures and workshops internationally, organizing Astrology Conferences, writing and publishing books, researching and occasionally doing private consultations

If you offer more than one service, what were the different reasons for you to expand the range of astrology services?

> I like to do all these different things, so this is how it goes…

Is your practice mostly for local clients or do you practice internationally?

> I think it's now probably 50:50, locally and internationally.

Can you describe how you studied astrology?

> I mainly studied by myself and I'm still learning by researching.

Were you certified for your astrology studies?

> Yes, I'm ISAR CAP

How long have you studied before you began your practice, and how old were you?

> I studied Astrology for about 5 years before I started to meet clients. Age 26.

If you are a full time astrologer, how long did it take you to transition from a part time to a full time practice?

> I believe it took me about three years, before I became a full-time astrologer.

How do clients usually find out about you?

> Students and clients usually find me online, or when I do public lectures, through my books, and by recommendations.

How long does it take you to prepare for a typical private consultation reading?

> It doesn't take any time for preparation after so many years. At the beginning it took me 2 - 3 hours preparation for a one hour consultation, and then it took just one hour, then half an hour and now it doesn't take any time. It usually just "flows."

How was your choice to become an astrologer received by your family and greater environment?

> I don't know, really. I think if you don't care about that and you are just honest with yourself, probably no one really cares if you are doing something unique and different...

How do you cope with the general credibility questions that astrology is subjected to by the mainstream?

> I've never felt any problem with that, but in order to avoid questions, I usually present myself as a publisher—which I am. I have an astrology publishing house and publish just astrology literature for professional astrologers.

What are for you the great rewards of having chosen to become an astrologer?

> Happiness of living a dream and discovering the mysteries of life and of your own existence.

What are your most important guidelines and insights for a person who now contemplates the opportunity to become a professional astrologer?

> Be honest with your feelings and if you still want to be an astrologer after that, let the magic be your guide and you will live as a happy person.

Aleksandar Imsiragic (ISAR CAP) is ISAR Education Director and founder of the Johannes Kepler Astrological Institute in Belgrade, Serbia. He has been an astrologer for more than 25 years, teaches meditation, wrote eleven books, and organizes annual International Astrological Conferences in Belgrade since 2001. His work synthesises Western and Eastern traditions, and his focus is in the fields of fixed stars, karmic astrology, and astro-healing.

Caroline W. Casey

Professional Astrologer Interview

Outside Washington DC
www.CoyoteNetworkNews.com

Are you practicing astrology part-time or full-time?

Full-time since 1978.

What are the components of your astrology practice? Please share information about the different services you offer:

Unique art of Astro - mytho - politico guiding, meta - storytelling in myriad multi-media venues.

Astrological readings, readings for the collective at innumerable conferences, (Robert Bly's Great Mother Conference, Ingenious Solutions Festivals: Bioneers, Green Festivals etc.)

MC-ing Gaia, to tease an astro-themed guiding story through a whole weekend with 6,000 people; presenting at Envision, Lightning in a Bottle, Symbiosis Festivals, Parliament of World Religions in Cape Town; working with delinquent kids, (Pisces, 12th house, those most exiled are those most mythologically literate, with much to contribute.

Mythological News Service:

2 Audio Books with Sounds True, "*Visionary Activist Astrology*," "*Making the Gods Work for You*", (audio and in print via Random House)

The Visionary Activist Show, 19 years on Pacifica Radio network KPFA in Berkeley, KPFK in LA, and web-cast, pod-cast and archived. A constantly evolving experiment in Radio astro*Magic.; providing the astro*Mythic News, proffered metaphoric opportunities...and hosting those contributing to Cultural Renaissance, for Dreaming, Conjuring and Implementing a more lovingly ingenious world.

Compassionate Trickster Experimental Mystery School, aka Trickster Training Council www.TricksterTraining.com

If you offer more than one service, what were the different reasons for you to expand the range of astrology services?

Now is perhaps the greatest time for astrology's great gift of guiding humans to join back in the choreography of Creation, to humbly collaborate with Nature's guiding evolutionary ingenuity.

What percentage of your overall income comes from your astrology practice?

100%

Is your practice mostly for local clients or do you practice internationally?

Global

Can you describe how you studied astrology?

She began studying astrology as a late teen, where she was the kid who got to hang out at a salon presided over by Dr. Andrew Weil, comprised of way cool intellectual political mystics, reading anything the Whole Earth Catalogue recommended including Carl Jung and Joseph Campbell, with whom she studied Grail legend and Animal Myths in later years.

Dedicating to astrology as one of the great meta-languages of antiquity, uniting everything of consequence: personal and collective change, ritual magic, esoteric philosophy, Quabbalah, she went on to study at the Astrological Lodge on Baker street in London, traveling though India, returning to Brown University, where she read long 18th and 19th century novels, and studied everything useful to astrology: The Grail Legend, Comparative Religion, Sufism, Voudoun, Oriental Theatre, Middle Eastern Dance, Film, Writing – all contributing to a degree in Semiotics.

During which time she lived at the Providence Zen Center, earning a Brown Belt in Shim Gum Do, Korean sword(wo)man-ship.

And studying with the late astrologer Isabel Hickey in Boston.

She continues her studies of magic, mythology, literature and social activism all over the world.

Were you certified for your astrology studies?

Sun, Neptune, Saturn square Uranus wary of out-sourcing to others the definition of what it is to be a great astrologer.

Let each define, in an on-going way, our own definition of what we should be perpetually cultivating to be agents of this beautiful language—the first environmental language of dynamic kinship.

How long have you studied before you began your practice?

In 3 ish years, I began to accept money for readings (in humble amounts), but still reading from Brit astro text books....But learn so much from each reading, in perpetuity.

How old were you when you first started to practice?

20 ish

If you are a full time astrologer, how long did it take you to transition from a part time to a full time practice?

Age 26

How do clients usually find out about you?

Reputation, 19 years + Radio, Speaker at many mega-festivals, conferences, TV, interviews, social media.

What makes it possible for you to be a professional astrologer— both in character and in practical terms?

Always learning, cultivating metaphoric agility, spiraling forth into the memosphere.

How long does it take you to prepare for a typical private consultation reading?

...varies, in the ancient pre-computer days, 2 hours...Then with computers 90 minutes, now an hour is a luxurious plenitude.

How was your choice to become an astrologer received by your family and greater environment?

Bewilderment

How do you cope with the general credibility questions that astrology is subjected to by the mainstream?

...a spirited training in crossing borders.

Did you initially, (or do you now) feel self-conscious to a degree about being an astrologer?

Sure, don't always mention to radio guests that the show has an astrological frame, lest it spook them and distract us from the conversation that wants to happen. Don't always have to mention astrology to practice astrology.

What are for you the great rewards of having chosen to become an astrologer?

A life in which every day has miraculous Mystery- wow - what a language! Worked again, for effective deep-delving. To be dedicated to a craft that no matter how much we know - there will always be more to learn-forever. Restring Mythological literacy to culture. Synchronicity speaks to us in whatever realm we cultivate. The deeper the cultivation- the greater the perceived synchronicities.

Contributing to innumerable venues, the sine qua non, of an all-inclusive guiding meta-story, at this time of Dire Beauty.

What are your most important guidelines and insights for a person who now contemplates the opportunity to become a professional astrologer?

All cultures grow their own astrology, appropriate
for their time. Now, all teachings, and practices are eager to
be tossed into Pluto's alchemical composting cauldron: Does
it guide each to their own wise autonomy? Is it equal, Mars
and Venus, Men and Women, humans and the rest of our
kin on the home planet? "Yes?" then we ladle it out. "No?"
we toss it back in for another round of bubbling, a Cauldron
of Cultural Renaissance, from which we ladle our
willingness to cahoot with Nature's evolutionary ingenuity,
aka "Trickster." Magic is simply a willingness to collaborate
with everything. (Let us be willing to be influential, not
necessarily famous, but influential.)

When culture's in big trouble it turns to its outsiders. Now *Use*
'tis time for all to spiral sane reverent common sense,
proffered by astrology,

...that we avert disaster, we gather to consider.

Caroline W Casey, *weaver of context for the Visionary Activist Radio Show,*
since 1995, author of Making the Gods Work for You (print and audio),
student of astrology since 1970 (Astrological Lodge of London, Grail legend
with Joseph Campbell, Brown University.)
Founder of Coyote Network News, a mythological news service for the
Trickster Redeemer within us all, and Trickster Training Council.
A rousing and frequent keynote speaker, and MC, offering Astro*Mythic
Guiding Meta-Narrative at myriad global conferences; Continuing her studies
of magic, mythology, literature and social activism all over the world, Caroline
invites us to imagine, conjure, and implement a more lovingly ingenious
world.

Madalyn Hillis-Dineen

Professional Astrologer Interview

Brewster, Massachusetts
www.capecodastrologer.com

Are you practicing astrology part-time or full-time?

Full-time.

What are the components of your astrology practice? Please share information about the different services you offer:

Marketing Director and User Support at Astrolabe, Inc.
Consultations
Lectures and Workshops
Writing

If you offer more than one service, what were the different reasons for you to expand the range of astrology services?

Prior to coming to Astrolabe in 1994, I was the Executive Director of NCGR, a part time paid position. I have always "multi-tasked" in astrology to make it more financially sustainable.

What percentage of your overall income comes from your astrology practice?

> I have derived my income solely from astrology since 1990.

Do you financially rely on one of your services more than the others, or do they all provide more or less an equal portion of your income?

> I think my case is unique and, yes, my job at Astrolabe provides about 2/3 of astrology income.

Is your practice mostly for local clients or do you practice internationally?

> For the most part, it is nationwide, though I have consulted with people in other countries from time to time.

Can you describe how you studied astrology?

> I first began my study of astrology with a private weekly class with a teacher. After that, I learned from attending conferences, NCGR meetings, books, talking with others, etc.

Were you certified for your astrology studies?

> Yes, I am a certified astro*carto*graphy interpreter, ISAR CAP, and NCGR-PAA Level IV.

How long have you studied before you began your practice?

> I began my study of astrology in 1979 and began to do readings in the early 1980's. I really didn't start to have a regular income stream (part-time) until the mid to late 1980's.

How old were you when you started your practice?

> 29.

If you are a full time astrologer, how long did it take you to transition from a part time to a full time practice?

> About 7 years.

How do clients usually find out about you?

> Referral from existing client, google, networking, calling Astrolabe.

What makes it possible for you to be a professional astrologer— both in character and in practical terms?

> An old time astrologer once said that the qualifications to be an astrologer are two: to have fixed opinions and a big mouth. While I probably do fall into that category, my clients tell me that I have an ability to translate the esoteric into very practical terms. I also have had a good deal of experience with 12-step recovery and I use those principles as well with people. I look at what I do as service and I recognize that I don't know everything and try to help people to figure out how to navigate their life journey.

How long does it take you to prepare for a typical private consultation reading?

> Half hour or less. In the old days, when I had to calculate and construct the chart by hand, it did take longer.

How was your choice to become an astrologer received by your family and greater environment?

> It kind of just evolved. No one really objected. I had an uncle, who was a Catholic bishop, who actually gave me a gift certificate to Staples to buy what I needed to set up an office. I think when my children were younger, they would have preferred for me to have been doing something more conventional. But, now, they think it's pretty cool and even refer clients once in a while.

How do you cope with the general credibility questions that astrology is subjected to by the mainstream?

> I don't think too much about it. For one thing, I don't believe in astrology, I use it. I also don't make it my life's mission for anyone else to "use" it or "believe" it. I pretty much follow the principle that what other people think of me is none of my business. I used to want to convert others but no longer feel that need.

Did you initially, (or do you now) feel self-conscious to a degree about being an astrologer?

> In situations where I am meeting new people, I sometimes wonder how the news will be met. I am often pleasantly surprised. Usually, people start gushing about how interesting it is, etc. and I just nod in assent.

What are for you the great rewards of having chosen to become an astrologer?

> First and foremost, the ability to help others has been the greatest reward. Aside from that, I've been fortunate to travel to many places, meet wonderful people and enjoy a

community of like-minded astrologers. As my husband likes to say, "Astrology—she's been good to you." Yes, Indeed.

What are your most important guidelines and insights for a person who now contemplates the opportunity to become a professional astrologer?

Study and stay open-minded but be consistent in your work. There are many techniques and I've seen many people get bogged down trying to use all of them. Find a system or tools and apply them consistently. This is key.

Also, remember that you are a messenger or guide of the heavens but that you are human. You will inevitably make mistakes but you can learn from them. Before I speak to someone, I always ask God or the universe to help me to be of usefulness to the person. There is no way you can cover absolutely everything in a session but, if you can give them what they need at that moment, you will have provided a good service.

Madalyn Hillis-Dineen, CA NCGR-PAA is a practitioner of symmetrical astrology for over 30 years as well as a certified Astro*Carto*Graphy interpreter. She is also the Director of Marketing for Astrolabe, Inc., and has written and lectured extensively. A leader in the astrological community, Madalyn is a co-coordinator of UAC 2008 and 2012, the former Chair of NCGR, Clerk of the NCGR-PAA and winner of the 1995 Marion D. March Regulus Award for Community Service and the 2012 NCGR Sisyphus Award.

Hakan Kirkoglu

Professional Astrologer Interview

Istanbul, Turkey
www.hakankirkoglu.com

Are you practicing astrology part-time or full-time?

> Full-time.

What are the components of your astrology practice? Please share information about the different services you offer:

> Astrological counseling, writing in several media, teaching Certificate and Diploma levels since 1999, organization of events.

If you offer more than one service, what were the different reasons for you to expand the range of astrology services?

> Different activities provide a set of practices for many interested participants in public domain, be it general readers and followers as well as more sophisticated ones, such as students.

> The increasing importance of social media and technological abilities bring further avenues of astrological practices and activities.

What percentage of your overall income comes from your Astrology practice?

75%.

Do you financially rely on one of your services more than the others, or do they all provide more or less an equal portion of your income?

It is more or less in equal portions.

Is your practice mostly for local clients or do you practice internationally?

I provide astrological counseling both nationwide and internationally.

Can you describe how you studied astrology?

I began studying astrology in 1983 through my own sources, and later I studied with the Faculty of Astrological Studies in London, (between 1994 -1997) and was granted a Diploma degree. Later I also became certified via ISAR. I have been studying astrology for more than 30 years.

How long have you studied before you began your practice, and how old were you?

I began to study astrology in 1983 and commenced professional work in 2000. So, I studied 17 years before doing any professional work. I was 16 when I began to study astrology and I was 33 when I became fully professional.

If you are a full time astrologer, how long did it take you to transition from a part time to a full time practice?

> I was already writing articles since 1989, so if you would count it as a partial work, it took 11 years.

How do clients usually find out about you?

> They reach me via several media and also word of mouth due to my clients.

What makes it possible for you to be a professional astrologer—both in character and in practical terms?

> A sound education with keen interest, long years of experience and practice, ethical behavior, privacy, empathy, responsibility as well as dedication to help people.

How long does it take you to prepare for a typical private consultation reading?

> Approximately it is one hour while taking notes.

How was your choice to become an astrologer received by your family and greater environment?

> It was received positively as I was quite ardent in practicing astrology. I was also praised in the media due to my courageous decision to leave engineering and economics background. I studied Management Engineering in bachelors and later gained MA degree in Economics. Currently I'm doing another MA in History and later probably a PhD in History.

How do you cope with the general credibility questions that astrology is subjected to by the mainstream?

> When it is asked, I give lectures and interviews in the media. A firm education always helps in tackling with this kind of misinformation, confusion and charlatanry.

Did you initially, (or do you now) feel self-conscious to a degree about being an astrologer?

> Yes I did but it was also due to my own curiosity in the subject.

What are for you the great rewards of having chosen to become an astrologer?

> It gives me a feeling of finding my true calling which reflects my capabilities, and leads me to find happiness in life.

What are your most important guidelines and insights for a person who now contemplates the opportunity to become a professional astrologer?

> Firstly, one's own character provides the most important ingredient and base for learning. Desire for discovery and understanding people are primary constituents. One needs to be "person oriented" in this process.

> Additionally, astrologers need to be well versed in many facets of astrology, it is the technical and analytical aspects that would provide a firm education. Along with education, one needs also to broaden his/her understanding via interacting with peer group. My own principle is to keep the quality of astrological practice above providing best of our expertise and being service oriented rather than superficial and quickie for only monetary gain. In order to do so,

professional astrologers ought to have a dedicated approach for long years of experience.

Hakan Kirkoglu began to study Astrology at an early age of 16 having interests in both mythology, philosophy and natural sciences. Despite his career in finance, he applied to the Faculty of Astrological Studies and gained his diploma with Veritas Award in 1997. After leaving banking in 2000, he moved to full-time astrology practise, both teaching and consulting, and has since then been presenting at international conferences in the UK, USA, Australia, Poland and Serbia and in the UAC mundane astrology tracks. His astrology school (School of Wisdom of Sky) has become one of the educational institutions in Istanbul. In later years, his main interests turned towards the traditional side of astrology, particularly Hellenistic astrology. He was the Turkish representative of the Faculty of Astrological Studies and later became ISAR VP for Turkey in 2003. He has three books published: Astroloji Zamanları (1991), Göklerin Bilgeli (2005), Ruhun Yolculu (2010).

Donna Woodwell

Professional Astrologer Interview

Austin, Texas
www.donnaphilosophica.com

Are you practicing astrology part-time or full-time?

Full-time.

What are the components of your astrology practice? Please share information about the different services you offer:

My current income streams include writing, teaching, private consultations and special event entertainment.

Writing includes daily horoscopes and other articles for hire.

I teach at Kepler College, the University of Texas' Informal classes program, and at various astrology associations and metaphysical venues.

I see clients in person at my home office, or via Skype.

I do mini-readings at special events such as store celebrations, bachelorette parties, graduation parties, etc.

If you offer more than one service, what were the different reasons for you to expand the range of astrology services?

> I use ancient wisdom to help people discover their unique genius. To do this I use astrology and other forms of divination, as well as hypnosis, energy work, business experience, referrals and a little magic. Whatever is necessary to help the client achieve their objectives.

What percentage of your overall income comes from your astrology practice?

> 100%

Do you financially rely on one of your services more than the others, or do they all provide more or less an equal portion of your income?

> It varies from month to month; the multiple income streams cover for each other.

Is your practice mostly for local clients or do you practice internationally?

> Local, national and international

Can you describe how you studied astrology?

> In the beginning, I read books, and attended a several week course at the University of Texas Informal Classes program (where I now teach). I've also attended a few intensive workshops along the way in specific areas. I learn more now from my clients and their lived experience than I ever could have from books.

> But I often find the other skills I've developed to be more important to my work. Listening skills, and business

coaching skills, hypnosis certification and years of metaphysical/shamanic training with teachers. Academic training, with a couple of Master's degrees. Astrology itself is mostly a language; it's the other areas that give the language depth, meaning and purpose.

For Writing + Profile

Were you certified for your astrology studies?

No.

How long have you studied before you began your practice, and how old were you when you started your practice?

I began studying astrology 1994 (23 years old), and launched my formal astrology business in 2003 (32 years old).

How do clients usually find out about you?

Referral, Internet Searches, Teaching.

What makes it possible for you to be a professional astrologer— both in character and in practical terms?

Empathy and emotional intelligence.

An excellent memory, knack for language and pattern recognition.

A spiritual practice of my own.

A sense of humor.

Business skills.

Determination.

How long does it take you to prepare for a typical private consultation reading?

> 15 minutes.

How was your choice to become an astrologer received by your family and greater environment?

> It's never been an issue. My parents only want me to be happy. And I've never met anyone who hasn't been fascinated by what I do.

How do you cope with the general credibility questions that astrology is subjected to by the mainstream?

> I love questions. I wish more people asked them. I truly have never met anyone who hasn't been fascinated by astrology and metaphysics, once I start talking with them. Actually, I think I have more questions about the credibility of astrology (really astrologers) than the general public.

Did you initially, (or do you now) feel self-conscious to a degree about being an astrologer?

> Self-conscious? Only in the sense that I considered that astrology might be too much for the "general public" to handle at first meeting. Now I don't worry about it. In fact, I'm rather shocked at the number of people who don't seem to understand the difference between "astronomer" and "astrologer" – I even get questions about what it's like to look through one of those big telescopes.

What are for you the great rewards of having chosen to become an astrologer?

I love to watch the lights turn on in my client's eyes and minds and hearts when they get in touch with that spark of divinity inside themselves. When they know they are brilliant and unique and here for a reason. That they have something precious to offer—themselves.

What are your most important guidelines and insights for a person who now contemplates the opportunity to become a professional astrologer?

Go beyond the superficial kind of astrology. Have some additional skills in counseling, coaching, or working with people in some way. Get some business skills while you're at it. Being a full-time professional astrologer is not for the faint hearted, nor the uncommitted. You have to want it, and be willing to put in long hours to make it happen, because you love it.

Though **Donna Woodwell***, MA, attended grad school to become a foreign correspondent, she had no idea how foreign she would get. An explorer of Western and indigenous philosophical, magical and shamanic practices, she brings ancient wisdom to re-enchant modern life. In addition to her private consultations, Donna has hosted a weekly call-in radio show and written daily horoscopes and columns for several major astrological websites. She teaches astrology and esoteric studies at Kepler College and at the University of Texas Informal Classes. Over the years, Donna's served on the boards of the International Society for Astrological Research (ISAR), the National Council for Geocosmic Research (NCGR) and as the founding president of the Astrological Society of Austin. Currently, she's working on a book about the modern-day applications of astral theurgy.*
Find out more at www.donnaphilosophica.com

Ray Merriman

Professional Astrologer Interview

Farmington Hills, Michigan
www.mmacycles.com

Are you practicing astrology part-time or full-time?

> Full-time.

What are the components of your astrology practice? Please share information about the different services you offer:

> Financial Astrology market analysis via subscription reports (daily, weekly, monthly, yearly).

If you offer more than one service, what were the different reasons for you to expand the range of astrology services?

> You have many skills, you gain more meaning, it is more financially sustainable.

What percentage of your overall income comes from your astrology practice?

> 100%.

Do you financially rely on one of your services more than the others, or do they all provide more or less an equal portion of your income?

Mainly subscription services and trading.

Is your practice mostly for local clients or do you practice internationally?

International.

Can you describe how you studied astrology?

I first began my study of astrology with a private weekly class with a teacher. After that, I learned from attending conferences, NCGR meetings, books, talking with others, etc.

Were you certified for your astrology studies?

AFA and ISAR.

How long have you studied before you began your practice and how old were you when you began your practice?

2 years. I started to study when I was 20 years old and by 22, I was doing consultations/readings, and teaching.

If you are a full time astrologer, how long did it take you to transition from a part time to a full time practice?

About 5 years.

How do clients usually find out about you?

Word of mouth, internet.

What makes it possible for you to be a professional astrologer—both in character and in practical terms?

> Love of research and desire to help others; knowledge; skills at consulting; rigor with research; sincerity.

How long does it take you to prepare for a typical private consultation reading?

> About 30-45 minutes, but I can read the language, so I could consult without any preparation

How was your choice to become an astrologer received by your family and greater environment?

> As long as I was able to provide for myself, parents were fine with it. I think people I went to university with were surprised and thought I would go in another direction.

How do you cope with the general credibility questions that astrology is subjected to by the mainstream?

> I try to avoid it as much as possible. If not possible, I can debate it well. But mostly, I think it is a waste of time dealing with skeptics. I am not going to change their minds and they aren't going to change my mind, and I really don't have any interest in the waste of time with those who don't know and think they know. You can tell if there is a sincere interest, and if there is, I am there to discuss it with passion.

Did you initially, (or do you now) feel self-conscious to a degree about being an astrologer?

> Yes, but I also feel proud to be an astrologer.

What are for you the great rewards of having chosen to become an astrologer?

> A deeper understanding of man's relationship to the cosmos, to the infinite. It creates a sense of faith, belief in an orderly universe of which I am connected, and for which I can find the meaning of experiences—all experiences. It makes me tolerant of others and my own limitations as well as unlimited possibilities for joy.

What are your most important guidelines and insights for a person who now contemplates the opportunity to become a professional astrologer?

> You will need courage for this journey because it is not for everyone, and many people will both support you and criticize your choice, but in the grand scheme of things, you will find a greater purpose to your existence and a capacity to help and understand others.

Raymond Merriman is a financial market timer whose reports have served traders throughout the world since 1981. He has written several books on the correlation of financial markets to geocosmic studies, including a five volume series of books titled "The Ultimate Book on Stock Market Timing" (1997-2011). At UAC 1995, he received the Regulus Award for "Enhancing Astrology's Image as a Profession." At UAC 2012, he received the Regulus "Lifetime Achievement Award." He has served as ISAR president 1994-2000, 2002-2008, and 2015

References and Resources
for the Astrologer

Compiled by

Nancy Beale

Astrology Organizations

AAGB   Astrological Association of Great Britain
             www.astrologicalassociation.com

AFA   American Federation of Astrologers
             www.astrologers.com

AFAN   Association for Astrological Networking
             www.afan.org

ANS   Astrology News Service
             www.astrologynewsservice.com

AYA   Association for Young Astrologers
             www.youngastrologers.org

BAVA   British Association for Vedic Astrology
             www.bava.org

CVA   Council of Vedic Astrology
             www.councilvedicastrology.com

EAN	Evolutionary Astrology Network
	www.evolutionaryastrology.net
FAA	Federation of Australian Astrologers
	www.faainc.org.au
ICAS	Indian Council of Astrological Sciences
	www.icasindia.org
ISAR	International Society for Astrological Research
	www.isarastrology.com
NCGR	National Council for Geocosmic Research
	www.geocosmic.org
OPA	Organization for Professional Astrology
	www.opaastrology.org

Astrologer Directory

You can find a list of practicing astrologers on these websites:

www.findastrologer.com

www.findanastrologer.com

Schools of Astrology

Academy of AstroPsychology
www.astropsychology.org

> *Glenn Perry offers a Certificate in AstroPsychology and a Diploma in AstroPsychology and Conscious Evolution.*

American College of Vedic Astrology

www.acvaonline.org

> *Located in Sedona, Arizona, ACVA offers both online and one-on-one education and training in Vedic Astrology. Certification is offered through symposia, research and online education.*

American Institute of Vedic Studies

www.vedanet.com/courses

> *Pandit Vamadeva Shastri (Dr. David Frawley) is the founder and director, offering extensive distance learning in Ayurveda. Included is a specific astrology course called Ayurveda Astrology. No previous experience in Vedic astrology is required.*

Amsterdam School of Astrology in the Netherlands

www.asastrology.nl

> *Located in Amsterdam, Holland, the school is run by Faye Cossar and offers a variety of programs, from workshops, to webinars, and an apprenticeship.*

Astrological Psychology Association

www.astrologicalpsychology.org

> *Formerly known as AP-UK, the APA offers a Diploma Course based on the Huber Method, developed by Bruno and Louise Huber.*

Astrology College

www.astrologycollege.com

> *A correspondence course written by a group of UK professional astrologers, with one-on-one support of a personal tutor and a Diploma Course is offered.*

The Astrology Company

www.theastrologycompany.com

> *Bob Mulligan offers a Mastery of Astrology Correspondence Course.*

Astrology and the Evolution of Consciousness – The Complete Course

www.mauricefernandez.com

> *Directed by Maurice Fernandez. Part by correspondence, part on location. Participants are educated in the skills of diagnosis, synthesis, and effective counseling with a focus on identifying the evolutionary journey of the soul. A Comprehensive Certification Program in Evolutionary Astrology.*

Astrology Home Study Course

www.astrologycourse.net

> *Anita Burns offers an Astrology Home Study Course through the Metastudies Institute.*

Astro*Synthesis

www.astrosynthesis.com.au

> *Brian Clark offers a Certificate in Applied Astrology through his distance-learning program.*

Australia Academy of Astrology & Cosmobiology

www.astrologycosmobiology.com.au/courses

> *Pamela Rowe is the main teacher. The program accreditation overlaps with AFA certification.*

Avalon School of Astrology
www.avalonastrology.com

> *David Cochrane teaches the Professional Astrologer Certificate.*
> *The Diploma Program is Theoretical and Applied Cosmic*
> *Cybernetics.*

Centre for Psychological Astrology
www.cpalondon.com

> *Founded by Liz Greene & Howard Sasportas, the CPA changed to*
> *a more creative approach to astrological education in 2011. No*
> *Diploma Course is offered, instead, seminars at Regents College in*
> *London, online courses and webinars are taught by staff members*
> *such as Lynn Bell, Darby Costello and John Green.*

Deborah Houlding's School of Traditional Horary Astrology
www.sta.com

> *Offering various levels of study, including a Master's Level*
> *Horary Diploma. Based on William Lilly's techniques.*

Faculty of Astrological Studies
www.astrology.org.uk

> *Offering Foundation, Diploma Level 1 and Diploma Level 2*
> *(D.F.Astrol.S) by such noted faculty as Rob Hand, Liz Greene and*
> *Melanie Reinhart, as well as distance learning, and Summer*
> *School in Oxford.*

International Academy of Astrology
www.astrocollege.org

> *Ena Stanley pioneered this school of online astrological education.*
> *IAA offers two diploma programs: The Professional Training*

Department and The Classical Astrology Department. IAA
certification offers a degree of reciprocity with NCGR and ISAR.
IAA also hosts free monthly lectures with a variety of guest
speakers.

Jeffrey Green School of Evolutionary Astrology
www.schoolofevolutionaryastrology.com/school

*Astrology DVD comprehensive course that teaches astrology from
the ground up thru the prism of the Evolutionary perspective.*

Johannes Kepler Institute for Astrological Research & Education
www.keplerunited.org

*Founded in 2005 in Belgrade, Serbia by ISAR Certified
Astrologers Alexander and Lea Imsiragic. Offers certification for
all students completing studies at the Institute through Kepler
Association for Professional Astrology (KAPA).*

Kepler College
www.kepler.edu

*Kepler offers 3 paths of study: Continuing Education, Certificate
and Diploma programs online. Noted instructors are Donna
Cunningham, Gary Christen and Lee Lehman.*

The London School of Astrology
www.londonschoolofastrology.co.uk

*Offering accredited three-year courses in astrology in central
London, including an Apprenticeship Programme. Run by Frank
Clifford with various tutors and international guest speakers.
Additional short tarot and palmistry courses.*

Mayo School of Astrology

www.mayoastrology.com

> *UK based, Wendy Stacey is now the Principal. Exclusively a distance-learning format, offering a Diploma by correspondence.*

MMTA Financial Astrology Course

www.mmacycles.com

> *MMTA is the first in-depth on-line training course based on the principles of financial market timing developed by Raymond A. Merriman, (CTA), as a result of over 30 years of research and professional trading experience.*

Portland School of Astrology

www.portlandastrology.org

> *A physical school of astrology with a focus on embodied astrology with an inclusive framework exploring personal empowerment. Jaysen Paulson is founder and director. PSA offers year-long programs, quarterly classes, online classes, and events.*

Shamanic Astrology Mystery School

www.shamanicastrology.com

> *Daniel Giamario is founder and executive director based in Manila, Philippines. SAMS offers online and in person classes leading to certification.*

Astrology Bookstores

AFA Bookstore
www.astrologers.com/store/

Astrology et al Bookstore
www.astrologyetal.com/cat_home.html

Aurora Press
www.aurorapress.com

Ibis Press
www.ibispress.net

Midheaven Books
www.midheavenbooks.com

Astrology Magazines (in Print)

Dell Horoscope
www.dellhoroscope.com

Express Star Teller
starteller.com

Hexagon Astrology
www.hexagonastrology.com

The Mountain Astrologer
www.mountainastrologer.com

Astrology Software

AstroGold
www.astrogold.io

> *AstroGold for smart phones, tablets, and Mac*

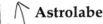

Astrolabe
www.alabe.com

> (Solar Fire)
> *Nova Chartwheels*
> *Jigsaw*

Astrologos
www.zyntara.com

> *Starlight*

Astrograph
www.astrograph.com

> *Time Passages*
> *(Basic, Standard, Advanced, Complete)*

Cosmic Patterns Software
www.astrosoftware.com

> *Kepler*
> *Sirius*
> *Pegasus*

Intrepid
www.intrepidastrologysoftware.com

> *Intrepid*
> *Sky Engine*

Matrix Software
www.astrologysoftware.com

> *Matrix*
> *Win*Star*
> *Blue*Star*

Time Cycles Research
www.timecycles.com

> *IO for Mac*

Astrology Conferences

American Federation of Astrologers Conference
www.astrologers.com

> Tempe, Arizona
> *Every 2 years*

Astrological Association of Great Britain Conference
www.astrologicalassociation.com

> London, England
> *Annually in September*

Astrology Student Conference (ASC)
www.astroconference.com

> London, England
> *Annually in late spring*

BAVA International Conference
www.bava.org

> London, England - *Annually*

Faculty of Astrological Studies Summer School
www.astrology.org.uk

> Exeter College, Oxford, England
> *Annually in August*

FAA International Astrology Conference
www.faainc.org.au

> Various Australia locations
> *Every 2 years*

Great Lakes Astrology Conference
www.greatlakesastrology.com

> Ann Arbor, MI
> *Annually*

Heaven and Earth Workshops
www.heavenandearthworkshops.com

> Bali, India, Mexico and Europe
> *Annually*

International Astrological Conference in the Balkans
www.keplerunited.org

> Belgrade, Serbia
> *Annually*

ISAR Conference
www.isarastrology.com

> Various locations
> *Every 2 years*

NCGR Conference
www.geocosmic.org

> Various Northeastern US locations
> *Every 3 years*

NORWAC – Northwest Astrological Conference
www.norwac.net

> Seattle, Washington
> *Annually Memorial Day Weekend*

OPA Retreat
www.opaastrology.org

> Various locations
> *Every year to 18 months*

The River of Stars Astrology Conference
www.theriverofstars.com

> Hawaii
> *Every 4 years*

Sophia Center Conference
www.uwtsd.ac.uk/sophia

> Bath, England
> *Annually*

SOTA Astrology Conference
www.donnavantoen.com

> Niagara Falls, NY
> *Annually*

UAC – United Astrology Conference

www.uacastrology.com

> Various locations
>
> *Every 4 years (usually)*
>
> Sponsored by American College of Vedic Astrology, AFAN, Council of Vedic Astrology, ISAR and NCGR

Local Astrology Associations
United States

ARIZONA

Arizona Society of Astrologers (ASA)

www.azastrologers.org

Phoenix/Scottsdale – Meets the 3rd Saturday of the month at Granite Reef Scottsdale Senior Center.

Tucson Astrologers' Guild (TAG)

www.tucsonastrologersguild.net

Tucson – Meets the 2nd Friday of the month at the Ramada Tucson Foothills

CALIFORNIA

Los Angeles NCGR

www.ncgrla.com

Tarzana – Meets the 3rd Thursday of the month Sept.-June at Coco's Restaurant

Sacramento Chapter of NCGR

www.ncgrsacramento.org

Roseville – Meets the 4th Sunday of the month at the Reserves at the Galleria

San Diego Astrological Society (SDAS)

www.sandiegoastrology.com

San Diego – Meets the 2nd Friday of the month at Joyce Beers Center in Hillcrest area

San Diego Chapter of NCGR

www.ncgrsandiego.org

Encinitas – Meets the 3rd Saturday of the month at the US Bank Building Community Room

San Francisco Astrological Society (SFAS)

www.sfastrologicalsociety.com

San Francisco – Meets the last Thursday of the month

San Francisco Bay Area Chapter NCGR

www.ncgrsanfrancisco.org

San Francisco – Meets monthly at the Fort Mason Center

Southern California Astrological Network (SCAN)

www.meetup.com/scanastro-com/

Laguna Hills

COLORADO

Denver Astrology Group
www.denverastrologygroup.com

Meets 2nd Saturday of the month at 3pm at the Mercury Cafe

Rocky Mountain Astrologers (ROMA)
www.romaastrologers.com

Boulder – Meets 3rd Thursday of the month at the Days Hotel, 3rd Floor

Rocky Mountain Chapter NCGR
www.geocosmic.org/chapters

Denver – Meets 1st Friday of the month from September to June at Isis Bookstore.

CONNECTICUT

Astrological Society of Connecticut
www.myasc.org

Wethersfield – Meets monthly Sept-May at the Keeney Memorial Center

Berkshire Fairfield NCGR
www.ctastrologers.org

Southport – Meets 2nd Sunday of the month Sept-May

FLORIDA

Astrology Association of St. Petersburg (AASP)
www.aaspfl.com

Florida Atlantic Chapter NCGR
www.astrologyfla.com

North Florida Astrological Association
www.nfaajax.com

Jacksonville – Facebook Group: North FL Astrological Association

South Florida Astrological Association (SFAA)
www.southfloridaastrology.com

Ft. Lauderdale/Miami/West Palm Beach – Meets 1st Thursday of the month with an all day workshop the Saturday following at the Courtyard Marriott

GEORGIA

Metropolitan Atlanta Astrological Society (MAAS)
www.atlantaastrology.com

Tucker – Meets the 3rd Thursday of the month at Harobi House at 7:30pm

ILLINOIS

Northern Illinois Chicago NCGR
www.chicagolandastrology.com

Chicago – Meets 1st Friday of the month at Wilson Park Fieldhouse

Friends of Astrology (AFA affiliate)
www.friendsofastrology.org

Chicago – Meets 3rd Friday of the month
Oak Brook – Meets 2nd Friday of the month
Oak Lawn – Meets 4th Friday of the month

INDIANA

Indiana Federation of Astrologers
Indianapolis – Meets monthly

Ohio Valley Astrological Society
Newburgh – Meets 2nd Monday of the month

KANSAS

Aquarian Organization of Astrologers
www.astrologykansascity.com

Kansas City

KENTUCKY

Astrological Society of Kentucky (ASK)
www.meetup.com/Astrological-Society-of-Kentucky

Facebook Group: Astrological Society of Kentucky

MARYLAND

Annapolis NCGR
www.geocosmic.org/chapters
Meets 2nd Saturday of the month at The Country Inn & Suited
10:30am

Baltimore Astrological Society
www.baltimoreastrology.org
Meets 3rd Friday of the month at 7pm various locations

MASSACHUSETTS

Boston NCGR

www.ncgrbostonastrology.org

Belmont – Meets monthly at Belmont Town Library

MICHIGAN

Smart Michigan NCGR

www.meetup.com/SMART-and-GLAC/

Ann Arbor – Meets 4th Sunday of the month

MINNESOTA

STARS Chapter of NCGR

www.mnstars.com

Minneapolis – Meets 3rd Saturday of the month

MISSOURI

Aquarian Organization of Astrologers (AOA)

www.astrologykansascity.com

Kansas City – Meets 2nd Monday of the month at Community Christian Church

Astrological Association of St. Louis (AASTL)

www.aastl.net

Brentwood – Meets the 2nd Sunday of the month at the Brentwood Recreation Center at 2pm

NEVADA

Las Vegas Stargazers Chapter of NCGR
www.meetup.com/Las-Vegas-Astrology-Meetup

Las Vegas – Meets the last Tuesday of the month at East Las Vegas Community Center
Facebook Group: NCGR Las Vegas Stargazers

NEW HAMPSHIRE

Seacoast Astrological Association
www.seacoastastrologicalassociation.blogspot.com

Portsmouth – Meets the 2nd Tuesday of the month March-December at the Roundabout Diner

NEW JERSEY

Astrological Society of Princeton
www.aspnj.org

Plainsboro – Meets 2nd Saturday of the month October-June at the Plainsboro Public Library

Cosmic Circle Astrological Association (CCAA)
www.meetup.com/Cosmic-Astrology

Northern New Jersey Chapter of NCGR
www.geocosmic.org/chapters

Montclair – Meets Wednesday and Sunday monthly from Sept to June

Willingboro Stargazers (AFA affiliate)
Meets 4th Tuesday of the month at the Willingboro Public Library

NEW MEXICO

New Mexico Enchantment NCGR
www.swcp.com/~nmncgr
Albuquerque – Meets 1st Wednesday of the month at 7pm

NEW YORK

Long Island NCGR
www.lincgr.com
Contact: astro-info@lincgr.com

Mid-Hudson Upstate NCGR
www.midhudsonupstatencgr.net/

New York City NCGR
www.astrologynyc.org
Meets monthly – days vary at Joanna Shannon Library, 39 Fifth Avenue, NYC.

NORTH CAROLINA

Asheville Friends of Astrology
www.ashevillefriendsofastrology.org
Asheville – Meets on the 3rd Friday of the

Queen Charlotte Chapter of NCGR
www.geocosmic.org/chapters
Earth Fare, Pineville

Network of Triangle Astrologers
www.ntastrology.org
Raleigh – Meets 3rd Thursday of the month Sept-May

OHIO

Lake County Astrological Association (LCAA)
Facebook Group: Lake County Astrological Association (LCAA)

Ohio Valley Chapter of NCGR
www.ncgr-ohiovalley.org

Cincinnati – Meets the 4th Friday of the month

OREGON

Astrology in Ashland aka Southern Oregon NCGR
www.astrologyinashland.org

Oregon Astrological Association (OAA)
www.oregonastrology.org

Portland – Meets 3rd Friday of the month Sept-June at the SUBUD Center

PENNSYLVANIA

Philadelphia Chapter of NCGR
www.geocosmic.org/chapters

Meets the 3rd Sunday of the month

TEXAS

Astrological Society of Northern Texas
www.asntx.com

DFW - Meets every 2nd Sunday of the month

Astrological Society of Austin
www.astrologyaustin.org

UTAH

Salt Lake City Astrology
www.meetup.com/The-Salt-Lake-City-Astrology-Group

VIRGINIA

Northern Virginia Astrology Group (NOVA)
www.novaastrologygroup.com

Richmond Chapter of NCGR
Richmond

WASHINGTON

Washington State Astrological Association (WSAA)
www.washingtonastrologers.org

Seattle- Meets 2nd Thursday of the month at Puget Sound Yacht
Club 7:30pm
Contact: Karen Wennerlind 206-362-2712

WISCONSIN

Milwaukee Chapter of NCGR
www.geocosmic.org/chapters

Astrology Associations International

BRAZIL

Centro de Estudos de Astrologia Psicologica (CEAP)
www.astrologiaceap.com.br

AstroBrazil

www.astrobrasil.com.br/site

CANADA

Astrology Calgary

www.astrologersofcalgary.com

Contact: Donna Young: youngestdonna@gmail.com

Astrology Toronto

www.astrologytoronto.ca

Meets various Saturdays at 1:30pm at The Centering Space

Edmonton Astrological Society

www.astrologyedmonton.com

Meets 2nd Friday of the month Sept-May at 7:30pm at the Homefire Grill

Fraser Valley Astrological Guild

www.astrologyguild.com

Vancouver, BC – Meets 2nd Thursday of the month Sept-Jun 7:30pm

Montreal Astrology

http://www.meetup.com/astrologymontreal/

OPA Satellites

Montreal - Contact Kate Rusko: katerusko@videotron.ca

Calgary – Contact Donna Young: youngestdonna@gmail.com

GREECE

Friends of Astrology in Greece

www.filoi-astrologias-ellados.blogspot.gr

OPA Satellite

Athens - <u>Contact</u> Smaro Sotiraki: smarwsotiraki@gmail.com

HOLLAND

AVN Astrology (Dutch Astrological Association)

http://avn-astrologie.nl/

ISRAEL

OPA Satellite

Tel Aviv - <u>Contact</u> Boaz Fyler: boazfyler@gmail.com

Urania Astrology

www.urania.org.il
Urania releases publications, and organizes conferences annually.

MEXICO

Mexico City Chapter NCGR

www.geocosmic.org/chapters

OPA Satellite

Mexico City – <u>Contact</u> Ursula Stockder: urstockder@yahoo.com

MONTENEGRO

Astrological Association of Montenegro (Academy of Astrology)

www.radioastrolog.com & www. radiohoroskop.com

NORWAY

Norsk Astrologisk Forening

www.astrologiskforening.no

OPA Satellite

Bergen - <u>Contact</u> Sol Jonassen: sol@sol-with.com

RUSSIA

Academy of Global Astrology & Metainformation

www.astrol.ru

OPA Satellite in Russia

AstraLife (Dmitriy Paramonov)

www.opa.astralife.net

SERBIA

Kepler Association for Professional Astrologers - KAPA

www.keplerunited.org/KAPA

SOUTH AFRICA

AstroLight (Johannesburg)

<u>Contact:</u> Cindy Lubner: cindyl@astrolight.co.za

Astrology Society of South Africa (ASSA)

www.astrologysociety.org.za

Johannesburg monthly meetings

OPA Satellite

Johannesburg - <u>Contact</u> Heitlje LeRoux: heiltjelr@gmail.com

TURKEY

NCGR Turkey

www.ncgr-turkey.com

UNITED KINGDOM

Aquarius Rising

www.aquariusrisingwsaa.co.uk

Glasgow, Scotland – Meets on the last Tuesday of the month at St.
George's Studio
<u>Contact:</u> Pamela Blair: pamela.blair@virgin.net

Aquarius Severn Astrology Society

www.aquariussevern.com

Gloucestershire – Meets on Thursdays from 8-10pm at Isbourne
Holistic Center in Cheltenham
<u>Contact:</u> Kris Lee: kris@aquariussevern.com

Astrological Lodge of London

www.astrolodge.co.uk

<u>Central London</u> – Meets Mondays from 7:00-9:30 at the
Theosophical Society, 50 Gloucester Place in Marylebone, London

Bath Astrologers' Forum

www.bathastrologersforum.co.uk

Bath – Meets on the 1st Monday of the month 7:30-9:30 at Waterfront
House, Lower Bristol Road, Bath
<u>Contact:</u> Jill Shearer: jillshearer@btinternet.com

Brighton and Hove Astrology Circle

www.brightonastrologycircle.com

Sussex, Scotland

Meets weekly on Thursdays
<u>Contact:</u> Phoebe Wyss: astrophoebe@btinternet.com

Exeter Astrology Group

Exeter – Meets monthly at the Friends'Meeting House

<u>Contact:</u> Louise Vergette-Lynn: astrolou67@gmail.com

Full Circle Astrology Group (Southport, Merseyside)

www.exeterastrologygroup.org.uk

OPA Satellite

London - <u>Contact</u> Wendy Stacey: wendya@psilink.co.uk

Oxford Astrology Group (OAG)

www.oxfordastrologygroup.blogspot.co.uk

Oxfordshire - Meets 3rd Wednesday of the month at 7:30pm

Plymouth Astrology Group (PAG)

www.plymouthastrologygroup.org

Plymouth – Meets 3rd Wednesday of the month at Unity House

Scottish Astrological Association

www.scottishastrology.co.uk

Edinburgh, Scotland – Meets 3rd Wednesday of the month

<u>Contact:</u> Mark Cullen: karmiccelt@aol.com

Suffolk Astrological Society

www.sasnews.wordpress.com

Suffolk – Meets 1st Wednesday of the month

<u>Contact:</u> Glenda Cole: astrogroups@gmail.com

Wessex Astrology Circle

www.wac-uk.blogspot.com

Important Astrology Resources

Astro Data Bank

www.astro.com/astro-databank/Main Page

The collection of birth Information of public figures – rated by level of reliability for the source of data.

Astrodienst

www.astro.com

Website with a wealth of articles, free chart generator, and ephemeris of asteroids and many other celestial bodies.

Asteroid Ephemeris Generator

www.true-node.com/eph0

Generate an ephemeris for any celestial body.

RUDHYAR Archival Project

www.khaldea.com/rudhyar

The best and most important of Dane Rudhyar's lifelong work is made freely available through the Rudhyar's archival project.

Urania Trust

www.uraniatrust.org

Founded to offer support through grants to individuals and organizations for publishing, translation, research and other work.

Join OPA

Make Astrology Stronger!

Unique programs to support astrology students and professionals

Peer Group Work / I-Astrologer /Free Monthly Talk/ Question of the Month / The OPA Retreat

Find out more about OPA

www.opaastrology.org

OPA International Satellites

Contact the Satellite in your country

- **Canada Satellite**
  Donna Young (Calgary) Email: youngestdonna@gmail.com
  Kate Rusko (Montreal) Email: katerusko@videotron.ca

- **Greece Satellite**
  Smaro Sotiraki (Athens) Email: smarwsotiraki@gmail.com

- **Israel Satellite**
  Boaz Fyler (Tel Aviv) Email: boazfyler@gmail.com

- **Mexico Satellite**
  Ursula Stockder (Mexico City) Email: urstockder@yahoo.com

- **Norway Satellite**
  Sol W. Jonassen (Bergen) Email: sol@sol-with.com

- **Russia Satellite**
  Dmitriy Paramonov (Izhevsk) E-mail: paramonov@astralife.net

- **South Africa Satellite**
  Heiltje LeRoux (Johannesburg) Email: heiltjelr@gmail.com

- **UK Satellite**
  Wendy Stacey (London) Email: wendy@wendystacey.com

New to Say   Synthesis

AIT + PL Reg + NDE + Synchron + Newton + Techs to heal + QF
& Phil (H, T, B) + Panentheism + PP

CPSIA information can be obtained at www.ICGtesting.com
Printed in the USA
BVOW06s1831260716

456914BV00014B/56/P